Winning Not Fighting

Winning Not Fighting

*Why You Need to Rethink Success
and How You Achieve It with the
Ancient Art of Wing Tsun*

JOHN VINCENT AND
SIFU JULIAN HITCH

BUSINESS

PENGUIN BUSINESS

UK | USA | Canada | Ireland | Australia
India | New Zealand | South Africa

Penguin Business is part of the Penguin Random House group of companies
whose addresses can be found at global.penguinrandomhouse.com.

First published 2019
001

Copyright © John Vincent and Sifu Julian Hitch, 2019

The moral right of the copyright holders has been asserted

The publisher is grateful for kind permission to reprint on p. 179 an extract from
p. 21 of *The Way of Zen* by Alan Watts, Vintage Spiritual Classics
(New York: Pantheon, 1957; Reprint Vintage Books 1985).

Illustrations by Kit Liu

Set in 11/13 pt Dante MT Std
Typeset by Jouve (UK), Milton Keynes
Printed and bound in Great Britain by Clays Ltd, Elcograf S.p.A.

A CIP catalogue record for this book is available from the British Library

ISBN: 978-0-241-31837-9

www.greenpenguin.co.uk

From John

For Natasha and Eleanor.

And in memory of my Dad
Leon who lent us his name.

From Julian

For Joan 'Peggy' Pyke-Lees,
who had the soul of a philosopher, and was a beacon of
positivity, love and laughter.

Contents

A Note on the Text

Though we have authored this book together, we have in fact each written our own distinct sections that join together to make the whole. Julian has written about Wing Tsun, its philosophies and techniques. John has written about its application in business and in his own life.

We have often been sitting beside each other as we write, stopping to ask questions and to debate. We have frequently paused, to train in Wing Tsun, or go for a walk together to get our heads round a particular topic that has been confounding us. Breakthroughs have come at different times – sometimes while training in specific Wing Tsun techniques, or through late-night chats after one of us has had an epiphany that we want to share.

We have attempted to convey the wisdoms of Wing Tsun and the relevant experience of Leon in the simplest way. And we have challenged ourselves and each other in the process.

We hope that the book will be helpful to anyone and everyone, and that its subjects are universal: for young people who are trying to find their direction; for people already at the start of their career; for leaders; for people who are about to retire; for people who have retired; and for those looking for a new challenge.

The book describes the four forms or four 'Doors' of Wing Tsun. We advise that you read them in the order they are experienced by the student of Wing Tsun – from one to four – rather than dipping in and out of the book. They contain the wisdoms of 3,000 years of civilization and of many Wing Tsun masters.

Neither of us feels that any book can do justice to the oral traditions and depth of knowledge that exist. And the direct experience of Wing Tsun, and of Leon, will go further than what we can achieve between these pages. But we are happy to say that we think this book is a worthwhile way to help you – and us – along the way.

Books are never finished, they are only wrestled from the authors as the final deadline for submission is reached. There will be many ways in which your input will help improve the book and extend and enrich our thinking. We have created a website at winningnotfighting.com, and we would like to warmly invite you to share your thoughts, and your own stories, there.

Thank you so much for reading this book.

John and Julian

Introduction

*'What Do You Mean I'm Not
Actually a General?'*
By John

It was the Year of the Dragon. Not in astrological terms; more in terms of ceiling art.

It was 2006 and, despite training for the London Marathon, I wasn't feeling well. Henry Dimbleby and I had started Leon, our healthy fast-food chain, with our friend Allegra two years previously, and we were exhausted. I was working too hard. I had high blood pressure. And I needed help.

A friend recommended a five-element acupuncturist called Wendy Mandy (a woman with two first names, like me, I thought – *we've got loads in common already*). So I called her.

'I can't see you for two months,' she said.

'Hold on a second,' I replied. 'What if I die in the meantime?'

'What will be will be.'

That made me smile. 'Fair enough,' I said.

Eight weeks later, I found myself still alive and lying on a treatment couch in her flat in Notting Hill, staring up at a ceiling adorned with a magnificent hand-painted dragon.

How pretty, I thought. A few minutes later, I found out why it was there. It was a grown-up version of the Disney posters that dentists put on the ceiling (in vain) to distract kids.

'Ouch!'

'Yes,' said Wendy, withdrawing the needle she had just inserted into me. 'It doesn't not hurt.'

I

Five-element acupuncture is not like the traditional Chinese medicine (TCM) acupuncture you can find almost anywhere. TCM acupuncture does not hurt. Five-element, which is actually older than TCM despite the latter's name, doesn't not hurt.

Over the last few years I have endured needles through my tear ducts and parts of the body that don't see much natural light. The needles are one thing; the pinpoint accuracy of Wendy's insights is another. Within a few minutes she is able to tell the specifics of your relationship with each parent and at what age you suffered any traumas of particular significance.

When she told me in our first session after feeling my pulses* that I am driven by the need to avenge my dad, I thought to myself, *Don't give me that psychobabble cliché.* Then I reflected that I had named Leon after my father. (I owe you one, Henry.) That I was driven every day by stories of how Dad failed his finals at the London School of Economics because he walked out when his own father died . . . and on and on.

Wendy has a brilliant ability to understand people. And so I have had some enlightening moments under that dragon's watchful gaze.

'What Do You Mean I'm Not Actually a General?'

In 2014, Wendy rang me and said, 'John, one of my clients is finishing a course in coaching and needs to coach you for free to qualify.'

I agreed. And then Aimée and I had session 'zero' of our programme over coffee near the Leon office in London's Borough Market – a session in which she was supposed to suss me out, see

---

* Whereas in Western medicine, we speak of 'the pulse', Chinese medicine recognizes 29 pulses to offer a more comprehensive picture of a patient's overall health.

the cut of my jib. She asked me what makes me laugh. I told her. It made *her* laugh, and I knew we were going to get on. There was no attempt to advise or find solutions in this initial session. She asked me questions and listened.

Session one was very different.

It was immediately clear that Aimée had done a huge amount of thinking and preparation for this meeting. She had recorded our first encounter and listened to it over and over, pondering our time together deeply.

'John, the biggest thing I noticed in our earlier conversation was the extent to which you use military analogies. You talk about commanding an army, about battles, about deploying the troops, and you seem to think about yourself being in a "fight".'

She paused, giving me time to reflect. She was right, I thought to myself. It was how I felt about the challenges and opportunities facing us, and how I needed to lead Leon.

'I'm not saying that there's anything wrong with that,' Aimée continued. 'I'm just wondering if that might come at too high a cost to your health.'

That got my attention.

I had for some time been feeling that the price of my desire to achieve had been my health. That was why I had gone to see Wendy Mandy in the first place. In addition to high blood pressure, an irritable bladder and gut had been adding to my unease for years. Wendy had done a huge amount to help me manage this, but I needed to do more to fix these things for good.

Eternity

'I thought it might be helpful if I gave you an alternative metaphor to think about,' Aimée then said.

An alternative metaphor, I thought to myself. *Really? What sort of an alternative metaphor?*

I felt as though I actually *was* fighting, that I really was using scarce resources to win battles. And suddenly Aimée was suggesting that the army and fighting stuff wasn't . . . *real*? That it was somehow a map I was creating to explain the terrain of my business – and perhaps even my life.

'There was a man in Sydney, Australia . . .' she began. (She had me at 'Sydney, Australia'; I've always liked Australians.) '. . . who heard his pastor say, "Eternity, eternity, if only I could preach the word to all of Sydney." Now this was in the 1930s, and this was an uneducated man who had fought in World War One, acquitting himself well. But when he came back, he got in trouble with the law. He realized he needed to change his ways, and he decided he would help his pastor achieve his goal.

'He'd get up early every day, before most of Sydney was awake, and write the word "Eternity" in chalk. On pavements, on walls, on famous buildings – anywhere he could – in copperplate handwriting so unmistakable that, when people started to notice, everyone knew each word had been written by the same man. And everyone started to wonder: who was this person writing "Eternity" everywhere? Why was he or she doing it? What did it mean?

'Every day for thirty-five years, he wrote this word – the only word he could write, because he was functionally illiterate – all over the city, until everyone was talking about what it meant. With this single action, he prompted everyone to ponder the meaning of Eternity. He changed an entire city's conversation, so much so that, at the 2000 Sydney Olympics, they lit up the word "Eternity" in fireworks on Sydney Harbour Bridge.'

Ah, okay, so that wasn't a perfume advert.

'The moral of the story,' Aimée said, 'is that one man was able to achieve something big in a way that was within his own resources. It was something simple that he could do without stress, without fighting or overstretching himself. And without making himself ill. His name was Arthur Stace.'

I liked what she was saying. But how could I really apply it?

Over the next ten sessions, Aimée helped me rethink and re-feel my approach to Leon and my life. She introduced me to *The Great Work of Your Life*, a Western exploration of the Hindu scripture the *Bhagavad Gita* that is rich in examples of people who have lived their lives according to their sacred mission or Dharma; which prompted another friend to recommend *Mastery*, by an Aikido master called George Leonard. And between these two books I discovered the joy of committing oneself to one thing, and practising it now, in the present moment, without emotional or physical distraction – and in so doing, allowing oneself not to be fixated on the outcome.

I had grown up being reasonably good at a number of things and driven by a can-do approach to new hobbies and opportunities. But I realized I needed to focus. And *Mastery* convinced me I needed a martial arts instructor to help.

Lot No. 8

In a roundabout way, Wendy Mandy also introduced me to Julian. She had invited me to a race meeting and auction at Newbury Racecourse in aid of a charity called Key4Life – which, among other ways, uses horses to help young offenders rehabilitate. And Lot No. 8 in the auction was for a Wing Tsun Kung Fu lesson with a man called Julian Hitch.

I had briefly met Julian earlier that evening, and had had an inkling we would be friends. But all I knew of Kung Fu was what I'd seen in Bruce Lee movies . . . oh, and the song. And so although Carl Douglas had tried to convince us all in 1974 that 'everybody was Kung Fu fighting' (and that it was a little bit frightening), the only person I knew who was Kung Fu fighting was my cousin Kate.

We were holding a Leon 'well-being' event at my house two

weeks hence, and it occurred to me that we could book Julian for the event. So I stuck up my hand at the right times and ended up with the prize: Sifu Julian Hitch.

Julian came to our two-day Summer Well-being event and was an instant hit. He told the story of his martial art, taught people how to punch, how to get out of an arm grab, and trained us in Chi Gung, which literally means 'life energy cultivation' and underpins all Chinese martial arts. Then he sent Adam (my friend and the Leon property director) six metres across the grass with one punch. And all in a way that left Adam laughing about it. I knew then that this was the person I wanted to be my teacher.

I didn't realize how important a teacher he would be.

One Kwoon, Many Sticky Flip Charts

Julian agreed to train me twice a week. Each time we trained he would write up more principles and techniques on giant flip-chart sheets and stick them on the walls – until all four walls of the big loft room where we trained (our 'Kwoon') were full.

- Take the shortest line.
- Never attack but always hit first.
- Whatever happens is to your advantage.
- Don't force.
- When you start moving forward, keep moving forward.

And there are hundreds more.

As I stared at them, it was clear that so many of these ancient principles – some of which date back to before the Ming dynasty of 1368–1644 – were applicable both to my private life and my business life. And they echoed the lessons I had learned from Aimée that I had started to apply to Leon.

Throughout the following year, Julian taught me the philosophy behind Wing Tsun. We set to work formalizing a way to apply its ideas to business and to the world of Leon. We created a blueprint for how I could lead Leon without burning out and without burning out my colleagues, and in a way that allowed me to get up every morning and metaphorically write the word 'Eternity' in chalk.

Since then, we have woven these principles into life at Leon. We have recognized their alignment with our founding purpose and with our values, and consciously adapted our strategy and culture to Wing Tsun and its approach of Winning Not Fighting. We have had many sessions with our 'Leaders of Leon' – people from the support team (aka head office) and all of the restaurant managers – to explore Wing Tsun's ideas and how they change the way we work.

Because we want it to be a practical and physical tool too, not just a tool for management, Julian has begun a programme of training the baristas (and the team members who work in the kitchen) in Wing Tsun, with remarkable results for their coffee-making speed and quality, as well as for their heart rates and stress (now relaxation) levels. And all Leaders of Leon have practised the first form on multiple occasions and have incorporated it into their work and home lives as Chi Gung.

Have You Got a Problem?!

For most of us, our minds and bodies are not built for the lives we live today. In fact, the very things that made our species successful in a pre-industrialized world are slowly killing us now. Our operating system – the way our conscious and unconscious mind functions within our environment – which evolved over tens of thousands of years, is not designed for the modern world.

Thousands of years ago, we lived a life that was not separate

from nature. As hunters and gatherers, we ate fruits and vegetables in season. We ate meat rarely, because most animals could
run faster than us. We learned to work together to hunt more
efficiently, gather more effectively, to build, to farm. We had a
physical relationship with our environment.

Since then, we have invented the wheel, the city, literacy. We
have fired a small machine beyond the confines of our solar system. And yet our bodies, brains and impulses – our DNA – have
hardly changed. And we know a lot about a lot of things, but very
little about ourselves.

At a physical level, our basic concerns remain the same: to
survive long enough to reproduce, and to have enough energy
to provide shelter and food for our children. But human existence cannot be reduced purely to such functional or rational
considerations. At an emotional and spiritual level, we have a
sense of wonder and curiosity. We create myths and stories to
try to make sense of the universe around us, and these are part
of our ability to thrive.

Occasionally, something happens to make us afraid, trigger-
ing the 'fight or flight' response. This biomechanical reaction to
outside stimuli helps us avoid and respond to danger.

You know how this works . . . You are walking in a forest.
Maybe you're picking berries or hunting rabbits. Or maybe you're
just enjoying walking for the sake of walking, and noticing the
details of your immediate world. But you are increasingly aware
that you're not alone. There's a tightness in your stomach and
you're breathing a bit faster, oxygenating your system. This is
your adrenal gland preparing your body, raising your blood
pressure and your heart rate, dilating your pupils to make you
focus on what is right in front of you so that when that tiger
strikes, you are ready to run. Or fight. Or freeze.

This is very useful. But it was never meant to be the norm. Our
bodies are built to spend most of their time digesting our food
properly to provide us with energy, to be relaxed and imaginative,

to be able to have sex without the distraction of being eaten by a wolf. (Unless that is your thing.)

The adrenaline and cortisol, and lots of other chemicals, produced by the fight-or-flight response interrupt and confound these processes, compromising digestion, making the body function less well, and laying us open to disease. And the big problem – the one which so many of us think we don't have – is that we have built a world in which our fight-or-flight response is constantly activated to greater or lesser degrees. Dr Lissa Rankin, who has worked on understanding the power of the mind on our overall health, describes it like this in her book *Mind Over Medicine*:

> When this hormonal cascade is triggered by a thought or emotion in the mind, such as fear, the hypothalamic-pituitary-adrenocortical (HPA) axis activates, thereby stimulating the sympathetic nervous system to race into overdrive, pumping up the body's cortisol and adrenaline levels. Over time, filling the body with these stress hormones can manifest as physical symptoms, predisposing the body to disease.

Rankin then goes on to explain what happens when we are winning, not fighting:

> stress hormones drop, health-inducing relaxation hormones that counter the stress hormones are released, the parasympathetic nervous system takes over, and the body returns to homeostasis. Only in this rested, relaxed state can the body repair itself. Anything that reduces stress and elicits a relaxation response not only alleviates the symptoms the stress response can cause, but frees the body to do what it does naturally – heal itself.

What was once meant to be an occasional or intermittent response has become a constant, affecting us mentally and physically.

Twinned with fight-or-flight is the inflammatory response, triggered by the immune system. It is a reaction to physical stress at a cellular level to a joint, a muscle or an organ. The body creates inflammation to protect the injured area and to help it heal. It is a useful short-term response, but again it is not intended to be a constant state. Constant or chronic inflammation confounds our normally healthy processes – including not allowing our bodies to realize when we are full, which is just one of the many things that go wrong when we are inflamed.

Along with the Industrial Revolution, the scientific revolution – which for simplicity's sake we'll say began with Sir Isaac Newton – replaced many of the religious beliefs that spawned during the agrarian age with a mechanistic view of the world. And in medicine this led to a belief that the symptoms we experience as a result of the ill health caused by constant stress can be fixed by intercepting the mechanical processes. Painkillers can suppress pain and inflammation at the very time that we *need* that inflammation.

Antibiotics have successfully intercepted the growth of bacteria, but the longer we rely on them, the more bacteria evolve a resistance to them – including those that are used as the drugs of last resort.

This is not to say that these medical breakthroughs have not had major benefits, but rather that they are in part responding to diseases that are themselves the product of our industrialized environment. And second, that they mask and confound the real healing that we need.

In a series of lectures available online as a collection called 'Training the Mind, Healing the Body', Deepak Chopra and David Simon go further. They argue that we are in a post-Newtonian 'information age', where we understand that our thoughts create information – aka energy – that directly influences the chemicals and cells in our body. Positive or negative thoughts create molecules that can either support or debilitate our immune system and can cure or create disease. An inflamed mind creates an inflamed body. Chopra and Simon also explain that, in this way, fighting comes with a big cost for all of us.

You get to choose whether you want to change your life. To do so, you are going to need to start by changing your mind. Or rather, by letting your mind go.

Let us take a moment to understand how this state of constant fight-or-flight has become so deeply embedded within us.

The Power of Language

Look at the media and pick one British newspaper at random. You will see the recurrence of the words 'fury' and 'anger' and 'shame' and 'chaos' in its headlines. Disagreements in politics will describe a 'FURIOUS ROW' or a 'TRAITOR TO BRITAIN'. Even a serious broadsheet, several years ago, described a day when two things went against Prime Minister David Cameron in one day as a 'DOUBLE HAMMER BLOW'.

More recently, a headline described a conflict between the politician Boris Johnson and the Chancellor of the Exchequer Philip Hammond as 'HAMMOND GETS BOTH BARRELS FROM JOHNSON', conjuring up a nice image of Boris Johnson holding a shotgun and standing over the splattered remains of his victim.

This is the language of fear and aggression – language used to manipulate the ego.*

And it is used to sell us things.

---

* *Ego*, in terms of Wing Tsun, is something different from the Freudian or Jungian use of the word with which you may be more familiar. When Julian and I use the word, it is to refer to that part of ourselves that can be emotionally manipulated by fear, shame or anger, creating conflict within us, which we then project outwards. We will explore this more fully in due course.

Once upon a time, I worked for Procter & Gamble, the American consumer products company. It was my first proper job (other than running dance events), and right away I was struck by the formula we were given to develop TV adverts. Step one: *Create the Fear.*

For example, 'Isn't it embarrassing when you get dandruff on your shoulders? No one will want to date you if you have *dandruff on your shoulders.* How can you possibly be "good-looking" with DANDRUFF ON YOUR SHOULDERS? You will never have children and you will die alone.'

Then, of course, we went on to show how buying our shampoo was the solution to this fear, and how, by implication, using our product could help you get laid.

It's basic stuff. Primally so. And it goes beyond advertising. The language of fear – of aggression – pervades our lives, especially in business.

A recent report from PricewaterhouseCoopers stated that 'Apple is beating Google in the fight to become the world's biggest company'. Which begs the questions: is it really a *fight* to become the world's biggest company? Does it need to be? And are the long-term interests of both companies best served by being in a constant state of fight-or-flight?

And it is not just the reporting of the competition between two huge companies that employs such warlike vocabulary. We must all be aware of and careful of the language we use. Does your company really need to call the place where strategy is conducted the 'war room'? Do we need to 'kill' the competition?

And it's not just business. In modern politics – certainly in Britain and America – adversarial party-versus-party conflict creates more heat than light. When Henry and I worked on a major project for the UK government we were dismayed by the attitude of some politicians who were more keen on bashing the opposition than finding a solution. Some argue that the fighting is necessary to keep democracy alive. But my experience working with Her Majesty's Government has shown me that more can be achieved from positivity and consensus, as we shall see.

But How Can You Have a Martial Art That's Not About Fighting?

In the next chapter, Julian will share the story of Wing Tsun and its central thinking. But, in essence, it believes that fighting is fundamentally bad. It teaches us how not to create conflict, by putting aside fear and ego, and how to carry ourselves with calmness and confidence, safe in the knowledge that – if conflict truly cannot be avoided – we will prevail. And we will prevail by using the minimum force and causing minimum harm.

So Why Write This All Down?

We live in a world faced with significant economic and ecological problems that cannot be divorced from each other. And the solutions require a significant shift in culture that has to start with each of us looking inside ourselves.

I believe that Wing Tsun offers us the way through. Its unique approach runs entirely contrary to much of what is taught in business – and, indeed, in education – today. But Wing Tsun has practical lessons and a philosophy that can help us meet the challenges we face as a species. And in a way that works *with* the reality of humans' true nature rather than fighting against it.

We have a chance – or rather a vital responsibility – to remember our right relationship with ourselves, each other and the planet.

I have applied the lessons outlined in this book in my private life and in Leon. Not perfectly. And not without twists and turns. But I believe they are the bedrock of the fact that we have performed well, and grown in a market which has not.

These lessons are intended to equip us for the inevitable fact that something, at some stage, will go wrong. They are both practical and philosophical. They require you to see the familiar in new ways. And they work.

Winning Not Fighting
By Julian

What is Wing Tsun?

Wing Tsun Kung Fu is an ancient martial art which contains wisdoms to teach you how to succeed in life: at home, at work, in combat. And it does this by revealing that, ultimately, winning cannot be achieved by fighting.*

It is, at its heart, the study of the human condition. It offers an understanding of our own true nature and how we can relate to the world in the healthiest way.

Wing Tsun approaches winning from a completely different perspective from any other martial art. Its objective is to *not* create conflict – and, if conflict arises, to address it with the minimum of force in the fastest time. It provides the skills to prevail against a larger, stronger opponent. And it understands that the toe-to-toe trading of blows cannot succeed.

It does all this because of its specific historical origins.

Wing Tsun is not a combat sport. Unlike boxing or Taekwondo – where the objective is to fight within a constrictive set of rules – it instead focuses on *not fighting*. Its purpose is opposite to that of a combat sport.

Some writers have taken sports like tennis and football, and

---

* This paradox, which lies at the heart of the martial art, is resolved by Wing Tsun's definition of winning, which we explore on page 19.

written books that look to apply their principles to life. But Wing Tsun is not an activity to be used as an analogy. It is a thoroughly practical and philosophical approach to life developed over many centuries.

In the next chapter, John is going to explain why war is an unsuitable metaphor for business and life. So it may seem contradictory that we will use a *martial* art, which contains aspects of combat, as a guide to life. But there is no contradiction here. Wing Tsun is not a metaphor.

Fundamental to the art is the teaching of how to win at life. To avoid fighting, and instead to flourish.

The Philosophical Influences

Wing Tsun is not a religion. It does, however, draw on the wisdoms and insights of four Eastern traditions: Taoism, Confucianism, Mahayana Buddhism and Zen.*

In simplistic terms, Taoism is a philosophy that teaches harmony with oneself and with nature, and is principally an oral tradition supported by a number of texts including the *I Ching* and the *Tao Te Ching*. The *I Ching*, written around 900 BCE, is a guide to accessing one's unconscious brain, whereas the *Tao Te Ching*, written by Lao Tzu around 500 BCE, is a fuller guide to Taoist philosophy.

Confucianism was created by Confucius around the same time as the *Tao Te Ching* was written, and Confucius and Lao Tzu knew of each other. In many ways, however, the two philosophies could not be more different. Whereas Lao Tzu and Taoism

---

* Throughout this book, we have used the term Zen where the Chinese would say *Chan*. Zen is in fact the Japanese pronunciation, and has become the more commonly used term in the West. Both derive from the Sanskrit word *Dhyana*, meaning 'meditation'.

encouraged freedom and spontaneity, Confucius promoted a set of rules and hierarchies that aimed to create social harmony through imposed structure.

Buddhism originated in India around the same time as Taoism in China, and Mahayana Buddhism is the form of Buddhism that spread across northern Asia and which celebrates the practical application of the religion in everyday life.

Zen is the product of Taoism and Mahayana Buddhism coming together. Zen teaches that much of what we think is true is, in fact, illusion.

Wing Tsun is a powerful combination of these contrasting philosophies. And, more than that, it applies them to a physical art that has a coherent structure and methodology. All four traditions offer insights we can use in our everyday lives, but only Wing Tsun translates these wisdoms into practical actions, as we shall see.

Where Does it Come From?

Wing Tsun's roots can be found in northern China, where in 495 CE the Shaolin Temple was founded on the sacred Songshan Mountain. One of the ancient centres of Buddhism, the temple was located far from the hustle and bustle of everyday life. However, this was a time of constant warfare, and the secluded location left the monks open to bandit attacks. Worldly dangers were very real to the founders of the Shaolin.

In 520 CE the Indian mystic Bodhidharma, an expert in combat and the founder of Zen Buddhism, arrived at the temple to help spread its teachings. Recognizing the link between physical and spiritual well-being, he set about training the monks in physical exercises to strengthen the body, mind and spirit – and, crucially, to enable them to protect themselves against attackers.

And so they became the first community of combat monks, who used the medium of their physical training to achieve spiritual enlightenment. The 'martial' aspect provided structure and discipline, and the 'art' brought freedom and creativity.

From that point onwards, the Shaolin Temple quickly became a rare beacon of acceptance and community, with people of different sexes, races, classes and faiths all mingling together in one complex. So potent was its teaching that, by the seventeenth century, four further such temples had been founded across China. Wing Tsun emerged from the southernmost of these temples, in Fujian Province.

However, in 1644, the Ming dynasty was overcome by the incoming Qing dynasty. The Qing armies pushed into the south of China and – searching for Changping, the last princess of the Ming dynasty – destroyed the Fujian temple. Thanks to the bravery and sacrifice of every other monk, five top masters escaped – Changping among them. And through them, the teachings of the temple survived, put together in an art.

Three women stand at the heart of the development of Wing Tsun, among them Princess Changping, who became known in the Shaolin Temple as the formidable nun Ng Mui. This female influence created a special balance and perspective which allowed Wing Tsun to be powerfully different from all other martial arts. And, through these women, Wing Tsun was passed on. Indeed, the art was named after Ng Mui's first student, a young woman called Wing Tsun, which means 'beautiful springtime'.*

From 1644 on, Wing Tsun was taught in secret to protect the five masters and their disciples from the Qing dynasty's wrath. And for centuries this secrecy became almost integral to the art. It wasn't until the 1940s and Grandmaster Yip Man (now famous for being the teacher of Bruce Lee) that it became available to the wider public.

---

* Ng Mui saw a young woman being forced into marriage by the local bully, and taught her the martial art so she could defend herself. The young woman, Wing Tsun, proved its efficacy by defeating him.

To understand the depth of Wing Tsun's teaching and its wisdom, it is perhaps helpful to put it into a wider perspective. Most other martial arts are surprisingly modern, and they were all created by men: Karate (which also originally came from the Shaolin Temple) was created in the 1880s, as was Judo (1882); Aikido was born in the 1920s, Brazilian Jiu-Jitsu in 1925, Krav Maga in 1948 and Taekwondo in 1956.

Wing Tsun's feminine influence created a vastly different approach to conflict. Recent studies have shown that having women involved in government increases the likelihood of peace – indeed, just a 5 per cent increase in the presence of women in representative government results in a five-times reduction of the likelihood of war. Similarly, negotiations and peace talks that involve women are 35 per cent more likely to have a lasting result. Women peacemakers have famously had an impact in Burundi, Rwanda, Sudan, Liberia, South Africa, Northern Ireland and Colombia.

In the modern world, Wing Tsun takes this natural wisdom to its zenith and provides a much-needed counterbalance to the male-dominated – and commonly accepted – attitude to force.

To make this possible, the Wing Tsun masters created a simple but particular definition of winning. It's a combination of three elements, all of which are needed for us to live a truly contented life:

1. Enjoying the present
2. Achieving longevity
3. Being yourself

These are guiding principles rather than rules that you must follow. For winning is not about comparing yourself to or competing with others. It is personal. Wing Tsun has always been interested in the empowerment of the individual, and these wisdoms will allow you to live the life that *you* define as successful.

In *Winning Not Fighting*, you will learn how to master winning and make these three elements your way of life. However, before that, it helps to know what *fighting* means to you in reality.

The Fallacy of Fighting

Conflict is diametrically opposed to winning. It's easy to romanticize fighting as 'glorious' or 'noble', but any war veteran will tell you that's far from the truth. There is no such thing as a 'nice fight'. People are injured or killed.

Conflict creates stress and trauma, drains your energy and resources, and takes your focus away from your intended goals. The reality of fighting – whether in actual combat, combat sports or heated arguments – is high-risk but low-reward for those involved. It leaves you at a significant disadvantage. It puts you in a place where you are open to manipulation and exploitation – emotionally, mentally, physically and financially. Fighting cannot be a long-term strategy, because it is almost impossible to create a sustainable positive result from negative actions. Furthermore, fighting can be addictive, creating destructive patterns.

The foundation of your learning in Wing Tsun, therefore, is developing the ability to deal with conflict efficiently and effectively and to not create conflict in the first place. But if there is no option other than the use of force, then you need to end a situation quickly, proportionately and with the minimum consequential damage.

The Shaolin monks summed this up with their saying:

It is better to move away than grab;
It is better to grab than hit;
It is better to hit than hurt;
It is better to hurt than kill;
It is better to kill than be killed.

As surviving is an essential prerequisite to thriving, Wing Tsun teaches basic self-defence skills straight away. It allows you to face and overcome your fears, and takes away the tendency to overreact when you are faced with an unexpected or challenging situation.

The masters of old realized that – once you have progressed past this initial stage of learning survival skills – sustained success is fundamentally a continual journey of development. Over many hundreds of years, they created a simple system in Wing Tsun to progress you in the fastest possible manner. While structure normally implies rigidity, in Wing Tsun it implies flexibility. The whole point of this art is to give you back complete freedom in your life.

To help you achieve this success, Wing Tsun is divided into four separate developmental stages. Each stage – known as a 'Door'* – contains key wisdoms to help you progress to the next stage, and so enables you to create a winning pattern in your life. We have also chosen eight of the most powerful wisdoms of the art of Wing Tsun, which we will share with you under the corresponding Doors.

These eight wisdoms have been ordered in the best way to help you progress the fastest. Each is a standalone wisdom, the application of which will increase your success in life. The more often you apply these wisdoms, the more successful you will be. Apply them all and the benefits will be exponentially increased.

The Four Doors

In summary, *Winning Not Fighting* contains four Doors to guide your development, with a total of eight wisdoms supporting them. These are structured sequentially as follows.

---

* Or 'gate' – this term is interchangeable depending on the translation.

THE FIRST DOOR:
SIU NIM TAO — BECOME CONSCIOUS

Key theme: *Understanding who you are, why you do what you do, and how you work.*

- Wisdom 1: Know Yourself
- Wisdom 2: Staying Relaxed

THE SECOND DOOR:
CHUM KIU — CONSCIOUSLY CONNECT

Key theme: *How to build effective relationships with others.*

- Wisdom 3: Don't Force
- Wisdom 4: Positivity

THE THIRD DOOR: BIU JEE — SELF-REALIZATION

Key theme: *How to step into, and utilize, your innate power.*

- Wisdom 5: Simplicity
- Wisdom 6: Freedom and Responsibility
- Wisdom 7: Expect to Be Punched

THE FOURTH DOOR:
MUK YAN CHONG (WOODEN DUMMY) — BEYOND SELF

Key theme: *Understanding your wider connection to the world around you.*

- Wisdom 8: Mastery

The Gateway to Winning

Although we can't physically teach you the movements in this book, we will share the key concepts of each one. We will also give you illustrated examples to bring the physical aspect more to life, which in turn will help bring out the relevant learning and wisdoms.

So, what are these forms and how do they create 'doors' to development?

Every traditional martial art has 'forms' – an ordered series of movements and sequences which contain key techniques to help you learn, practise and improve your skills. Some martial arts have over a hundred forms, but Wing Tsun has only three forms and a quasi-form in the Wooden Dummy. It is through these forms that the Doors are structured and taught.

Not only are there relatively few techniques, but thanks to Wing Tsun's principle of 'simultaneity', one technique provides a multitude of different applications, teachings and wisdoms. Crucially, every physical technique also has a spiritual connotation. Masters of the Buddhist wisdom called this 'one method to open two doors', and this was adopted in Wing Tsun from the outset.

Although easy to ignore as an impractical 'nicety' for those seeking pure physical winning, the spiritual aspect of the form is far from a side effect. It provides the background, substance, tactics and strategy for winning. Each form is there to 'open doors' to your development – transporting you to new ways of how you view, engage and live in the world. Through a sequence of simple steps, each Door creates a paradigm shift for you, your perspective and your consciousness. Thus we speak about these forms being the 'Four Doors to enlightenment'.

That being said, Wing Tsun is not religious. It has no cult, no creed, and no code of conduct. Instead, it aims to free you from dogma.

Nothing in Wing Tsun is there by accident. Everything has meaning. Zen talks about 'doors to liberation' and 'doors of the senses'. The reason for Wing Tsun's four Doors is not just to teach the relevant martial skills, but also to reinforce the implicit meaning of the art. Taoism talks of the Four Cardinal Virtues, which enable you to know the truth of the universe. Buddhism teaches the Four Noble Truths. Indeed, the number four is itself significant and has several meanings, among them stability, grounding and security – exactly what you are looking for when you start your developmental journey, and essential when practising a martial art.

Finally, the wisdoms of each of these Doors involve physical, spiritual and well-being (health) aspects. Simply stated in Wing Tsun, in the maxim 'three levels, four Doors', this triad is a powerful combination, and one that reinforces success in all areas of your life.

The beautiful feature of these Wing Tsun Doors is that they teach you wisdom that is timeless but also relevant for you today. These Doors are a method for profound positive change in your life, and can be done on either an individual or group basis. You also don't need to be physically trained in Wing Tsun to pick up the wisdoms the forms contain. Indeed, it was this revelation that first led to the development of this book.

Finally, there are no barriers to entry with Wing Tsun. You can start incorporating it into your life now. It can teach you the courage, knowledge and self-belief that will enable you to start new roles, careers, businesses and relationships that work *for you*. Similarly, it will improve whatever role you are doing right now. To facilitate this, we have put simple action summaries at the end of each of the Doors and wisdoms.

Overview of the Four Doors

1. The four physical forms in Wing Tsun create the Four Doors. These will guide your self-development.
2. Each Door contains key wisdoms for success in life and business.
3. Each Door contains physical, spiritual and well-being aspects.
4. These wisdoms are immediately useable in your everyday life.

The (St)Art of War
By John

We need here to ask a fundamental question: if winning is not fighting, then how did fighting and war become the predominant metaphor for business?

Sometime in the early 1970s, the sixth-century BCE Chinese general Sun Tzu was sitting on a cloud in the big commander's tent in the sky when he received a telephone call. It was from his agent in Los Angeles, and it went something like this:

'Sun, baby, how's it goin'? I got great news. Did I say great? It's better than great! Some guys out here have started writing about your book. They've applied it to business and it's gonna be huge!'

'They've applied it to business . . . ?' Sun replied.* 'I don't understand. My book is about war.'

A Generalization

It turns out that the 'me as a general' metaphor I had created for myself was, although I had not realized it, a direct result of the work of American business scholars from the mid-1960s and early '70s.

The word 'strategy' itself comes directly from the Greek word *stratēgia*, meaning 'generalship' or 'pertaining to the general'. In 1962, Alfred Chandler published *Strategy and Structure*. An

---

* This is the Oliver Stone biopic version, so it is not historically accurate.

analysis of America's industrial multinationals, the chemical company DuPont among them, it was the first book to introduce the concept and the term 'strategy' into business. It was closely followed by Igor Ansoff's *Corporate Strategy* (1965), and Kenneth Andrews's *The Concept of Corporate Strategy* (1971). If you had asked in a meeting before the mid-1960s 'What is our strategy?', the reply would have been 'What is our what???'

All three writers served in World War Two, the conflict interrupting both Chandler's and Ansoff's postgraduate education. All three were influenced by the hierarchical organization and command structure of the American military. And the thinking they outline is so accepted in business today that we find it very difficult to imagine corporate rhetoric without it.

In fact, there has been such agreement that the ideas of generalship and war can be translated to life in business that this state of affairs has almost never been challenged since Chandler, Ansoff and Andrews introduced it. We talk today about price wars. Project headquarters are often called the 'war room' – including the office Amazon sets up each year to cope with the Christmas rush. Let's think about that: to celebrate the birth of Jesus, the bringer of peace, people buy lots of stuff; and because the company that sells them that stuff can't quite cope, they launch what they describe, without recognizing the irony, as a 'War on Chaos' and create what they of course describe as a WAR ROOM. Beautiful. Just what Jesus would have wanted.

It is only when you begin to question these constructs that you realize how strange they are. We differ from other animals in our ability to tell stories and to create metaphors. On the one hand, these provide us with maps that make some sense of the world, and help us to share knowledge. They are a shared lens, through which we can see the world. However, this lens is ultimately inadequate. It starts to shape and distort reality. A metaphor can create a new reality, so the more we style business as war, the more it will become so.

We hold 'Winning Not Fighting' workshops with the Leon restaurant managers and the support team, and part of the session involves covering flip charts in military analogies that are commonly used in business, such as:

- Let's divide and conquer
- Plan of attack
- Choose your battles
- We'll need more ammunition
- Smash your targets
- Let's keep our powder dry
- Annihilate the competition

You get the idea . . .

They have become the everyday way of describing what we do. As a general rule.

'War – Huah! – What is it Good For?'

We have become so hypnotized by the business-as-war metaphor that most of us are not even conscious of its effects. The business world and the Internet are so full of its adoring followers – many of them Sun Tzu fans – that I have often wondered whether I am the mad one. So, like all people in my position, I have sought to find others who share my contrarian views – Sir Lawrence Freedman, Emeritus Professor of War Studies at King's College, London, among them.

When I contacted him about the subject, he emailed back within the hour. And in one short sentence was confirmation I was not alone: 'The War metaphor is dodgy for business.'

Even before I met Sir Lawrence, his excellent book *Strategy: A History* made clear that he understood the spell that *The Art of War* has cast, and how the adoration for and adoption of its ideas accelerated during the 1980s, with a helping hand from popular culture. In *Strategy*, Freedman draws our attention to two powerful 'popular culture' references to Sun Tzu.

The first is the movie *Wall Street* (1987), in which *The Art of War* is the handbook by which the financier Gordon Gekko (of 'Greed is good' fame) conducts his working life. Gekko tells his younger associate Bud Fox, 'I don't throw darts at a board. I bet on sure things. Read Sun Tzu, *The Art of War*. Every battle is won before it is ever fought.'

Bud Fox later outfoxes Gekko (to protect the airline his blue-collar father works for from Gekko's asset-stripping), turning Gekko's own favourite book back on him: 'If your enemy is superior, evade him. If angry, irritate him. If equally matched, fight, and if not, split and re-evaluate.'

Meanwhile, in the TV series *The Sopranos*, Tony's shrink Dr Melfi advises him, with a slight sense of sarcasm, 'You want to be a better mob boss, read *The Art of War*.'

So he does. 'Been reading that – that book you told me about,' he says. 'You know, *The Art of War* by Sun Tzu. I mean here's this guy, a Chinese general, wrote this thing 2,400 years ago, and most of it still applies today! Baulk the enemy's power. Force him to reveal himself. Most of the guys that I know, they read Prince Machiavelli.'

As Freedman explains in his book:

Soprano claims to have found Machiavelli, whom he read in a study guide, no more than 'okay'. Sun Tzu, however, 'is much better about strategy.' As a result of Tony Soprano's endorsement, Sun Tzu became an Amazon bestseller in New Jersey.

Once war had been introduced into the business bloodstream, it was only a matter of time before people turned to Sun Tzu. Beyond war's appeal to our competitive instincts, Sun has much to say on stealth and deception. And this certainly spoke to the business and finance culture of the 1980s and '90s, where greed, cunning and subterfuge were all good.

But it is our fault, not Sun Tzu's, that we have adopted his book about war as a manual for how to do business.

Sun Tzu Wasn't Stupid

There is an emotional reason why Sun Tzu's work has gained a following. War appeals to the ego. To our fears and insecurities. To our desire to conquer. To the compensating mechanism of blaming others. And Sun Tzu appeals to people who like to think of themselves as cunning and clever and devious. The romanticized characters of Tony Soprano and Gordon Gekko are strong heroes (or anti-heroes) to many viewers, because they appeal to our inner (insecure) gangster and tycoon.

More substantively, however, Sun Tzu offers very good advice to the modern general – advice that, to paraphrase Tony Soprano, is just as relevant today as it was 2,400 years ago. Michael, Leon's head of food in Washington DC – who served in the US Navy and spent five years on submarines – explained at a recent workshop that *The Art of War* remains recommended reading across the US military.

You probably won't be surprised to hear that I think the use of the war metaphor in business is unnecessary – and, more than that, it's dangerous.

Since I began my training, I have been struck by how *The Art of War* is both consistent and inconsistent with the principles of Wing Tsun. And Julian and I have come to a simple conclusion that has only strengthened as we have tested it – *The Art of War* is consistent with the first two Doors of Wing Tsun and no more.

The opening sentences of *The Art of War* say: 'The Art of War is of vital importance to the state. It is a matter of life or death. A road either to safety or to ruin. Hence it is a subject of inquiry which can on no account be neglected.'

Embedded in this beginning and throughout the rest of the book is the presumption that war is a necessary extension of the political affairs of the state – a recurring recourse to violence when non-violent (at least in the physical sense) political problem-solving breaks down.

The Art of War is, by its very approach, about an enemy. About separateness. About beating 'them'. Wing Tsun, in contrast, is about self; about looking inward at what *we* are doing to create conflict. By the time we reach its Fourth Door, we learn to put aside the need to fight and realize that the only potential enemy we have is ourself.

This is not to say that *The Art of War* is without practical wisdom. But it is incomplete. By its very subject matter, it cannot go far down the path of Wing Tsun and of Taoist philosophy, and thus it never espouses their main message – that we can free ourselves from the need to fight, and in so doing discover a wholeness that connects us to the planet and each other. That rather than projecting anger or blame outwards, we must look within. Where Sun Tzu suggests that war is the presumed norm, Wing Tsun encourages us to rethink this.

And, of course, as a reminder: Sun Tzu's book is about war, NOT about your life or your company.

Where Sun Tzu and Wing Tsun Do Agree

Before I explain the dangers of applying Sun Tzu's teachings specifically – and the war metaphor more broadly – to business, let us take the first step and explore where there *is* shared thinking between *The Art of War* and Wing Tsun, and examine what is worth taking away from Sun Tzu's work. For it contains hard-fought wisdom from a general who learned about human frailty, the reality of war, the dangers of hubris and the need for strong character. The book contains a pragmatic wisdom, presented with a healthy lack of ego and foolhardiness, which is not always reflected in modern interpretations and uses.

The four wisdoms you will read about in our discussions of the first two Doors of Wing Tsun are Know Yourself, Staying Relaxed, Don't Force and Positivity. Each of these can also be found in Sun Tzu's teachings.

First, the armchair business warrior should understand that Sun Tzu warned against the dangers of prolonged war, and praised the general who obtains victory without bloodshed. Sun Tzu shares the belief inherent in the first two Doors of Wing Tsun (Siu Nim Tao and Chum Kiu) that a short battle is better than a lengthy battle, and no battle to defeat the enemy is better than a short battle.

The elements of Winning Not Fighting introduced in these first two Doors are most simply described in Sun Tzu with the single sentence: 'In war, then, let your great object be victory, not lengthy campaigns.'

Elsewhere, he writes: 'To fight and conquer in all your battles is not supreme excellence. Supreme excellence consists in breaking the enemy's resistance without fighting.' And:

The skilful leader subdues the enemy's troops without any fighting. He captures their cities without laying siege to them. He overthrows their kingdom without lengthy operations in the field . . . Without losing a man, his triumph will be complete.

Long wars deplete the resources of the state and wear down your troops. 'If you engage in actual fighting and the victory is long in coming, then men's weapons will grow dull and their ardour will be damped.' And: 'If the campaign is protracted, the resources of the state will not be equal to the strain.'

Second, Sun Tzu is firm on the need to know yourself, and know your enemy:

> If you know the enemy and know yourself, you need not fear the result of a hundred battles. If you know yourself and not the enemy, for every victory gained you will also suffer a defeat. If you know neither the enemy nor yourself, you will succumb in every battle.

Third, Sun Tzu warns – just as Wing Tsun does – of the danger of being driven by ego: 'A good general does not send his troops into battle to satisfy his own spleen.' In addition, Sun Tzu offers us five vices – manifestations of ego – that a good general must avoid at all costs: recklessness, cowardice, a hasty temper, delicacy of honour, and over-solicitude for his men.

And just like Wing Tsun, Sun Tzu warns against dancing on the enemy's grave – of celebrating their defeat. If you have beaten an enemy and killed many combatants, do not gloat. Do not brag. Do not fly a big banner reading 'MISSION ACCOMPLISHED' even as your forces continue to take casualties. Take a moment to remember the dead on both sides. 'Those who celebrate victory are bloodthirsty and the bloodthirsty cannot have their way in the world.'

The fourth area where Wing Tsun and Sun Tzu agree is the need to not force. Just as Wing Tsun and Taoism use water as a metaphor (we'll get to that), *The Art of War* uses water to describe how a good leader is 'in flow' and how they avoid the trap of 'forcing'.

Sun Tzu advises the general to take the easy road that makes his victories look easy – which, ironically, will bring him no lasting fame. He must give up the spoils of his success. 'A clever fighter not only wins but wins with ease. Hence his victories bring him no reputation for wisdom nor credit for courage.' He also explains the need for patience:

> The good fighters of old first put themselves beyond the possibility of defeat. And then waited for an opportunity to defeat the enemy. To secure ourselves against defeat lies in our own hands, but the opportunity of defeating the enemy is provided by the enemy himself.

Thus the good fighter is able to adapt to circumstance.

This need for fluidity is inherent in my favourite statement by a more modern general, Dwight Eisenhower: 'Plans are useless but planning is essential.' And you may well have heard the related wisdom from the Prussian general Helmuth von Moltke: 'No plan survives contact with the enemy.'

Sun Tzu concurs. He is clear on the need for preparation ('The general who loses a battle makes few calculations beforehand'), but equally clear on the need to be flexible and fluid once the conflict has begun: 'Water contains no constant shape. There are no constant conditions in war. They are always changing. Water takes the easiest route . . . according to the ground over which it flows.'

This is why, at Leon, I am keen on scenario-planning but less keen on having prescribed dogmatic and rigid plans – or single scenarios – that the organization *must* stick to. But I don't describe all this planning as preparation for war. Mostly because it is not.

Where's the Harm?

The writers who adopted *The Art of War* as a valid methodology for business, and the ardent theorists and practitioners who followed, looked at a few superficial familiarities in Sun Tzu's text and thought, *Yep, that fits.* War and business have objectives; in war they have resource allocation, they have tactics, and they have leaders. And competitors can pass very easily for 'enemies'. Looks like a match, right?

Not necessarily. And it is certainly worth a second opinion.

Because at no stage did Sun Tzu suggest that he was writing about anything other than war. He made no intimation that his book be a guide for how to live, work or start a business – nor how to get along as a family or as teammates, or how to be a farmer, CEO, entrepreneur or doctor. It is us who choose to use it as such.

It is not his fault that modern business commentators have tried to apply his thinking to business.

At the most simple level – and I am sorry to have to break it to all the lovers of war metaphors out there – if you are the CEO of a business, you are not fighting a war. You are *not* a general. (It was a shock to me too, and you may need to take some time to get over it.)

Worse still, business has made war an ongoing activity that drives every annual plan and every quarterly plan to the point that it becomes a constant mindset. And yet, even in *The Art of War*, war is described as an activity of last resort with dire consequences. So, if even Sun Tzu saw war as occasional, what metaphor is the CEO supposed to use between business 'wars'? Does she or he go beyond even Sun Tzu and make war the everyday activity? That is certainly what seems to happen in most businesses today.

It begs a lot of questions: how do they know when they are at 'war' or not? How are they supposed to act when they decide they are *not* at war? Should they sit in their metaphorical barracks and have ceremonial dinners? Or play metaphorical polo? Or clean their metaphorical uniforms and polish their metaphorical medals?

I ask in all seriousness, if even in *The Art of War* battles should be rare, then what is the business person supposed to do in business when they are not metaphorically fighting? How can it be that a business bases its entire annual cycle and everyday mindset on war when a) it is not at war and b) even Sun Tzu's advice was to avoid fighting (or if that fails, then to fight very occasionally and for as short a time as possible)?

And even if you win the 'war' – what then? Do you seek another? Are you sure you know what you wanted in the first place?

And how did businesses thrive before the adoption of the war metaphor, in the 1960s? The answer is actually: *very well, thank you.*

Beyond its high level of inconsistency, at Leon we have come to the firm belief that not only does the business-as-war metaphor have severe limitations, it also has extremely dangerous consequences – and not just for businesses and the people who work there, but for society as a whole.

But let's begin with the negative impact on the long-term health of the company.

You've Only Gone and Shot the Customer – How War is 'Dodgy' for a Company

In war, where is the customer? One's focus is on killing the enemy. And the idea of fighting and beating an enemy focuses energy outwards, not inwards.

Does the quite crucial lack of a customer in war explain why, through some strange Shakespearean mix-up, we end up equating the customer with the enemy and 'targeting' them? Is it really a good idea to 'target' the people we serve? (*Hey, Sally, what's that red dot on your forehead?*)

Instead of focusing on the customer, a lot of businesses dissipate their energy by fixating on the competition. Now, we're not saying that having a peripheral view of what the competition is up to isn't helpful. But the competition should not be the constant focus of a business's effort, as it is in war.

At Leon, we seek constantly to innovate our menu. And in doing so, we are never inspired by the competition. At the same time, the actions of other companies in our industry make it very clear that they are focused on us. We created the category of 'good fast food'; we were the first to serve halloumi wraps, porridge, egg pots and triple-certified coffee (organic, Fairtrade and World Land Trust); we created the superfood salad which is now everywhere; and the Leon breakfast menu has inspired many Leon lookalikes.

One of my (excellent) board members, Rodrigo Boscolo, once said to me: 'I feel like Leon's is at its best when we stay true to our purpose and focus on making tasty healthy food accessible to everyone. Focusing on this means our energy is directed towards the customer (what do they want, what is the right price, how fast can we be, etc.) and not against competitors (we don't care that much about what they do, so we're not "fighting" them). To serve the customer, by definition we need to connect to them; to innovate, we need to put aside fear and ego, to allow ourselves to try many things, fail and try again (recognizing that we don't always have the answer . . .).'

In making this simple case, Rodrigo is in accord with Peter Drucker, who said quite simply: 'The purpose of a business is to create a customer.'

By focusing on the enemy, or the competition, a company's leadership is failing at one of the most important requirements of a healthy and successful organization: a sense of responsibility. If we are fighting a war – and competitors' actions – funding and luck have such an impact on our success that we can too readily blame the competition for what happens to us. Annual reports which pin results on the fact that 'the competition have been particularly aggressive' should be read with some care.

Kind and Concerned, or Devious and Cunning?

The company who sees itself as fighting a war (i.e. most companies, in my experience) creates a hypocritical culture with a confused sense of identity. To the customers, they must project a friendly 'Hey, we're nice guys, come buy our products' culture. Meanwhile, back at the office, they are pouring efforts into crushing the competition with the ultimate aim of putting them out of business. Then their customers will no longer have any choice, and will be forced to buy from the company out of necessity.

I would not like to invest in or be led by a CEO who is attracted to the perceived cunning of *The Art of War*. How would you ever know where you stood? How closely would you have to read the contracts for all possible future interpretations? How could you entrust the company's – or the world's – precious resources to them?

Wing Tsun, on the other hand, teaches openness and not cunning.

I contrast the temptation to be devious shared by many business people with the traditional 'Midwest' industrial and corporate approach typified by people like my friend Brad, who spent the formative years of his business career at General Mills and Darden Restaurants. This is a business where the long term mattered; where relationships and trust mattered; where the quality of the product and the welfare of people mattered. And this is an approach that allows a business to prosper in a broader community.

The Sacred Feminine (It's a Thing)

It is very rare to find a female CEO or businesswoman who uses *The Art of War* as her guiding philosophy (despite the publication of *The Art of War for Women*). In contemplating this chapter I have asked myself whether the adoption of militaristic and aggressive thinking engenders a hard and arguably masculine culture that women can find instinctively dubious. This of course raises more questions about what constitutes masculine and feminine energy, about whether any differences are based on nature and/or nurture – but the fact that these questions are complex should not prevent us from having the conversation. We know that, on the one hand, there are innate differences between male and female energy. We know that such natural differences are important to understand. (Kirsty, who was Leon brand and marketing director, has studied how, for example, medical research and medicine have failed to recognize that women present different symptoms when having a heart attack.) And we know, too, that we need to question whether the way we raise our children creates differences that are not inherent in nature. In researching the mostly fanatical support for Sun Tzu and the war metaphor, I read a comment on one website that said 'a female student in my MBA class questioned the war metaphor'. The comments that followed pitied the 'wet and naive people' who don't realize that business truly is war.

And it can be subtle too. Consider a statement made by someone who runs an investment company that owns many well-known coffee brands and coffee shops. When explaining that his job is to find challenges for his young (seemingly male?) executives, he phrased it thus: 'There were all these young guys with the knife between their teeth, and ready to fight the next war.' Is this really the energy that is compatible with your favourite little coffee house?

We are making business a place that is more about fighting than it is about nurturing – or what the East might call the 'Sacred Feminine'. We need to let her in.

Carl Jung concluded that we achieve a psychological harmony ('psychic totality') over our lifetime by balancing our female and male energies. As such, female energy is not seen as the preserve of women – any more than male energy is the preserve of men. Notwithstanding this, we need to create an environment in which the number and prevalence of female role models increase – for the benefit of men as well as women.

I was recently looking at the life of one male UK politician and was struck by the paucity of female role models in his life. Boarding school from ages 7 to 18, with almost exclusively male schoolmasters, followed by a career in a male-dominated bank.

I myself have been particularly lucky to have had a large number of female role models. Although I ended up at a private school in North London, my first school was a 1970s state school full of brilliant and interesting women teachers. They included Miss Kirk, my teacher from the key ages of 5 to 7 (who had to cope with my inability to sit still); Miss Bland (who let me take her rather attractive daughter Holly to see *ET* – with Holly's brothers sitting in the row behind us); and Miss Harper, who taught me maths as well as anyone ever did. Thank you, all of you.

In business, too, I have been shaped by many female role models. At P&G, in the early 1990s, there were a number of senior women who served as role models for all of us, not just the women graduates. Karen Higgins, who latterly has become versed in shamanic teaching, was a very popular and extremely effective sales director; and the marketing director, Ann Franke, led her department with flair. And at Bain, the global chair was Orit Gadiesh – famous for her wisdom and memorable sound bites.

Compare this with the experience of my wife, Katie, who was told by the accounting firm where she was doing work experience that she would be welcome to join but had to understand that partnership was not something that the firm's female employees could aspire to.

There are still far too few women in most businesses. And even if women fill the graduate ranks of a company, there is a big reduction when some women have children. Rightly, much has been spoken of the practical support that women need after childbirth: maternity leave, paternity leave to allow their partner to share the childcare or more support to leave their job to take the lead in childcare, flexible working hours, at-work crèches. But I believe that focusing solely on these practical challenges masks another big reason for the problem: the energy created by businesses acting as if they are fighting a war, which results in an energy and culture that many mothers have told me they have come to instinctively reject.

Why? Here are some clues. My daughter Natasha helped direct and choreograph a musical at her old school. Helping make costumes was a retired detective sergeant who had served in the Met Police – Heather Rook – and she would captivate Natasha with stories from the front line. DS Rook had, it seemed, been involved in most of the notable events in the last 30 years of the Met Police – she had among other things found and arrested the Croydon riots arsonist and the perpetrators of the Millennium Dome robbery.

She had also been one of the first women in the force (if not *the* first) to be given a firearm. She came top in her firearms course, but the (male) head trainer pulled her aside to tell her that in private – because he didn't want the men to know in case it became an issue for them. Are you thinking *WTF??* I am.

But here's the rub: after having her child, Heather decided to turn her firearm in. 'Something changed,' she said. 'I didn't want to take a life. It could be someone's child. I struggled with that.'

While an extreme example, female colleagues tell me they have experienced similar responses after having children. Something changes, they explain. And perhaps this is something that many feel without being able to articulate it precisely to themselves.

The people who represent our financial investors are mostly male, but I have sought the outside counsel and input from as many women as I can in building the Leon culture, in addition to that of the many women who help run Leon internally. Aside from the female role models I had at school and in my first job, I talked at the start of this book about the role that Wendy Mandy has played in my journey of personal and professional discovery, and how – thanks to Wendy – Aimée was an important part of that at a key moment too.

Wendy, and someone called Donna who you will meet a bit later, have been key influences on our culture at Leon. As was of course Allegra, as a co-founder. And in the last seven years Jane Melvin, who has held senior roles at Starbucks, Olive Garden and elsewhere, has been a huge influence. I hope, and believe, that the energy we have all created is one where women flourish after starting a family.

Not by any design, as I type this, exactly 50 per cent of our restaurant managers are female. And the majority of the senior team (known as the Pirates of the Med after a memorable boat trip to Greece) are women: the directors of operations, food, marketing, people, purchasing, commercial and UK operations support. And Leon as a total company has a 0.0 per cent – i.e. zero – gender pay gap.

Perhaps one day soon one – or many – of these Leon women will write about their experiences and insights. My two favourite business writers, James 'Jimmy' Allen (and co-author Chris Zook) and Jim Collins, are male, as well as both being Jims. The fact is that of the published business writers, many more are male than female – Jeff Haden makes the point in a great *Inc.* magazine article and hands over to Rachel Happe, co-founder of a company called Community Roundtable, to share a list of business books written by women. Happe compiled the list, with the help of those who contacted her, after Richard Branson produced a list of recommended business books that was notable for its lack of women authors. It is worth looking at the article and the list for inspiration. Seek '60 Great Business and Leadership Books, All Written by Women', and you will find.

Change has not happened quickly in the last half-century. As with most of us, the first woman I came into contact with was my mum, Marion. Marion has been a consistent source of love, inspiration and support not only for me but also for the thousands of children she has taught. Mum began her career at a company called the School Travel Service in North London. She led a team of four brilliant women, two of whom, Corrine and Glenys, became her bridesmaids.

'It was a great team. We organized hundreds of school trips a year and had to be on top of every detail. We worked hard and laughed a lot. It was a time when women were being given opportunities and we were taking them.'

Later, Mum became a teacher, and she still teaches now at the age of 82. (When her own mum, Edith, went to her employers in North London in 1972 to explain that she was retiring, they said, 'Ooh Edith, congratulations on being sixty!' She replied: 'Thank you, but I am seventy-two.')

I recently spoke to Mum about the progress that is being made, or not being made. She told me that, given the hopes that had existed in the 1960s – while she and her colleagues were working at the School Travel Service – she would have expected and hoped that 60 years later things would be in better shape. But Mum does not allow it to bring her down. 'I am still hopeful,' she explained. But we owe it to ourselves, and to future generations, to increase the pace of change.

So, Mum, how can I help? And how can Wing Tsun, the only martial art created by women, help? Perhaps we can begin right here, in this chapter, by recognizing that the war metaphor has a dangerous grip on our minds and therefore on our reality. And by asking whether this is contributing to the unhealthy overall representation of women in business – and therefore causing great harm, for individuals and for society, resulting in great economic cost and grave waste of human talent.

Bye-Bye to the Future

A business that is fighting a war in its mind will inherently focus on the short-term outcome and compromise on the future. After all, war is a 'do or die' fight to the death, where long-term considerations are put to one side.

This mindset encourages destructive, short-term decisions

that compromise the long-term health of the company. It puts the company off balance. In our sector, this is characterized by short-term cost-cutting and asset-stripping (see the ownership of Romano's Macaroni Grill in the US by Golden Gate Capital) or overly rapid store roll-out (of brands like Gourmet Burger Kitchen in the UK).

When a company chases short-term outcomes and aims to please the reactive metrics of the stock market, it will take short-cuts that will not help to build its capabilities for the long term.

Winner Loses All

The proponents of using war as the guiding idea for commerce fail to appreciate that the nature of war is such that the 'winner' often loses. Remember Sun Tzu's words: 'If the campaign is pro-tracted, the resources of the state will not be equal to the strain.' And think of the toll of World War Two on Britain, which meant that the country was severely economically weakened.

So we must ask: what does it cost a business to engage in 'war' incessantly?

Both the US and the UK provide examples of business leaders who have built businesses on aggression that have not stood the test of time. Karma always catches up with these people in the end.

And the long-term success of businesses built by communities opposed to war – such as the Quakers or Methodists – shows that a warlike approach is not a requirement. Think of Quaker Oats and Cadbury's chocolate, to name but two. Or Rowntree's, whose former CEO and owner Joseph Rowntree said at the begin-ning of the twentieth century: 'The real goal for an employer is to try to seek for others the fullest life of which an individual is capable.'

Narrow Vision

In a state of constant war, creativity and empathy suffer too. Our fight-or-flight instinct – our natural response to aggression – shuts down our peripheral vision. While necessity can be the mother of some types of invention, people tend to be far more creative (and aware of other people's feelings and views) when they are in a more relaxed state.

In war, our egos lead us to believe that we must and can control our situation and our environment. Plans become rigid and controlling, and less adaptable. Wing Tsun, in contrast, has taught me to become much more fluid in my management of Leon, and much more realistic about what I can and can't control.

As a result, I am much less surprised when things happen that I did not foresee. I have let go the war mindset and the subconscious bias to dominate or control that stems from it. As you progress through the stages of Wing Tsun the 'martial art', you will experience less 'martial' and more 'art'. You will increasingly stop trying to control the uncontrollable. And you will also become less angry and less surprised when you fail. Wing Tsun teaches that being responsible for your success is not the same as being able to control your current or future environment.

Command and Control

Another consequence of the warlike mindset in business is that it reinforces a top-down command and control management structure that slows down decision-making and stifles creativity. Or worse.

A friend of mine, who used to run a store for a clothes and food retailer, once told me: 'When the senior executives visited my store, it was like the top brass were visiting. Everything had been prepared for their visit, and I was warned by my own regional managers not to speak the truth or tell the top bosses what I really felt. It was a culture borrowed straight from the military. It meant they saw a fantasy world; that they did not hear the truth; and that good ideas were not fostered.' I am sure that even at Leon we are not immune from this.

As we will explore in the Third Door of Wing Tsun – Biu Jee – this kind of culture is influenced by an overemphasis of the rigid structures of Confucianism, and is contrary to the more free and fluid principles of Taoism that we at Leon seek to follow instead.

A bellicose approach to business throws up other consequences, as well. For instance, in 'war', how do we decide who is friend or foe? Is your supplier someone to 'beat up' on pricing (you hear buyers talk like this all the time) or an 'ally' to cosy up to?

If you own a consumer product brand, how do you propose to deal with your retailers? Are you going to 'fight them for every bit of margin you can get' or are you going to treat them as a partner with whom you'll delight the customer? In the UK the biggest supermarket in the 1990s and beyond built itself on very aggressive buying practices. But forcing, as we will discover, does not last. They are still repairing the impact this rightly had on their reputation.

The People Suffer

There are not many dissenting voices on all the comment pages that accompany the many articles and blogs lauding *The Art of War* and its seemingly unchallenged place in corporate life. However, I recently found an online comment from a retired US Army major that said: 'People who say that business is like war clearly have never been to war.'

War has a human cost. If the adoption of the war metaphor

hurts companies, as we have seen, we must also consider its impact on the people who work at those companies.

You know – real humans.

To commemorate the 100th anniversary of the end of World War One, the Imperial War Museum (IWM) commissioned the documentary *They Shall Not Grow Old*, which took hundreds of hours of footage from the IWM archives, colourized it to make it more accessible and vivid for the viewer, and overlaid it with audio of the first-person accounts of survivors recorded a few years after the war. Watch it and ask yourself this question: do you *really* want business to be like war?

Alternatively, you could speak to a veteran.

In war, both the winners and the losers suffer. And yet I often hear CEOs talk about the need to 'create a war to motivate the team'. This is like a monarch going to war against an 'enemy' to maintain control over – and the loyalty of – their people. It doesn't take the people into account.

So before we choose to make business *like* war, or argue that it *is* war, let us consider the effects – and take our *people* into account.

War doesn't sleep. People need to. And yet we are expected to function in a culture of relentless emails and work WhatsApp groups. In phases where I lose my discipline, the last thing I do before going to sleep – and the first thing I do upon waking – is check my messages or sales results on the phone that I keep on my bedside table. That's not good, is it? It's certainly not healthy.

Work in the twenty-first century is becoming more unhealthy and more inflammatory – not less. In Japan, 'overwork' is an officially recognized cause of death. That is to be expected, isn't it? Because business is war, right?

Regardless of the fact that we have sought to banish the war metaphor at Leon, the company exists in a difficult and operationally intense industry. Leon has big aspirations, it is at a critical stage of its growth, and it lives in a country that has burdened the restaurant industry with huge costs. The number-one area of well-being that our people score themselves lowest on is being 'relaxed and free from stress'. Imagine what it would be like if we talked all the time of war? Or didn't invest so heavily in our employees' well-being?

We get the leaders we deserve – so let's tell our leaders, in business and politics, that we can find reasons other than war to get excited. Like sex and hugs and rock 'n' roll.

While the Planet Suffers

Lao Tzu says in the *Tao Te Ching*: 'A land ravaged by war is a place where only brambles grow.' In war, we use landmines, napalm, depleted uranium and nuclear weapons, and have adopted scorched-earth policies. Not one of these is good for our environment.

So how will a business treat the planet when it adopts the framework of war? Is it any surprise that, in destroying their competitors, such businesses are destroying the environment too? Do we intend to do to our competitors, their people and the planet what the Allies did to Dresden?

A recent World Wildlife Fund report stated that 60 per cent by total mass of birds, mammals, fish and reptiles have been wiped out by humanity since 1970. Whether or not we can lay this at the door of the business-as-war metaphor is a matter for debate, but what we can say is that this statistic shows bluntly how destructive our species is when we go for short-term 'wins'.

If 60 per cent of your village had been eaten by lions, you'd be damned sure that you were going to do something about it. But the destruction isn't being done by lions. It's being done by us. And we have to take responsibility for our own actions. By not looking after the planet for future generations, we are committing 'generational theft'.

Recently, I was asked by the government to create a new organization called the Council for Sustainable Business. It exists to help the UK Government and business sector to support the (at time of writing) current administration's 25 Year Environment Plan, which was published in 2018.

One of the plan's fundamental principles is based on the concept of 'natural capital'. A business today does not have to formally account for its depletion of our shared natural resources. If a company uses up old barrels of whisky, or uses a machine in a factory, by accounting rules it has to record annually the cost of using or depreciating these assets. But the destruction or use of natural resources is 'free'. Thus the economic model that we have created – or rather, the means by which we measure economic success – does not take into account the fact that we are dependent on the planet to create value.

Businesses must start to account in financial terms for such 'externalities': their use of resources not directly owned by the company, like shared natural assets such as water; or the destruction of natural habitats and ecosystems, or the pollution of air or the oceans. But at the same time this means that they can tell their customers and the communities they are part of about any positive contributions they are making to the common good – for example, replanting rainforests or supporting new habitats and biodiversity.

In this way, the net impact a company makes on nature and the common natural assets we all share will become a core part of doing business. My hope – and I am not alone in this – is that when businesses account as best they can for the impact they have on these precious natural resources, then customers, employees, investment funds and the people who fund them with their pension contributions will start rewarding businesses that make environmentally sound decisions.

Of course, ultimately, nature cannot be 'bought'. We can't swap our planet for a thousand trillion dollars and sit on the money. But not putting any value on the planet or on the ecological impact of certain actions doesn't seem to be going that well either. So, although the methodology will never be perfect, we nevertheless need to do our best to show in financial terms the ecological impact that each business has.

There are people and movements arguing that it is time to replace capitalism. Until they have a viable alternative to offer, we must begin by creating capitalism incorporating both a conscious agency and an accounting framework that acknowledges the basic truth: that this planet and its resources are all we have.

Proper accounting plus mindful leadership will lead to better decisions.

But as long as businesses think of themselves as at war, with all the focus on the short term which that involves, we will continue to compromise the planet. And that won't be good, cos we won't have anywhere to put all our stuff.

Beyond Business – the Contaminating Effects Elsewhere

We live in a world where we have a 'War on Terror', a 'War on Drugs', a 'War on Crime' . . . The metaphor of war has not just impacted business – it has polluted many elements of our society.

When Henry and I were developing the School Food Plan, which set out to improve school food and schoolchildren's diets throughout UK state schools, we presented a solution to a minister whose response was: 'Brilliant. We can use this fact to kill the opposition's plans.' I had to remind this person that our goal was to feed children better, not to be engaged in a sideshow of petty conflict.

Many things about our society have become based on fear. School league tables have resulted in head teachers and teachers living in a state of perpetual fear, which they are passing on to their students. Lessons have become about outcome. And outcome is not necessarily the joy of curiosity and learning. Outcome is more often success in exams. So the focus of the curriculum is not on widening the eyes of students, but on coaching them on exam tactics and the specifics of the mark scheme.

I created Leon's purpose to be about the 'now' – to be about the present. This is fundamentally different from chasing short-term rewards for your shareholders and from defining one's business purpose as achieving a far-off goal. It shifts our purpose, allowing our future to take care of itself while we focus on the one thing we can actually change – the present moment and our practice within it – all of which we will explore when we reach the Fourth Door of Wing Tsun and the practice of Mastery.

The Leon purpose – to nourish people's journey towards wholeness every day – is something that we can do *today*. These are not the words we use in advertising but they are understood internally to mean that we recognize that we are here to help people with their most fundamental urge – to understand and reconnect with themselves, with others and with nature. We often simplify this as 'Make it easier for everyone to live and eat well today' or at other times '. . . to feed the human spirit'. Those are present-moment activities and practices that at the same time enrich the future. We are not putting off happiness or contentment. We are creating them now.

Alternative Metaphors

Those who advocate using *The Art of War* as a guide to business argue that it fits so well because it considers leadership, deployment of scarce resources, decision-making, context, etc. But all these facets can be found in other areas of life and nature too. Be it farming or sailing, not only do they fit better, but they do so without the downsides, and they offer a framework in which businesses and people can thrive.

In our training courses on Wing Tsun and Winning Not Fighting, Julian and I invite people to offer up and discuss alternative metaphors for how we might think about business more broadly and their own company specifically. We explore the validity of sporting metaphors, and discuss whether they are just gentler formulations of the war metaphor. (We also acknowledge that it takes time to shake off the instinctive use of the war metaphor, so ingrained is it in most of us.) We talk about conducting, jazz bands and space missions. But it is nature metaphors that keep recurring most.

They fall into four areas:

1. Animals
2. Family
3. Water
4. Gardens and trees

Before I share these in a little more detail, I would like to tell you the story of a woman who was given a seemingly impossible task.

It involves cute animals. Bear with me.

Squirrel, Beaver, Goose

When we say that someone is 'gung-ho', we generally mean they are too enthusiastic or overzealous. The term, however, is an anglicization of the Chinese *gong he*, which means, literally, 'to work together'.

In their book *Gung Ho!*, Ken Blanchard and Sheldon Bowles answer one of the most complicated questions of them all: how can you get the best out of your people? How can you make them more productive and more profitable?

Blanchard and Bowles say that the best way to increase output is to motivate your people. And the best way to do that is to watch the habits of three animals. And then they tell this story . . .

Peggy is tasked with turning around a failing factory. The task seems impossible until she notices one department outperforming all the rest by far. Peggy befriends the manager of this department, a Native American called Andy.

When Peggy asks Andy about his secret to success, he takes her into the forest to watch nature at work. He explains to her that he follows the philosophy of his grandfather, which is based on the Spirit of the Squirrel, the Way of the Beaver and the Gift of the Goose.

In the autumn, squirrels are busy all around the world, rushing about collecting acorns in preparation for the winter ahead. The squirrels know their goal. Without these acorns, they will not survive the winter, so the work they are doing could not be more worthwhile.

Knowing the value of your contribution as well as its wider purpose brings a level of motivation that cannot be faked. If everyone understands how their job fits into the big picture and how it helps to achieve a common goal, self-esteem will skyrocket and your team will work together without effort.

Meanwhile, from the beavers, we can learn how to let go as a manager. When beavers build a dam, there is no Boss Beaver telling all the others how to swim, or where to place branches. Each beaver can decide for itself how and where it will contribute.

As a manager, after setting up the goalposts and drawing out the pitch, you need to get off that pitch and set your teams free to operate based on their own best judgement. This breeds confidence and self-reliance among your people.

And finally, while all this is going on – goals and purposes being set; teams free to achieve their targets – keep an eye out for the good news. Whether a big win or a small achievement, everything deserves big and heartfelt congratulations. This is the Gift of the Goose.

When geese fly south for the winter in a V formation, they honk all the way. They honk when they take off, when they fly, and when they land. They honk because they are working together and want to encourage the 'leader', who is currently taking the brunt of the wind at the front. They are cheering each other on with a big bag of noisy joy.

Sometimes, modern humans find teamwork tricky. But nature shows us how to do it effortlessly, day in and day out. These three principles will make everyone feel confident in their role – valued, fulfilled and (hopefully) happy.

I successfully used this simple and naturally inspired approach in September 2017. Our industry had just suffered a very difficult summer, following a slowdown in consumer confidence and a rise in fears resulting from the terror attacks in London. But no company that has a healthy culture likes to blame external events for its own results. We set about taking things into our own hands.

Instead of launching a range of 'strategic initiatives', I set the company one simple challenge: to achieve positive like-for-likes (a growth in same-restaurant sales* as compared to the previous year) on my birthday. In the Spirit of the Squirrel, everyone knew the goal.

I then gave each department and each restaurant full freedom to choose how they would approach it (the Way of the Beaver), while cheering them on from the sidelines (the Gift of the Goose) as they did so.

Restaurants did whatever they thought might work. They put hosts at the front to bring in customers. They spent the day before giving out vouchers for people to come back the next day. They focused local marketing on local offices. The central marketing team did a promotion for our club members. And all of the people in the Leon support team went out into their 'buddy'

---

* This describes the sales growth of all restaurants that existed the previous year, so all our sites excluding the new ones.

restaurants (that they had been twinned with) to help clean the tables and to generally provide extra labour and support. Everybody focused on one very clear outcome, and provided their own ideas and hard work to make it happen.

We achieved our specific goal (the sales we achieved that day set a new Leon record) but the impact went way beyond this. It gave the teams a new confidence, and a suite of tools that they could use again and again in the coming days, weeks and months.

Families

Families – the basic unit of human existence – allow humankind to survive and thrive. They exist continuously, in times of peace and war, and demonstrate the power of love, nurturing, teamwork, freedom and responsibility, and of learning and adaption. They are just as powerful a metaphor as that of war.

And family is a comparison that is very much part of the Leon culture – Leon managers are called 'Mums' and 'Dads', and to those on the inside it feels natural – though I am conscious of not overplaying this metaphor or making Leon sound like a cult.

Water

Water will be a recurring theme in this book, as it is in all forms of thought influenced by Taoism and Zen Buddhism. But groups in Leon workshops come to the conclusion that it is a useful metaphor, because of its clear intent to get to the sea, its ability to adapt as it flows around objects, and its lack of ego and readiness to be as low as the sea.

Water overcomes hard things through softness. It can morph between solid, liquid and gas without changing its fundamental essence – its transparency. And it is essential to all life, sustaining and serving the earth's plants and animals as it flows. It is always constant, and yet – as the saying goes – you will never walk in the same river twice. It offers a metaphor for how a company must stay constant even as people in it change or move.

Be it a drip or a tsunami, water will always effect change.

Gardens and Trees

The CEO who lives the principles of Winning Not Fighting will find much to apply in the metaphor of the garden. A gardener recognizes that it is not she or he who grows the plants, but the plants themselves. Yet there is still a role for the gardener – to select the plants, to provide them with an environment in which to flourish, to provide water and nutrients. I am sure you can add to this yourself.

At the management consultancy Bain & Company, where Henry and I worked in our pre-Leon days – and where we met – the principal construct for describing strategy required the CEO to identify 'battlefields'. (The company even created a set of slides showing how one could use the Gulf War as a model to explain strategy.) But just as powerful as choosing which 'theatres of war' to fight in, if not more so, is the idea of choosing where in the garden to plant the seed, given the light, humidity, type of soil and any neighbouring plants.

At Leon, we often use the metaphor of a tree – an image that has a particular recurring significance in my own life. In this example, we'll be using an oak tree.

The acorn has within it a very clear intention. It knows its job is to grow into a big oak tree – just as any good business ought to know what it is and what it intends to be. The oak tree has a longevity far beyond any battle or war. It lasts for a century or more, and it sees many seasons and many cycles. Its roots provide a strong base, and are adept at finding the sustenance it needs to grow – the water and nutrients in the soil that can be readily equated with money and 'human capital' (aka people).

In *Great by Choice*, Jim Collins shows the power and importance of sustaining steady growth rather than expanding in fits and starts. And although a tree does not grow at exactly the same rate (no company does either), the rings on an oak tree show that its growth is – within a reasonable range – consistent.

The tree provides a visual symbol too, for how good businesses grow. From a strong core – the trunk – and then outward into closely related branches, or what businesses have come to call 'close adjacencies'.* CEOs who have leapt into businesses without a strong core could do well to pin a photo of an oak tree onto their wall.

Unlike war, trees are a metaphor that encompasses customers and shareholders and society more broadly. A tree produces fruit or acorns or seeds that feed the particular fauna in its environment. And it produces oxygen that sustains all life. It lives sustainably (until humans come along and chop it down) within an ecosystem, thanks to its symbiotic relationship with animals and plants and other trees in the forest. Trees positively influence the weather – heat, cold, rainfall and humidity. And, crucially, trees cooperate and communicate. They tell each other where the best water and soil is, and they have Snapchat.

Okay, that last bit isn't true. But read Peter Wohlleben's *The Hidden Life of Trees* and you will discover things that are just as surprising.

Minimizers, Maximizers and Mindsets

Newly appointed Leon restaurant managers attend a two-day workshop where, among other things, we offer people an opportunity to learn to know themselves. To go through the First Door of Wing Tsun.

---

* Sectors, or areas of business, in which a company is likely to prosper because of the capabilities it has already developed at its core.

The first exercise we do aims to understand whether they are a Maximizer or Minimizer, and what that means for them and those around them. A Maximizer is somebody who, when under stress, exerts energy outwards; a Minimizer is somebody who draws their energy inwards.

Once everyone has identified their predominant reaction, they split into the two groups. And then they are invited to discuss the pros and cons of being a Maxi or a Mini, listing all the things that annoy them about having to work with their opposite types, and answering the question 'What would Leon be like if it were just run by Maximizers or Minimizers?'

Maximizers tend to let you know how they're feeling. They may appear aggressive, and exaggerate their feelings and, most of the time, their needs. They can act impulsively – taking action without too much planning and adjusting quickly when they hit obstacles. They may not finish all projects they start, and may depend on others to do so.

Minimizers can appear passive-aggressive, and often withhold their feelings and thoughts, sharing little of their inner world. They will plan before acting. They are slower to begin, but the job is likely to get done. They are compulsive rather than impulsive.

Minimizers consider Maximizers rash and foolhardy. Maximizers consider Minimizers broody and even dishonest. A Maximizer will blow up and then quickly get over it. They'll say, 'The argument finished five minutes ago, why are you still in a bad mood, Mr Grumpy Pants?'

In the most recent workshop, having just written the previous section about alternative metaphors, it suddenly struck me that these two groups would most likely each choose a different metaphor. So I tested my thinking and asked them.

And to a person, they each chose the metaphor I thought they would. The Maximizers chose the metaphor of water – beginning right away, with the intent of reaching the sea but with no fixed plan of how to do it, flowing or raging round or over boulders on its way downhill. The Minimizers chose the metaphor of the oak tree. Deep intent within the acorn, taking time to appear above the top of the soil, setting firm roots, preferring the comfort of staying in one place and growing steadily rather than constantly adjusting.

Both the tree (in the form of the Tree of Life) and the watercourse play an important role in our inherited memory, but we will come to this later, in the chapter on Know Yourself.

As you would expect, the Maxi/Mini exercise reveals that we need both types of people. Most marriages or partnerships have one Maxi and one Mini. Where there is a Maxi–Maxi or Mini–Mini relationship, it can last, but these combinations come with challenges: fiery burnout or simmering, unspoken resentment, respectively.

Trees and water, Minis and Maxis – we need each other. In the Lake District, where the trees have been removed the rivers flood, but where they have not, the rivers stay within their banks.

And we need the metaphors too, so long as we are not wedded to any one of them. (Which is itself a metaphor, because under current legislation you cannot marry your metaphor – even for tax purposes.)

The Pushback

By now, some of you may be thinking, *Yes, John, that's all very well, but isn't life just a war to survive? It's a dog-eat-dog world. Didn't Darwin say something about 'survival of the fittest' and all that?*

No, he didn't. Darwin observed that creatures with advantageous characteristics were more likely to survive in a given environment, and thus the next generation would be genetically better adapted to their surroundings. His theory is based not on competition or fighting within the species, but on adaptation over time.

The phrase *survival of the fittest* was coined by Herbert Spencer in 1864 as he tried to adapt Darwinism to societal development. In so doing, he was arguing that some people are superior to others, which served to 'justify' colonialism, eugenics, racism – things that should have no place in today's world.

But if we are to look seriously at the advantageous characteristics of the human animal, cooperation must be chief among them. Humans are reliant on social learning: most of our behaviours are not based on biology; most of our knowledge comes to us from other people. We learn through imitation, and through creating a set of stories and beliefs on which we seek to agree in order to have a common way of interpreting the world around us. Every social unit created by humans relies on cooperation. As does every action – be it raising a family, starting a business or even fighting a war.

More than anything else, this allows humans to thrive. An episode of the BBC's documentary series *Human Planet* features a remarkable piece of footage in which three Masai warriors steal a leg of wildebeest from a pride of lions, armed only with self-confidence and spears. We show it to new people joining Leon.

First, the warriors track the lions until they find the pride with a fresh kill. Then they advance. Slowly. Determined. As a team. Until suddenly the lions back off, and they have a brief window of opportunity to thieve the meat.

Alone, any one of them would be dessert. Together, they bag a prime roasting cut of gnu, and the lions have the rest.

Cooperation and coexistence, then, are critical not just to survival but success. As, in this case, is the Masai warriors' preternatural calm – a taster of the upcoming wisdom of Staying Relaxed.

Wherever I have worked – be it at P&G in various categories; at Bain for many clients in many industries; at the spirits business Whyte & Mackay; in the Ethiopian beer business; and at Leon – I have seen cooperation deliver more results than annihilation.

In our industry, CEOs meet often and share how we're performing and what we're seeing and learning in the marketplace.

When one company faced a serious health and safety challenge, we at Leon offered to help. I hope that if we were to find ourselves in a similar situation, others would do the same.

Restaurants and retail businesses huddle together like pack animals. You see this in many cities all over the world, be it the garment district or the meatpacking district. London's Hatton Garden is an area where jewellery businesses nestle together – better off as one than they would be spread across the capital.

A shopping centre or a well-managed high street creates an ecosystem where shopkeepers work together rather than looking to destroy each other. And yet despite this reality, the rhetoric still tries to push us towards conflict.

My friend Fred was writing a script for a film about 1950s auto racing. The producers wanted to show the rivalries between the teams. But the more Fred researched the topic, the more he discovered huge levels of cooperation. If one team's gearbox went, another team would lend them one. The teams needed each other – and the drivers respected and liked each other. More than that, they had to trust each other with their lives. More than 100 drivers died racing in the 1950s alone.

Businesses are rarely wiped out by their 'competitors'. It is normally a new player offering a new product or substitute. The celebrations of the 'number one' milk bottle company in the 1970s turned sour when Tetra Pak turned up and they were no longer the cream of the crop. When someone makes a pill that provides the physical and emotional benefits of naturally fast food, we at Leon will have to have our wits about us.

The Art of Peace

As an antidote to *The Art of War*, consider the lessons of *The Art of Peace* – a small book that collects the teachings of Morihei Ueshiba, the founder of Aikido, a martial art that shares some similarities with Wing Tsun.

Ueshiba was a great Japanese warrior. As an infantryman in the Russo-Japanese War, he battled pirates in Mongolia and mastered a number of martial arts before creating Aikido. He also taught in Japan's elite military academies.

He wrote: 'The world will continue to change dramatically, but fighting and war can destroy us utterly. What we need now are techniques of harmony, not those of contention. The Art of Peace is required, not the Art of War.'

As you read this book, you will be invited to consider the validity of another of Ueshiba's statements – one that is consistent with the teachings of Wing Tsun:

> The Art of Peace is medicine for a sick world. There is evil and disorder in the world because people have forgotten that all things emanate from one source. Return to that source and leave behind all self-centred thoughts, petty desires, and anger.

At Leon, I take pains to explain to my colleagues that we have no competitors, no enemies. We are fighting no one. When others copy our menu, our imagery or our marketing, they are attempting to do something that is impossible – they are trying to *be* us.

Our job is to live every present moment as our true selves, consistent with our purpose of nourishing the journey towards wholeness. This is not fighting. It requires no 'aggressive' business plans or 'taking a stab' at anything. No price wars – just offering the best value we can every day.

Our customers are guests who, we know, will shop elsewhere. They are not consumers to be 'targeted'.

We are the same inside as we are outside. We do not have an external face of love and an internal face of fighting, of destroying the competition. How could we explain to our guests that our purpose is to destroy the alternatives and create a world where they have to use us because we are the only offer? I mean, I love our food, but I want to go out for Thai food from time to time. If we ever have 'competitors', it will be because we have forgotten how to be us.

Ueshiba wrote: 'Opponents confront us continually, but actually there is no opponent there.' Whenever I have ignored the competition, we have flourished. Whenever the competition has copied us (and they do it incessantly), they have not. Whenever I have strayed, karma has caught up with me. Whenever I have tried to keep our competition out of sites by taking them ourselves, we have paid too much – in rent or in key money – and I have made expensive mistakes.

In *Strategy*, Sir Lawrence Freedman cautions against companies placing too much belief in their ability to control the future, or in the notion that one can plot a single path through the chaos to achieve a certain outcome. Strategy, he concludes, needs to focus on the actions we choose *right now* – given all the potential unpredictable outcomes that life provides. The advent of science and reason, he explains, gave us the belief – the illusion – that we can control both our environment and the outcomes of our actions. It's true that we may have some things to show from this self-confidence, but we tend to overstate our abilities to affect the world around us.

Strategy is, in reality, much more a response to current problems than it is a predictable route to success. We never really achieve the single outcome, or reach the promised land, because 'decisive' battles are only decisive to a point.

This, then, is a fundamental flaw of the military metaphor. And it stems from thinking such as that of the Prussian general Carl von Clausewitz, who believed that the key goal was to win the battle so decisively that an unmistakable political and moral victory would follow. The kind of victory that so blinded American and Coalition forces in the Iraq War.

In reality, victory presents you with a brand-new set of problems. For example, how do you secure the peace? And it continues: you win an election – *terrific* – but now you're in government, what happens next? You pull off a successful takeover – *congratulations* – but how do you merge two companies that may have fundamentally different corporate cultures?

Strategy doesn't stop. It's not a three-act play, it's a soap opera. It goes on and on, scene after scene. The Queen Vic will always need another landlord.

Many of the Japanese martial arts have a series of planned, choreographed moves that are meant to be followed in sequence. By contrast, in Wing Tsun, while the forms structure our learning, in practice (and reality) we focus merely on the next – or current – move.

I apply this to Leon by asking: *What is the thing that we need to change next?*

Yes, we need to have a sense of the various options that may ensue. And yes, we should have one eye on the competition. But we must focus on the one thing that *we* are going to do, without giving in to distraction.

From the 1960s, and accelerating through the 1980s until today, the love affair with war has come to dominate the world of business, with a widespread belief that lessons can be drawn from the exploits of Alexander the Great, or Caesar, or Napoleon. There are management books devoted to the strategic wisdom of Attila the Hun, Sitting Bull, Robert E. Lee, Ulysses S. Grant and George C. Patton.

In *Strategy*, Sir Lawrence Freedman points out a list of maxims and quotations contained at the back of one such book. What, he asks, is a business manager supposed to make of the following?

1. 'War is cruelty and you cannot refine it' – General W. T. Sherman (him of the tank)
2. 'Shoot them in the belly and cut out their living guts' – General George C. Patton
3. 'War, by definition, means a suspension of rules, laws and civilized behavior' – General Robert E. Lee

The author of said book then goes on to deride 'smiley-face, win-win, love-thine-enemy kinds of business thinking', writing later that business, 'like war, is basically a zero-sum adversarial game with economic and professional stakes of the highest order'.

We have shown that this kind of macho thinking doesn't work. Moreover, much as it might appeal to your ego, the examples such books choose from military scenarios are all too often taken out of context. And in such books, Sir Lawrence warns, strategy becomes 'collections of aphorisms and analogies, often contradictory, trite, and at most pithy restatements of best practice'.

Sun Tzu, as we have seen, presented an approach to war and not to life. His wisdoms encompass only the first two Doors of Wing Tsun, which will teach you not only how to deal with people you encounter who think like this, but also how to move beyond them.

More importantly, giving up the war metaphor leaves a question: what do you really want to do?

I want to serve my customers fast food so good it's as though it were made in heaven. If you really want to 'cut out someone's living guts', I suggest you need medical help.

The Dutch psychiatrist Joost Meerloo argued that war is often a 'mass discharge of accumulated rage, where the inner fears of mankind are revealed in mass destruction'. War, therefore, is the product of an individual's frustration at his or her incapacity to understand and master themselves. We hope that this book offers an antidote to this – for you, for your business and for the planet.

The First Door

Siu Nim Tao – Become Conscious
By Julian

The First Door is named Siu Nim Tao, best translated as 'the Way of the Little Idea'. Its overriding message is one of becoming conscious – physically, mentally and spiritually. It teaches you to see clearly the patterns of your life, your unconscious habits and thought processes, and shows you how to change these into ones that support your sustained success. It does this through two fundamental wisdoms: Know Yourself and Staying Relaxed.

Physically, Siu Nim Tao contains 108 movements and teaches you how to stand, punch and move to best effect. It introduces the concept of natural movements, and starts to combine physical stillness with calmness of the mind. Here it teaches: 'Never move without reason; never delay when you have to move.' Fundamental from the outset is an understanding of the strong link between the mind and the body.

Siu nim means 'little idea'. Like everything in Wing Tsun, the meaning behind these words is layered, and thus so is our interpretation:

1. It can indicate this is a small part of the whole, to get you started on the martial art.
2. It can mean start small and simply, as it will be the basis of everything you do.

The First Door in Wing Tsun is no normal door, for its spiritual name is the 'small door'. It requires you to bend down to see it, symbolized by the bow we make before we start the form.

The small door pays tribute to Chinese Confucianism. On the surface level, it advises you to avoid conflict by bowing rather than squaring off, and it teaches you the practicality of learning from a teacher. Confucius's overemphasis on position, etiquette and rituals meant that he didn't take the ideas behind this much further, but if you have a more enlightened teacher it goes much deeper. It is humbling. It reminds you, as my teacher once told me, that you need a 'clear mind and a strong heart' to learn Wing Tsun and to succeed in life.

The small door also introduces the concepts of 'being present' and 'beginner's mind' – sometimes called 'the mind of a child'. This is the ability to look at everything as if it were brand new, so that you can comprehend and assimilate knowledge and skills properly. In physical conflict, you need to see the world as it really is – not how you would like it to be. While sometimes similar, no situation is ever the same as another, and it is only our preoccupation with our mind that makes us think it might be. This is so simple, but it is one of the most challenging aspects of our life to change. Recognizing it is a first step towards winning.

Wing Tsun tells us 'our thoughts are not reality', although they contribute to what happens to us. Our overreliance and misuse of the mind and memory cause us all sorts of problems – and are arguably the cause of almost all our conflicts.

The small door has a big opening because it also introduces you to the concept of ego. When we say 'leave your ego at the door' in martial arts, what is commonly understood is not to be arrogant, competitive or unkind with fellow trainees. And, if you go a bit deeper, perhaps to actively accept others and not judge them.

But while all those things are true, it really means 'let go of your identity'. For your identity is both a false understanding of yourself and a real hindrance to your progression. This First Door is where you start to truly know yourself.

It's also a small door because not many people enter. The old teachers had another saying to reflect this: 'It's hard to find a good master, but even harder to find a good student.' It's arguably the most difficult level of Wing Tsun (and life) because, like starting anything new, the first step requires you to overcome many of your fears and inhibitions. In this case, it's also one of the hardest steps because you start to move from being unaware of what's going on to becoming conscious of your impact on the world around you. It's beautiful, but often painful. It forces you to re-evaluate your life, and challenges what you think and how you act. But it's only then you can start to relax and let go of your strongest and most destructive habits and patterns. To improve your personal effectiveness, negotiation and influence has to start with complete self-awareness.

Finally, the First Door has an aspect of well-being; this is about opening up and tuning into what is happening to you. The fact that there are 108 movements in Siu Nim Tao is highly significant. It is the same number used in Buddhist prayer beads and symbolizes that you are beginning a deep meditation.* Wing Tsun uses this sacred number because *you* are sacred. It's about being able to feel your present-moment experience, and listening to what is going on in your body. You start to understand your current state, without having to judge what you perceive or think you should be feeling. You accept that you are where you are.

When you have embraced this present moment, this Door then gives you practical tools to change your state. It shows you how to pause in stressful situations, and teaches you how to reset your mind and body and regulate your energy levels.

---

* It is also a highly significant number in Hinduism – the product of 12 months multiplied by 9 'planets'.

Breathing exercises in Wing Tsun.

Breathe in through the nose. Let the stomach fill with air. Slightly bent knees.

Breathe out through the mouth. Squeeze air out of the stomach.

Through the breathing and Chi Gung exercises incorporated into the form, you experience mindfulness in motion, as well as how to feel where your tensions are in your body and how to relax them. The more you do this, the more you will understand the internal loop between mental and physical tensions. Practising the form becomes a great source of meditation and focus, which you can then apply to any area of your life.

In this way, you will start to take responsibility for your own health – both mental and physical. No matter how skilled an expert someone else may be, it's only you who can truly know what is going on inside your body.

Overall, this Door provides you with all the keys you need for high performance. By the end of the First Door, you will have a far better understanding of your own processes – mental, physical and spiritual. By delving into your motivations – your innate skills, desires and patterns – you will understand far more about your time, energy and self-management. And when you combine this with your new ability to unleash your inner calm, it gives you a wisdom and clarity beyond most other people.

The most powerful part of all of this is that you don't need to spend any money doing it – you just need to listen to yourself. You already *are* it.

Lessons of the First Door

1. Understand the interconnected nature of your mind and body.
2. Calmness is power.
3. Take complete self-responsibility for your own body and way of life. No one else can.
4. See clearly. Don't let your thoughts cloud what is actually happening.

3.

Know Yourself
By John and Julian

Julian

The first wisdom of Siu Nim Tao is Know Yourself. Sustained success requires you to be you. Over time, if you attempt to be something you are not, it creates huge internal tension and conflict. In Wing Tsun, self-knowledge allows you to gain a far deeper internal understanding, awareness and perspective, which has immense power to transform every aspect of your life.

Know Yourself starts with the form. In Wing Tsun, the order and number of times we do an action illustrates its importance. After bowing, the first action we take is to stand up completely straight, and face forwards. Still facing forwards, with our shoulders square, we then create our stance.

This forward-facing motion is repeated at the beginning and end of each of the four forms, highlighting its continuing significance to our development and the ongoing process at each Door.

While seemingly insignificant at first glance, this is in fact one of the most powerful physical and spiritual strategies in the

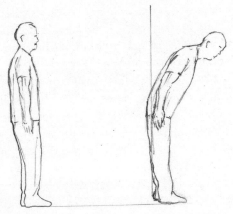

Facing yourself and letting go of your ego through physical movement.

whole of Wing Tsun. In Chinese this is known as Chu Ming and provides a deep understanding of the wisdom of Know Yourself.

Translated as 'face to face', Chu Ming has two meanings, representing the Yin and Yang (internal and external) aspects of Wing Tsun. The first is that you need to 'face yourself' – for it is only by knowing yourself that you can ever achieve sustained winning. The second is that you always physically face your opponent squarely, never covering your head with a guard or turning sideways.

Both of these meanings are inherently connected; when you face someone physically it not only takes courage, it is a mirror of your own internal state. Under this kind of pressure, every internal stress becomes highlighted. This pressure is the 'martial'; the learning from this is the 'art'.

The reason that Wing Tsun begins by addressing physical concerns, rather than just the spiritual – as other traditions do – is that this allows you to address your primordial fears. You can then quickly move away from the need for safety towards a reality of self-actualization.

When you have these skills, safety becomes such an inherent state of mind and body that you automatically see the world, and those around you, differently. It no longer becomes a place full of threats or people 'out to get you'.

When you have physical safety, you can then work through understanding what it means to be psychologically safe. In work, as a manager or leader, creating this feeling is an absolute essential. No amount of financial remuneration or perks will make up for a pervading feeling of fear in the long run.

So, physically in Wing Tsun, the wisdom of Chu Ming allows you to be in a position where you never have to initiate force, but are covered if you are attacked. In Wing Tsun we call this principle 'leave last, hit first'. It creates much-needed clarity, as in potentially violent situations the 'grey area' for everyone is knowing if and when you have to use force to defend yourself.

Typically, people either resort to being too aggressive – either creating the conflict, or not allowing a non-violent solution – or too passive, putting themselves at risk of personal injury or worse. Chu Ming, therefore, creates a clear demarcation. You only move if you have to – when your opponent steps into your space with the capability and intent to hurt you. With training, you learn to recognize and respond to this instinctively and proportionately.

The way this strategy happens is simple. By standing square and facing your opponent, rather than with a leg forward, as in almost every other martial art, you take away a weak point that can be easily attacked. Having a leg forward leaves you vulnerable to being kicked, and is hard to defend as legs are longer than arms. By staying neutral, if an opponent wants to kick you, they must now step into your punching range. In short, it 'sets up' your opponent, making them stick to *your* strategy.

By stepping in to attack you, not only does this make your opponent's attack visible but it puts them at a significant disadvantage – a counter-attack with your hands is much faster than their step.

This is then combined with your own step-in through the

yourself. Similarly, what you like about others is what you like about yourself. You need to understand this because this is the creation of so much of your behaviour, interpersonal conflict, aggression (whether passive or overt) and unconscious bias.

The ego is created by a need to have a consistent 'identity'. Not only is consistency impossible – for we are, in reality, an ever-changing organism from moment to moment – but it is not desirable. It means we are for ever trying to hold on to what has gone, rather than embracing what is here in the present moment. And this is self-perpetuated by fear stemming from the need to conform and be what others want us to be.

It's not hard to see why this would stop you from being successful. 'People-pleasing' has never been a winning formula.

By way of contrast, authenticity creates a magnetic radiance. It transcends self-belief and self-confidence. People become irresistibly attracted to your presence. If you truly want to win in this life – both spiritually and in whatever field you choose to be in – this is how you do it. Know Yourself is, therefore, about transcendence. It teaches you to let go of the need to define yourself by other people's sense of identity. And simply to embrace and enjoy being you.

Know Yourself also gives you the opportunity to try a different approach to achieve success. One that is grounded within your own internal integrity and sense of purpose. In business, people buy *you*. It's well known that skills are easy to train but attitude and behaviours are far harder. A person who knows themselves and their motivations is rare and invaluable.

Know Yourself is about understanding where your fears come from and how to address them. When you feel your body being stressed in a work situation, it's the wisdom from Know Yourself that helps you understand your best next steps. This is the foundation of all great organizational cultures. When staff feel unsafe psychologically – and therefore are unable to develop – this is a serious challenge for the long-term stability of the organization.

Lastly, Know Yourself helps you stop the danger of self-selecting and only choosing people that are like you – another organizational risk – as all businesses ultimately thrive on natural diversity.

Lessons of the First Wisdom: Know Yourself

1. Winning starts with self-knowledge.
2. Know Yourself takes away fear and creates psychological safety for you and those around you. Harmony with others starts with harmony within yourself.
3. You are not what your ego says you are.
4. Authenticity is both power and influence.

John

In Which John Discovers He is Not Just a Labrador Puppy

Remember the metaphor discussion we had earlier? Well, here's another metaphor, this time about a garden. Followed by a swear word that I'm not sure I should have left in.

We explain to people at Leon that, by entering the First Door of Wing Tsun, by practising the physical and spiritual aspects of the first form, they will discover a unique garden that is their own conscious and unconscious self. Some of the landscaping and waterways of this garden you inherit at birth. These are the result of many generations of gardeners – your ancestors – who have worked on this garden before you. Then there are plants and trees and water features that have been added in your lifetime. And there are fresh flowerbeds that you have only just planted. You can continue to explore this garden in the dark, or blindfolded. Or you can take off the blindfold and start to become conscious. You will not be able to explore and understand this garden all at once. But we encourage everyone at Leon to do so whenever they can.

Read the Fucking Plan

'The thing is, for the most part there's the Labrador puppy John Vincent . . . and then occasionally there's the Rottweiler John Vincent.'

My friend Ed Percival was right in saying this. Much of the time I feel like a Labrador puppy. Paws slightly too large for my body, bounding around the office – or my house – with enthusiasm and ideas, looking for new toys or food. Curious, bouncy, positive, playful.

And people who have known me for a short time might think that this is all there is. Then they meet the Rottweiler.

When I went back to be full-time CEO of Leon in 2014 after a six-year break from the role, my American friend and business partner Brad Blum gave me some counsel, using a different analogy to describe the same thing that Ed had seen.

'John,' Brad said, 'you're like San Francisco. Most of the time, San Francisco is a lovely place to live. Sunny, picturesque, warm . . . good food, positive people, culturally interesting, and the odd cycling path for mountain bikes.' He paused for a moment. 'But every now and again, there's an earthquake. And people don't enjoy those so much.'

One of these personal earthquakes struck in 2013. Henry Dimbleby and I had been invited by the British government to write the School Food Plan in 2012. We had taken it on, in the first place, on the condition that we would report directly to the then Secretary of State for Education, Michael Gove.

During the process, we also received great input from Under-Secretary of State Liz Truss, especially concerning the inclusion of instruction on cooking savoury dishes to the national curriculum; and from the Minister of State for Schools, David Laws, regarding managing the implementation of free school meals

Aha!

In Wing Tsun, we use the expression *chu ming* to mean 'face oneself'. It is our opportunity to look at ourselves in the mirror. Most people never do so. They may not know how they come across to others. They may not recognize how they behave. And they are even less likely to know why they behave that way.

For many, the process of facing yourself brings an immediate benefit – an 'aha!' moment that allows people to be instantly more comfortable with who they are, and often even able to laugh at themselves.

It's a process that provides a map of yourself that helps you navigate your character. Both the sunny uplands and the darker valleys.

Into the Enneagram

Aimée's insight – that I act with anger when I see a lack of love – was a vital first step towards self-knowledge. And at our Leon Winter Well-being break a few weeks later, I made more sense of the terrain.

We hold both Winter and Summer Well-being events at my house for the now 120 or so Leaders of Leon, so that all our managers can spend time with the rest of the senior team, building and strengthening relationships. The summer session is all about bridging and connecting with others (Door Two). In part, it's a pool party. But it's also about long walks. It's about doing Wing Tsun together. Crawling around like we used to; learning how to move properly again. We spend time interviewing each other on the trampoline in my garden, finding out more about one another's hopes and dreams. We play rounders. We play tennis. And we make sure that there are activities which allow us to create a strong web – a strong network across everyone at Leon.

The winter sessions are very Yin to the summer's Yang. They are introspective, and about wrapping yourself in a blanket – both real and metaphoric. They go far deeper than any 'corporate' team event I have experienced.

On the first day of that session, each person received four treatments: reflexology with Jesse; a massage from 'Clean Chris' (he is always very well presented); Reiki with Ged; and an acupuncture session with Wendy. And on the second day, Wendy arranged for her friend Donna Lancaster to come along to teach us about something called the Enneagram.

The Enneagram is a model of the human psyche that uses nine interconnected types to describe personality, and it thus aids us with both self-discovery and our interpersonal relationships. When Wendy first told me about it, I'll admit that I was sceptical. I wasn't sure such a simple 1–9 structure could define . . . well, everyone. But, as Occam's razor teaches us, the simple explanation is frequently the best, and I have come to realize what a powerful tool it is.

The first day's treatments gave people the chance to break their normal patterns and reconnect their mind and body. For many, these treatments are rare opportunities to break from work and busy home lives. So, even without the Enneagram, this mirrors the effect of the first form, or Door, of Wing Tsun – allowing people to break from their everyday patterns and face themselves.

And the acupuncture session with Wendy and the Enneagram day with Donna gives people the best opportunity to look at themselves in the mirror – often for the first time.

Wendy's acupuncture stands alone – physically and emotionally – even without the chat. But the chat is arguably the most important part. For Wendy, acupuncture is a way into very deep conversations, and a route to insight. It is therapy. She has the ability to understand and 'see' people in a very short amount of time. People spend an hour with her, and often experience a lifetime of insight in those 60 minutes, providing them the chance to see themselves. And feel themselves too (in an appropriate sense).

Wendy does not share what goes on in the room during a treatment, but people do sometimes share their experiences with me. Some reveal that they have for the first time understood the impact of an abusive relationship, or the effect of a death of a family member, or the impact of an illness or separation. A session with her is more often than not the beginning of a more positive course in someone's life.

On at least two occasions, senior people in Leon have found out things so powerful about themselves that it has become apparent that they need to leave the company in order to 'process' their discovery. One person discovered how much the accidental death of his dad, when he was just a young boy, still affected him at home and at work. His relationship with anyone in authority, especially those who were male, was made much more complicated than it needed to be by his father's early exit.

We experienced the second day as a group led by Donna, a trainer who has huge experience working with people on their psychological make-up. Typically, she leads personal development courses that help people understand and resolve behavioural patterns that are getting in the way of their lives.

Donna distils as much as she can into the one day. People across the business have the chance to learn whether they are typically Maximizers or Minimizers, and they explore the difference between appropriate and inappropriate emotions – inappropriate being when you transfer your relationship with one person unfairly onto another person.

People start to think, *Ah, that's why I react like that . . . it's not because I'm evil!*

But the real meat of the day was a deep dive into the Enneagram . . . and we discovered something so powerful and so simple that we weren't sure how everyone hadn't heard of it.

The Enneagram recognizes its nine character types as follows:

1. Reformer
2. Helper
3. Achiever
4. Individualist
5. Observer
6. Loyalist
7. Enthusiast
8. Challenger
9. Peacemaker

While we may have characteristics of two or three of these character types, one will always predominate. They each describe not so much our true essence, but more the character that we have created for ourselves in this lifetime – the lens that we and our experiences have jointly shaped, and through which we see the world. This in turn shapes our behaviour, creating a self-reinforcing set of what one might call distortions, biases or predilections. So when we talk in this chapter about knowing yourself, we first explore the outer layer of who we are – as described by the Enneagram. As you progress through the Four Doors, you will explore what it is to move beyond this outer shell, into the shadows of your mind and the unconscious, and then deeper still to discover an innate and natural self that is your core.

All nine Enneagram types are influenced by three dominant characteristics of the ego (used in Wing Tsun terms, not in the strict Jungian sense) – fear, anger or shame. While each of us is influenced by all three, Enneagram numbers One, Eight and Nine are driven more by anger; Two, Three and Four by shame; and Five, Six and Seven by fear. This may sound negative, but it is our reality, and by understanding it and realizing the huge role it plays in our behaviour and our life's outcomes, we can find great positives.

Using the principles of the Enneagram, Donna guided us to

understanding who we were. She allowed us to face ourselves. And she reminded us that it's important to know that no number is better than any other. Each has its own characteristics. Through one lens, one might call them strengths and weaknesses, but this implies a level of judgement absent from the Enneagram's central concept. So don't do it.

It turns out I am an Eight. A Challenger. With Seven, the Enthusiast, coming in a close second. Which sort of explained everything. Well, a lot of things. As an Eight I could either be Nelson Mandela . . . or Saddam Hussein.

'The Labrador puppy and the Rottweiler!' I exclaimed to myself. Or maybe out loud, I can't recall. But a light had been shone onto my past. And it also explained my choice of university, college and jobs.

One training and coaching website (the Enneagram Institute) defines the character traits of those tagged with the Enneagram's number Eight like this:

> Overexpresses instinctual energy, using too much energy for the matter at hand . . . Focus of attention and energy is directed outward against the environment, so that nothing can get too close and control or hurt them. They repress their vulnerability and tenderness. They have tremendous vitality and a keen intuition. They are powerful and dominant, and not afraid to act out their rage.

Using too much energy for the matter at hand? Totally. I am 'passionate' (let's entertain that word for a while) about everything that I do and Leon does. I want everything that we do to be incredibly good. I want every guest to LOVE us. For every guest to be treated with love – as if they have travelled from Australia just to experience Leon.

Does this cause me ill health? Yes.

Have I learned ways to balance this energy? Yes. But it has taken time, and I need to constantly be aware of my tendencies.

Your Wingman, or Wingwoman

When you discover your Enneagram number you will discover too your 'Wing'. It will be one of the numbers either side of you. For me it is a Seven. The Enthusiast. Someone who loves life and new adventures. An Eight with a Seven-Wing is called the Maverick. It figures. It means that there are principally 18 key personality types (nine main types, each with one of two possible Wings). Understanding your Wing helps you go even deeper in knowing yourself.

An Eight Uncovered

When you look at your Enneagram profile (visit Eclectic Energies online for a good example of a free test to find your number), you begin to understand the link between your character and your physical make-up – as well as your well-being.

In addition to the Wings, which further refine your profile, each number is grouped into one of three categories: gut, head and heart.

Eights belong to the 'gut' group, which explained to me why I usually get to an answer quickly based on gut instinct . . . and then get frustrated when others work through the answer with spreadsheets or a list of pros and cons.

It also explained why my gut often hurt. By relying on and stressing my gut, my brain and my gut were making each other sore. Which may seem very touchy-feely, but three months ago, a leading gastroenterologist confirmed for me in medical, scientific terms how and why this model for understanding people and pain had actually got it right.

In all the processes of self-discovery we try, the Enneagram is the one that people at Leon find most fascinating.

I strongly suggest, therefore, that you go online, take one of the tests available and explore the different websites that offer explanations for who you are and what it means for you.

As a bonus, which will in no way be as interesting as your own profile, I am going to share with you what it means to be an Eight. To be me.

According to the Enneagram Institute and similar authorities:

> Eights are self-confident, strong and assertive. Protective, resourceful, straight-talking, and decisive, but can also be ego-centric and domineering. Eights feel they must control their environment, especially people, sometimes becoming confrontational and intimidating. Eights typically have problems with their tempers and with allowing themselves to be vulnerable.

(Are you going right off me now? Go and have a read of your own for context!!)

> At their best, [Eights are] self-mastering, they use their strength to improve others' lives, becoming heroic, magnanimous and inspiring.

Each Enneagram type is said to have a basic fear and a basic desire. For Eights, they are:

- Basic Fear: Of being harmed or controlled by others
- Basic Desire: To protect themselves (to be in control of their own life and destiny)

In the materials we share at Leon well-being days, we say of Eights:

> We have named personality type eight *The Challenger* because, of all the types, Eights enjoy taking on challenges themselves

as well as giving others opportunities that challenge them to exceed themselves in some way. Eights are charismatic and have the physical and psychological capacities to persuade others to follow them into all kinds of endeavours – from starting a company, to rebuilding a city, to running a household, to waging war, to making peace . . . An Eight may be a general or a gardener, a small businessman or a mogul, the mother of a family or the superior of a religious community.

But: 'Eights ignore physical needs and problems, avoiding medical visits and check-ups.' (So completely true.) And: 'Eights indulge in rich foods, alcohol, tobacco [my indulgence is definitely the food] while pushing themselves too hard, leading to high stress [totally], strokes and heart conditions.'

Level Best

As well as nine primary Enneagram types, each type has nine levels of development.* These describe how your type will be at your most positive and relaxed (Level 1), and how you could be at your most stressed and 'low' (Level 9).

Before I lay my lowest level on you, let's look at me in my optimum low-stress state, Level 1:

When Eights are emotionally healthy, they have a resourceful, 'can-do' attitude as well as a steady inner drive. They take the initiative and make things happen with a great passion for life. They are honourable and authoritative – natural leaders who have a solid, commanding presence . . . Eights are willing to 'take the heat', knowing that any decision cannot please everyone. But as much as possible they want to look after the interests

---

* According to the Riso–Hudson interpretation of the Enneagram.

of the people in their charge without playing favourites. They use their talents and fortitude to construct a better world for everyone in their lives.

When I first read this, it was like it had been written by a shrink who had been seeing me for years. (You will likely feel the same when you look at yours.) It explained why, even in primary school, I had ended up being captain of the football team; why at secondary school I had been captain of athletics and head of school, aka school captain. It also explained why I created, with friends, a massive party to rival my college's May Ball. At Cambridge, the May Ball is a big deal. In my first year, I applied to be on the ball committee but was turned down in favour of someone who I seem to recall was a friend of the committee president. The next year, I was asked to join the team but I declined and instead organized a giant dance event to rival the ball. It had huge projector screens featuring silhouetted dancers, search lights and intelligent event lighting all around the roof of the courtyard, a big central stage, and multiple bars and food stalls. For an entry price of £6. This was John the Eight in full swing. (As was the fact that the security was a total fiasco, and that I hadn't organized the cash management for the bar very well so we were stuffing money in plastic cups and trying not to lose them, and that, without having planned waste collection properly, we threw the trash down some long basement steps until it almost reached the top.)

I haven't changed a bit since.

When I visited a boat show at London's ExCeL in around 2006, I paid to get in then asked for a map of the event.

'There's one in the programme,' they told me.

'I'll have a programme then, please,' I replied.

'That'll be £15.'

I'm sorry, I thought to myself. *I've just paid £20 to get in, and now I have to pay another £15 to find my way around?!*

There are a number of healthy responses I could have had to this conundrum. Let's explore them together . . .

One, pay the £15. Two, don't pay it, and ask someone for directions. Three, find someone who was leaving and ask if they would give me their programme. Four, find the organizers' office and provide them with some helpful feedback.

Perhaps you can add some more. I think any of these would have led to a sound result.

Instead, my reaction was to organize a rival boat show back at Earls Court (where the London Boat Show had previously been held) with my friend James Brooke, who undertook the brunt of the work. I wanted no financial gain from the endeavour – I was driven by anger and by my fear of being controlled by others – but my business colleagues and I did use the noise and publicity the new event created to promote the whisky brand Whyte & Mackay, which I was helping to manage at the time.

A challenger, helping create a challenger event, with a challenger brand. Boom!

I walked in on the first day and asked for a map of the event. 'There's one in the programme and it costs £15.'

You are bloody kidding me!

My powers of organization once again proved less than my ability to lead. Can you see why Wing Tsun has helped me?

If you want to know what people's characters are likely to be at age 30, 40, 50, 60 – see what they are like aged 18–21. It's all there. The question is whether later in life they have learned to grow towards Level 1 of their development as opposed to sinking down towards Level 9.

Speaking of Level 9, mine is:

If they get in danger, they may brutally destroy everything that has not conformed to their will rather than surrender to anyone else. Vengeful, barbaric, murderous. Sociopathic tendencies. Generally corresponds to the Antisocial personality disorder.

Before you judge, read your own. No Level 9 is a pretty read. Though I would like to reassure those close to me that I have never got to the point of feeling like murdering anyone or anything other than an espresso martini.

If I Had Known Myself at a Younger Age . . . and How it Helps Now

So, hopefully you've read your Enneagram profile, and you thought to yourself: *Wow! That's so accurate. What now? What changes as a result?*

On the one hand, you don't need to force any changes. You have a map of yourself, and it will serve you in all sorts of situations where you need to know the lie of the land. Allow your less conscious brain to absorb it, and don't force it. As you read this book you will learn to put yourself aside, and to free yourself without forcing.

Tell others about what you now know about yourself too. Help them understand your fears or anger or shame. Tell them you're going to seek out the higher levels of your Enneagram number, but ask them to help you when you fail – and offer the same support to them.

I have made conscious decisions to change, and would have made them sooner if I had known me better at a younger age. I have learned to make it more explicit to people that when I become frustrated, I show it. To explain to them what's going on in the moment I say 'FFS!' to myself. To recognize that this is more likely to be about what is going on in my own head than it is about them.

By recognizing that my biggest fear is being controlled by others, I can decide whether my response (e.g. launching a rival boat show) is appropriate or inappropriate. I can more readily weigh things up, and understand the potential risks and downsides of having such strong reactions. I can discuss the fear with someone, rather than spending the effort to start a rival dance event at university . . . though that one was worth it, I think, so the question always needs proper reflection. With the boat show, though, next time I'll just buy a programme or ask for directions.

If in my earlier years I'd known me as I do now, I would have made sure that I partnered even more deliberately with people who would have allowed me to be (a good version of) me. Now, when I do take on big projects, I make sure I partner with a chief operating officer (COO) who is great at the everyday running of a company, with a chief financial officer (CFO) who can manage the financial administration, and with a lawyer who can make sure there is no ambiguity in the deal. I am indebted to the people at Leon, who put up with and provide the antidote to my Eight-ness.

And if I'd known what I do now, I would have appreciated what the Enneagram tells me about the development an Eight undergoes when they adopt the characteristics of the Two, the Helper. This is the number that the Eight moves to when positively developing and growing. Despite being a Challenger/Protector/Leader, as an Eight I understand now that I can also be very content supporting and helping and protecting another leader. It is why I chose to write the School Food Plan with Henry for the Secretary of State, and to chair the Council for Sustainable Business to help implement the 25 Year Environment Plan.

The Enneagram has also reminded me to focus more on my health. And Wing Tsun has provided me with a physical and emotional toolkit that I could have done with when I was younger. With hindsight, I would have put myself more often in situations where I was not contactable on my phone, and I think I would have become less exhausted because of this.

Most importantly, I would have chosen – as I choose now – restraint and no action when under stress. These days, I seek to inspire rather than direct.

As the Enneagram Institute recommends for us Eights:

> It goes against the grain, but act with self-restraint. You show true power when you forbear from asserting your will with others, even when you could. Your real power lies in your ability to inspire and uplift people . . . Few will take advantage of you when you are caring, and you will do more to secure the loyalty and devotion of others by showing the greatness of your heart than you ever could by displays of raw power.

Here, in this paragraph, you have my Wing Tsun journey. From the First Door to – perhaps one day – the Fourth.

The Wing Tsun journey will be different for everyone. For some Enneagram numbers, it is about shrugging off shame, and for some it is about opening up to others. Mine is about learning to yield to others. And, in moving from separation to wholeness, through the Doors, my job is to recognize that 'Eights typically want to be self-reliant and depend on no one. But, ironically, they depend on many people.'

By choosing anger, by seeking not to be controlled by others, I was creating an illusion of separation. And I have learned all this by studying the Enneagram and experiencing and applying the lessons of Wing Tsun.

You will have your own experiences – your own fears and growth potential – as you progress through the Four Doors of Wing Tsun. And the Enneagram is a great tool to have with you as you do so.

By studying the lives of other Enneagram Eights, and in learning Wing Tsun, I have learned to recognize that there is often no need to rush for a result. Wendy reminds me, as an Eight herself, that an Eight can take a very long-term view. South Africa's apartheid regime thought it had dealt with the 'problem' of Nelson Mandela by incarcerating him for 27 years, 18 of them on Robben Island. He was patient. And four years after his release, he became the president of a new South Africa. Not all Eights end up as presidents of course, though there are precedents. They more frequently end up running small businesses or being change-making teachers or doctors. I intend, one day, to regain a majority share of Leon. I am relaxed about when and how, but I will do it in a way that ensures my partners benefit.

Lastly, I think I would have been even more explicit with Henry and with my board about who I am and how best we can work together. Without Henry's strength of character, Leon would of course never have got off the ground. It needed both of us. Looking back to 2014 when Henry was still at Leon, and the ten years leading up to that, we could have better acknowledged the things that we are good at and those we're less good at. Especially in the early years, Henry would become frustrated at my lack of organizational skills – and he wasn't wrong. And I would become frustrated when I began sharing an idea with him and he would say, 'Yes, but what's the process for that?'

'Screw the process,' I'd reply, and jump up and down because I just wanted to see how big we could make the idea if we discussed it together.

And I would have invited the board to do the Enneagram too. Indeed, I need to give the board the same level of insight into the Winning Not Fighting principles by which we run the company. I will fix that.

What This Means for Leon

This process of exploring the Enneagram has transformed our Leon culture. When I walk into one of our restaurants, I know it is being run by someone who is at least on the first level of consciousness. Someone who has bent down to see and walk through the First Door. I know that this manager is aware of how they come across to their team and is conscious of how they may react in certain situations – and I know whether they tend to make decisions rationally, intuitively or emotionally.

When we have our quarterly Leaders of Leon full-day meeting, the shared understanding means that there is also so much more 'baseline' wisdom in the room. I know that I am leading a group of open-minded people who are aware of how they tick and who are comfortable in their own skin.

These Leon people can be true to themselves and not feel bad about who they are. They can find roles in the company that suit them. They can spot the signs of when they are slipping down a level or two on the nine-level ladder, and do something about it. They can avoid putting themselves in situations that make that worse. They can adjust their communication style to get the most out of others. And they have learned how to stop judging people who take a different approach or have different characteristics to them.

And when we form teams in the restaurants, we make sure that the personalities of the principal, deputy and assistant managers have complementary Enneagram profiles.

Once Leon people understand who they are, they are more honest with themselves and others about their skills and capabilities. When I offered one of my team the chance to stand in for me in a UK MD role while I was spending a few weeks in America, she was excited. She rang me the next day and said, 'I love Leon and want to be here for ever, and to assume as much responsibility as I can. But there is more I need to learn before I can be MD – let me do this in stages. I also need to spend some time running a restaurant so I'm completely up to speed.'

Only in a company where people know themselves, are honest with themselves and are open with others – without ego – can a team work together to create a magical whole. I often explain to people: 'Whatever size and shape jigsaw piece you are, be clear and honest about it – we cannot together create the picture of the mountains and lush valleys if not.'

Who's Who

At Leon, the senior leadership team know who they are and who each other is. Gemma, who looks after all purchasing and the supply chain, is an Eight; as is Shereen, the person on my team who helps make the restaurants work. So we need to make sure that we find people to balance our Eight-ness. Glenn, who was the UK operations director and who now runs the US, is a Seven, an Enthusiast. Which is pretty much all Labrador puppy – without the Rottweiler.

Nick, who looks after our franchise partners, is also a Seven, with indomitable positivity. Ottie, who started work as a team member in our Strand restaurant and now does internal comms and Leon social media in our London support ('head') office, is an Individualist – the only Four among 120 Leaders of Leon. (It reminds me of the Monty Python scene where the whole crowd cheer, 'We are all individuals,' and one person puts their hand up and says, 'I'm not.')

Rebecca, who runs marketing, is another Seven, enthusiastically telling the world about Leon and literally jumping up and down when she comes up with a new and fun idea for our social media. The marketing department is full of Sevens in Rebecca's image. It's like having a positivity bath every time I walk into that room.

Tim Smalley is one of the reasons Leon is – touch wood – currently prospering, and I feel blessed to have him as my chairman. He shares and adds to my vision, and keeps me sane as I work every day to focus on the things that I believe will one day achieve that vision. Tim is an Enneagram Three, an Achiever, the same as Julian.

Also a Three is my previous chairman, Nick Evans, who is still on the board. Nick was chairman at a critical time for Leon, and all of us at the company owe him for his strength of character at a difficult time. The fact that we were able to collaborate well as a Three–Eight combo possibly saved the day at a tricky time. A Three and an Eight 'can form highly effective affiliations'. They bring out the best in each other because they both want to make things better, but they do so in different ways. So when they see that they have a shared goal they can come together to achieve it – but putting ego aside is important in order to avoid competition or rivalry as they do so.

Cengiz, who was responsible for helping me codify the Leon strategy, is a One, a Reformer. The Enneagram Institute describes the Reformer as 'principled, purposeful, self-controlled, and perfectionistic'. And Cengiz certainly had the tidiest cabin on our Greece boat trip. Here's what else the institute has to say about Ones:

> Always striving to improve things, but afraid of making a mistake. Well-organized, orderly, and fastidious, they try to maintain high standards, but can slip into being critical and perfectionistic. They typically have problems with resentment and impatience.

At their best they are 'wise, discerning, realistic, and noble. Can be morally heroic.'

In many ways, here is my perfect partner. The antidote to my Eight-ness. At the same time, the Enneagram warns that 'what makes the relationship so powerful can also be the thing that puts the relationship under pressure'. When all of us work with someone who is our 'opposite', we will find great value in it. The key is to openly recognize that this will inevitably also create some tension. Cengiz has to put up with my impulsiveness and desire to rip up plans and start again, and I have to be patient if I feel Cengiz is digging his heels in.

As a One, here's what Cengiz, according to the Enneagram Institute, is at his best:

Level 1 (At Their Best): Become extraordinarily wise and discerning. By accepting what is, they become transcendentally realistic, knowing the best action to take in each moment. Humane, inspiring, and hopeful: the truth will be heard.

Level 2: Conscientious with strong personal convictions: they have an intense sense of right and wrong, personal religious and moral values. Wish to be rational, reasonable, self-disciplined, mature, moderate in all things.

Level 3: Extremely principled, always want to be fair, objective, and ethical: truth and justice primary values. Sense of responsibility, personal integrity, and of having a higher purpose often make them teachers and witnesses to the truth.

But the Enneagram also gives Cengiz clues as to the dark side he needs to avoid, when he is most stressed:

Level 7: Can be highly dogmatic, self-righteous, intolerant, and inflexible. Begin dealing in absolutes: they alone know 'The Truth'. Everyone else is wrong: very severe in judgments, while rationalizing own actions.

Level 8: Become obsessive about imperfection and the wrong-doing of others, although they may fall into contradictory actions, hypocritically doing the opposite of what they preach.

Level 9: Become condemnatory toward others, punitive and cruel to rid themselves of wrongdoers. Severe depressions, nervous breakdowns, and suicide attempts are likely. Generally corresponds to the Obsessive-Compulsive and Depressive personality disorders.

Because he has done the Enneagram, Cengiz, I know, has an operating manual for . . . Cengiz. Full of FAQs and trouble-shooting tips.

Remember to download yours.

The Energy of Your Company

After Donna has helped everyone understand who they are on one of her sessions, she asks people this question: 'What number do you think Leon (the company) is?'

It is a good question.

I have come to the conclusion that companies and organizations do, in fact, have an Enneagram number. And the more I have reflected on this and looked at companies through this lens, the more I think it is a very helpful question.

People tend to answer that Leon is a Seven (an Enthusiast) or an Eight, sharing the 'challenging' energy and character of the leader . . . i.e. me. The Labrador puppy in me is the Seven part of my character. And, as with all projects, Leon is in part my own 'therapy' in action, an attempt to balance my conscious and my unconscious. (We will come to this later.)

At the same time, I have in Leon manifested my weaknesses. Leon, like me, tends to apply more energy than is required for the matter in hand. Leon is an intense and sometimes unforgiving – if also often loving – environment. People work incredibly hard at Leon. At 11 p.m. on a Monday, and sometimes on a Friday or Saturday too, there are often times when many of us are working. We could be a teeny bit more organized.

We love winning. But we have had to learn how we define this and how to win without fighting. Leon the company is learning from the Four Doors of Wing Tsun, just as we all are.

Forever Jung

The Enneagram shares many similarities with the personality mapping developed by Carl Jung. Jung's work fascinates me. In fact, I love it.

The senior team at Leon have delved deeply and broadly into the map of the soul that Jung drew for us. But for this book, it is most helpful to describe the way in which Jung described personality and gave us the opportunity to face ourselves.

Jung outlined four principal ways in which we interpret the world around us. He called them 'functions of consciousness' – thinking, sensation, intuition and feeling. People, Jung concluded (and others have since confirmed), predominantly use one of these four ways to interpret their experiences.

Both thinking and feeling are, in Jungian terms, 'rational', as they each use judgements to discern. The rational (thinking) person uses 'true–false' judgements, while the emotionally led (feeling) person makes judgements based on whether a feeling is 'pleasant or unpleasant'.

On the other hand, intuition and sensation are in Jung's view 'irrational'. They are no less powerful than the rational functions, but they perceive, in quite complex ways, rather than judge. Sensation experiences the world exactly as it is (noticing details), while intuition draws inferences and conclusions without looking at the detail of a particular situation.

Thinking and feeling are opposites, as are sensation and intuition. Jung drew a circle with thinking on the top, feeling on the bottom, sensation on the left and intuition on the right. In any single moment, Jung explained, one cannot be thinking and feeling to the same degree at the same time. And the same is true of sensation (where someone will be noticing details) versus intuition (where someone will be seeing the bigger picture and drawing all sorts of conclusions).

As we develop our personalities, we will find ourselves developing one of these four functions of consciousness more than the others. It is useful to know which one.

Jung then adds a new dimension – extroversion and introversion. An extrovert will focus their energies onto external objects; an introvert focuses internally onto the subject, i.e. themselves. Whereas the four functions of consciousness are mostly the product of nurture – our life to date – Jung concluded that the bias towards extroversion or introversion is created at birth; it is a biological inheritance.

Everyone leans predominantly to one of the four functions of consciousness, then in turn will be either extrovert or introvert. So where the Enneagram creates nine principal personality types, Jung effectively created eight primary types (with a bunch of subdivisions).

These dimensions are mapped out on the Insights Discovery wheel that we use at Leon.* Not only does a leader of Leon know their Enneagram number; they also know where they are on the Insights Wheel. A Helper in Enneagram profiling will typically be a Helper in Insights. And an Enneagram Reformer will have the same name in Insights. Consistent with my Challenger (Eight) type, I am in Insights Discovery terms a Motivator/Director. If you think it would be helpful to see it, I have posted the full report of my character on our Winning Not Fighting website.

This process of learning to know ourselves requires each of us to be honest about who we are, who we have become and who we *think* we have become. Some might shy away from it – maybe from fear, or from a concern that it is self-indulgent. But

* Although the current version of the Insights Wheel introduces Extraversion and Introversion on the horizontal axis where Jung had sensing and intuition, and denotes sensing and intuition by creating adjacent segments in the section of the wheel, it is entirely true to the scientific discoveries and life work of Jung. Available at www.insights.com/products/insights-discovery.

reflect on Jung's assertion that 'Your visions will become clear only when you can look into your own heart. Who looks outside, dreams; who looks inside, awakes.'

The Shadow

When anything stands in the light, it creates a shadow. Jung recognized this. And you need to recognize this too.

Jung explained that there is an energetic flow between the conscious and the unconscious. If we are more 'thinking' in our conscious brain, our unconscious will provide balance by 'feeling' – often in the context of our dreams. If we live our conscious lives 'sensing', noticing the world around us, our dreams will provide the balance of 'intuition' to ensure our psychic totality. Often our dreams provide explanations of people and events we were not consciously aware of.

A similar dialogue takes place between our conscious ego – or persona – and our unconscious shadow.

The shadow represents our insecurities and inferiorities, which, if ignored, grow in power inside us. 'A mere suppression of the shadow is as little remedy as beheading would be for headache,' Jung wrote. 'If an inferiority is conscious, one always has the chance to correct it . . . but if it is repressed and isolated from consciousness, it never gets corrected.'

In Enneagram terms, the shadow's existence is outlined in the lower of the nine levels of behaviour. For an Eight, that's sociopathic, psychopathic (*Why, it's Greased Lightning!*) – in other words, dark stuff.

But the shadow goes deeper still. It is within our unconscious. The unconscious created in our own lifetime, and also the dark unconscious thoughts and archetypes (see p. 109) we have inherited from all the generations that came before us and the trauma they experienced.

In the folklore of the Algonquin peoples of North America, the *wetiko* (or *wendigo*) is the dark side of human nature – a cannibalistic spirit driven by greed and selfish consumption. To their minds, European settlers were so infected with *wetiko* that it was their defining characteristic.

To know ourselves, we must know the shadow and its effects on our conscious minds.

Jung distinguished between the personal shadow, accumulated in our own lifetime, and the collective shadow, the dark part of the collective unconscious.

When it goes unacknowledged and unaddressed, the shadow contains the fears that make us easy to manipulate in work, as consumers and as voters.

We discuss the shadow openly at our Leon Winter Well-being session, making sure to create a safe space to do so. It helps us to know ourselves as individuals and as an organization. And it helps us to stay true to our mission.

Wing Tsun and Zen Buddhism, as we will explore in the Fourth Door, believe that there is a true self that lies at our heart. We are not our conscious mind. Nor are we our shadow. Beyond both, as we peel back the layers, is a central energy, an essence that is what we are all here to remember and rediscover. But we shall leave that there for now.

Arche-Typical

At the most recent Winter Well-being session, we spent the afternoon exploring the maps that Jung drew for us to describe our unconscious. Jung used the term 'personal unconscious' for the product of all the experiences, stories and memories from our own lifetime. (We will discuss this more in the next chapter.) But perhaps even more fascinating is his notion of the 'collective unconscious' – the unconscious mind that we were born with and that we inherited from our ancestors.

While understanding how we have become biased to one mode of seeing the world (thinking, feeling, sensing or intuition) is very useful, it is even more intriguing and potentially even more powerful to understand the structures that strongly influence how we see the world subconsciously – the structures we have inherited even though we don't know it, from generations of human and even animal ancestors.

Jung described how we are affected by what he called 'archetypes' – empty vessels or inherited structures that provide us with ready-made constructs and ideas that we then fill up and colour in with our own experiences. These are constructs like 'good' and 'evil', 'mother' and 'father'. And they drive how we feel and what we think.

Once the group we were leading started to get the idea, we filled up a flip-chart page quite quickly:

– Heaven and Hell
– The Sacred Feminine
– The Snake (to tempt, as in Eden; or to heal, as per the traditional sign for a doctor or pharmacy)
– The Temptress
– The Tree of Life
– Brother and Sister
– The Night Sea Journey
– The Saviour
– The Virgin Birth/Immaculate Conception
– The Trials and Enlightenment

and many more . . .

Earlier that day, Marc – the Leon physical trainer – had shared a very emotional story about when his stepdad, who had been beating him and his brother, was challenged and displaced by his mum's new boyfriend. Marc was doing his homework (or, as he says, 'pretending' to do his homework) when his mum's new boyfriend came round and told the stepdad what would happen to him if he ever touched the boys or did anything to Marc's mum.

'I remember he wrote down his number and said, "Next time you're thinking of treating Janine like that, call me – I'll come round and we can see how it works out for you." I was so excited, so relieved, that I was just scribbling up and down repeatedly on the page in front of me.'

So what has this got to do with archetypes?

Marc's experience, for good reason, conforms to one of the most powerful archetypal stories, that of 'Villain, Victim, Hero'. As I mention later in this book, it is a construct frequently used by the press because it is wired subconsciously inside us as a narrative. Just think of headlines like 'GULF WAR HERO RESCUES INNOCENT PENSIONER FROM ATTACK BY EVIL THUGS'.

Archetypes are so strong that we will typically take a small amount of information and project the archetype onto the situation or people we're relating to. In the group, we considered the example of two divergent characterizations that we have for women inside our subconscious. We split the page down the middle. On the left-hand side we wrote: *The Sacred Feminine*. On the right, *The Temptress*.

The Sacred Feminine, according to the Leon people in that session, represents purity, fertility, kindness, wisdom, nurturing, the womb, birth, new life. The Temptress represents Eve, the siren, the mermaid, the whore, the witch. These are, of course, gross distortions.

In these two opposing and extreme views of the female, we can see how quickly we can create a caricature in our minds – driven by our fears, or by our shame, or by the confusion between the ideal of the mother versus the temptation of sexuality.

It is why humans have burned witches on the one hand and created ideals of the Madonna on the other.

How does this help a leader of Leon? First, it invites them to begin to explore their subconscious, opening up the riches of myth, fairy tale and mysticism and providing them with an antidote to the overly rational world we have created. And second, it provides some caution against seeing the world in black and white or in extremes. Life is not like a Disney movie, with goodies and baddies. And these conversations about archetypes help Leon people to understand how and where we may be distorting reality, thanks to the power of stories and tales that have been passed down for thousands of generations.

Few people are aware of the power of these subconscious archetypes or inherited structures and stories. This is an impediment to our development as humans and to our ability to find solutions for our problems (and to stop us creating more). Jung explained that 'Until you make the unconscious conscious, it will direct your life and you will call it fate.'

By the Fourth Door, Wing Tsun says you will become unconscious again, but you cannot leap straight to it. You need to experience the First Door, followed by the Second and Third, before you can experience the real richness of the Fourth.

Unlike Freud, who was more likely to conclude that dreams were representative of sexual or power urges, Jung provides us with a richer and more mystical interpretation and understanding of our subconscious. Dream analysis occupied the centre of Jung's therapy, and, for the last year, we have encouraged Leon managers to write down their dreams – or better, draw them – and begin to work out what they can learn from them.

At Leon we take time, too, to discuss transference and projection, and the difference between the two. Transference is inappropriately and wrongly seeing in one person the characteristics and traits that you have experienced in someone else. For example, your manager at work may remind you superficially of your mum, so (without consciously knowing it) you wrongly perceive her actions as those of your mum, and experience emotional responses driven by your relationship with your mum. Meanwhile, projection is wrongly assuming that someone else has the same feeling or emotional response as you.

Understanding both these ideas equips Leon people to handle difficult or even routine situations better. Given that I am a Challenger/Protector Eight, we need to watch out for people thinking I am their dad. People can sometimes get themselves down if they think they have in some way 'disappointed' me, so it is healthy to be aware of the potential for this and other father-related transference.

The process of knowing yourself is a rich journey of discovery. The Enneagram or the Insights Wheel provide a brilliant start, but the exploration of the garden can take many years.

Look Who's Talking – Why Businesses Need to Know Themselves Too

The movie opens with talking sperm. Bruce Willis plays a sperm. Or, at least, he provides the voiceover. He wins the race to the egg (it's Kirstie Alley's), gets through the wall and announces, 'I'm in!'

At some stage in the development of a business, there is a similar magic moment. It is not the point at which the destiny of the business is decided – no more than the genes created at your conception decide your destiny – but it does provide the coding that defines what the business will find easy or hard, the biases that it will have in how it responds to certain situations, its character, and many more important things.

I believe a business must have purpose, and if a business is conceived without one, I don't see how it can ever find its way. If your objective is purely to make money, it is unlikely that you will ever have a touchstone or direction to consistently inform what you do and how you do it. But with a purpose, you are most of the way to knowing what to do.

When we started Leon, I was keen to identify very clearly what it is we were trying to achieve. The image that came strongly into my mind was that of fast food in heaven.

If God Did Fast Food

Let's say that you die. Chances are that you will. You go to heaven because, let's face it, you've made a good start by reading this book, and there you have an art class with Michelangelo. He looks down at your attempt to try to master perspective and says, 'Not bad for a first attempt. Now let's go and grab some fast food.'

And you say to Michelangelo, 'I didn't realize you had fast food up here.'

'Don't worry,' he replies. 'It's not like down there. Yes, it's still in the middle of a busy high street. Yes, it has the same format and structure as McDonald's. But everything else about it is different. When you're in there, you feel a deep sense of hope. The food is made from fresh and flavourful ingredients, and the team serving you smile because they *want* to smile.'

This image remains the same one that we have in our minds today, 15 years on. It provides guidance and clarity for decision-making in situations where other companies might have to resort to focus groups, spreadsheets and PowerPoint presentations. Or even to paying third-party consultants to work out what they should be doing.

We know from this big, central, organizing idea of 'fast food in heaven' that we should always be in very busy locations where people need us. We know that our food must be flavourful, fun, functional and fast. We know that it must be kind to the planet. We know it must be affordable. We know we must create iconic fast food brands (dishes) like our LOVe Burger and our fish finger wrap. And we know that, when asked if we would ever do a drive-thru, the answer is absolutely 'yes' – with the proviso that it has charging points for electric vehicles, discounts for car sharers and incorporates a cycle-thru.

I believe that Leon very clearly knows what it is.

Our mistakes have come not so much from a lack of clarity about who we are, but from when we have failed to live up to that. Pretty much all of the mistakes we have made strategically with Leon have been when we've strayed from the principles the idea 'fast food in heaven' provides.

The single biggest structural mistake that we made, right at the beginning, was our failure to provide a simple operating model and kitchen. And the thing is, looking back on it, my gut, my instinct, my intuition knew that at the time.

In the intensity of establishing the company and managing all the moving parts to do so, I remember saying to Henry, 'You know, partner, the *Harvard Business Review* article about our success, if we ever get there, will not be because we have made some nice food with some nice branding with some nice PR. It'll be because we have created an engine – a kitchen model, an operating model – which is simple, smart and scalable.'

And I remember being grateful to Henry for spending some time adding some flow charts to the business plan to demonstrate that we had considered this subject. But the reality is that the system these flow charts represented was deeply complex.

Fast food requires dishes to be made at speed, and for them to be highly simple. Yet when we launched, we were hand-rolling meatballs downstairs at Carnaby Street, marinating chicken and cooking it on a gas grill. We had two sizes of soup. When you ordered a wrap, you could have it wholemeal or white bread. On a melamine plastic plate or to take away.

At the end of the first day, exhausted, we sat down and agreed immediately that we had to make changes. Some of those changes we could make the next day. One type of wrap (wholemeal only), not on a plate, and one size of soup. And so we were able to fix some of our mistakes before our second day had even begun. But, as for the rest of it, we have spent 15 years trying to rectify and rescue a complex model. It turns out that trying to reinvent fast food with fresh produce had not been done before and was not straightforward.

To use a sporting analogy, the way that you set your business up at the beginning is like the first shot in golf. If you end up in the rough or a bunker, you *can* get yourself out of it, but it takes time. Often a lot of time.

And you need to not over-innovate. Innovation is seen as a key source of 'competitive advantage', but it can be as destructive as it is valuable. We have often tinkered too much. When we opened our second restaurant, we created a sit-down menu that took us way off 'naturally fast food', and the paper menu that was designed (the only time we have used an agency) was a terrible pastiche of what we had created – full of inauthentic expressions and misunderstandings of what we stood for. We should have just left well alone. A journalist called Richard Johnson wrote an article pointing this out, and he was completely right. Thank you, Richard.

Whenever we've been truthful to the idea 'fast food in heaven', things have worked. And whenever we have strayed from it, we have paid the price.

Whoever You Are, Be That

Don't read management or leadership books that give you slavish blueprints for how to manage or lead. And do not try to be any of your role models. You are not Warren Buffett, nor Steve Jobs. As my friend Richard Cairns says to his pupils, be the best version of you, not a second-rate version of someone else.

Be a leader who is at the top of the Enneagram ladder. Lead

the way you naturally lead. Be your most authentic, relaxed, loving self. Anything other than that will create more conflict for yourself and for others.

Tell people your weaknesses, share your dark side. We all have one. And equip yourself and others with strategies and tactics to rescue things if you slip down your ladder. If it helps, use humour – which in my experience, it does. Tell people how to take the mickey out of you. Ottie says 'mangoes' to me if I get frustrated – it is not a joke anyone else would get, but rather based on a joke meditation my daughter Natasha used to say: 'Apples and bananas, kiwis and potatoes, mangoes, mangoes.' See, it's not possible to translate, but it works for us.

Angered by a Lack of Love

I explained earlier the revelation that came to me when Aimée pointed out that I value love but am angered when I see a lack of love. What a paradox. And what a lesson. I was once in a meeting where someone running an anti-ageing clinic said that his strategy was to sell customers a certain drug, and then after a while switch to a cheaper drug without them knowing. That really pissed me off. I was suddenly angry. In one moment, all of my fears about humanity – what we can do to each other, and what that means for us and for society – came to the fore. I exploded at him.

Do you see the irony? My anger was from frustration and fear. But it was therefore somehow love. What you will see as we progress through this book is the journey that I have come on – and am still on – to see the challenges of the world, and of humanity, without becoming angry or letting my frustration drain me or exhaust me. I have had to learn this. It has been fundamental to what one might call the process of healing. First comes anger, then ultimately release. And a decision to focus on what I can do and on that alone. To attempt a narrow mastery, not to solve all of the world's problems. To experience anger, to understand it, but then ultimately to put it aside.

But we cannot leap to this. It is of course a process. We must begin by becoming conscious, by knowing ourselves and being honest about the anger, fear and shame that we have. To see things rationally to begin with. To understand the lens we have created to perceive the world, and the character this has created. To understand the value but also the inadequacy of our rational thought. To bring our shadow into the view of our conscious mind. And, ultimately, to move beyond even this – to our true self that lies beyond.

Woken with a Jolt

Many shamans, healers and coaches have become conscious following a personal event that has caused them to 'wake up' and for the first time understand who they are. Wendy has a shaman friend who suffered from polio as a child and now walks with difficulty because of the effect on one of his legs. But he credits it with giving him new wisdom. Jorge, who helps us with our Winter Well-being events (through breathing and massage), was studying economics in Mexico when his face was paralysed to such a degree that he was unable to sleep and could barely eat. After doctors failed to help him, he turned to acupuncture after hearing that a Czechoslovakian acupuncturist was visiting nearby. He was healed. It set him in a new direction, and after meeting a Sufi man who taught him an exercise in how to breathe (yes, he had breathed before, but not *this* way) he had an out-of-body experience. 'As clear as day, I felt and saw myself floating up and away from my body. I floated up and up until I was able to explore and see the stars.'

Jorge decided to stop his economics course to study breathwork practices from all cultures – Chi Gung, Vipassana, Pranayama. We at Leon benefit from this decision immensely today. (If you haven't tried it you might be sceptical – but don't let that stop you trying it.)

You, however, don't need anything so dramatic to happen in your life. You have this book. You can start now.

4.

Staying Relaxed
By John and Julian

Julian

The second wisdom teaches you the importance of Staying Relaxed. By tuning into your natural state of being, it gives you the ability to face any unexpected situation with clarity, poise and assurance. It takes your quest for self-discovery and empowerment a level deeper.

The wisdom of Staying Relaxed creates an interesting first response for most of us. We all know we should be capable of a state of relaxation, but it seems a nicety rather than a necessity most of the time.

Stress is linked to the six leading causes of death, and you just have to look at the slightly scary statistics about high achievers, and how soon they die after retirement, to realize that inherent tension is not all it's cracked up to be. There has to be another way to win. And there is . . . It's Staying Relaxed.

Having now discovered the First Door, you won't be surprised to learn that Wing Tsun takes a far more practical approach to Staying Relaxed than many other disciplines. It shows you how to achieve immediate and sustained results by doing less than you think is necessary.

Wing Tsun starts with this physically, so you can tangibly grasp the effects of Staying Relaxed. In short, the more relaxed you are, the faster and more powerful you become. It's just like throwing a ball. The more tense your arm, the less power you can throw the ball with. You need all the power to 'flow through the fingers' – an important Wing Tsun concept. Combine this with other Wing Tsun principles such as always using the 'shortest line' and 'punch from where the hands lie', and you have a strike so fast that it is almost impossible to see.

Staying Relaxed not only gives you speed, it also gives you far more control, efficiency and dexterity. You can change direction in a split second (this is known as a 'direction-changing punch') and respond to an attack before the other person has even been able to process it. Within two or three seconds, a physical confrontation should be finished.

Crucially, relaxation takes out the brain's feedback loop. This means that you can respond instinctively, without any prior conscious thought. This is absolutely essential in a potential combat situation, where even the shortest delay can be the difference between life and death. Relaxation also allows you to

Boxing fist.

tap into your natural intuition and 'gut feel', which shuts off when we feel tense. In Wing Tsun we call this connection 'when you train the hands, you train the brain'.

The power of the Wing Tsun punch is equally astonishing. It twins relaxation with natural body movements to create a force that goes straight through the opponent. It is like being hit with a wrecking ball. There is a strong contrast between this and a boxing punch, for example. In boxing, the way you structure a punch forces you to be tense, otherwise you damage your hand. You generate force from the shoulder and hit with a horizontal fist, using the top two knuckles.

In Wing Tsun, you use the natural movement of the body to generate force from your elbow and strike with a vertical fist, using the bottom three knuckles.

Wing Tsun fist.

Not only does this enable you to be more relaxed – making it a heavy rather than a tense punch – but it also ensures you are completely supported by the ulna and radius bones of the wrist, using the whole structure of your body to support and amplify your power. We call this the Iron Fist in Wing Tsun, because the effect is like hitting someone while wearing a metal gauntlet.

Furthermore, the power of this relaxed force allows you to employ a completely different tactic. Whereas other martial arts aim, in effect, to batter an opponent into submission, Wing Tsun looks to break the person completely with just one punch. It sounds brutal, but if you are attacked it is your only chance.

Finally, being relaxed also increases the distance you can punch because there is no shortening of the muscles and joints through tension. With training, you can safely add 30 centimetres to the reach of your punch – a substantial advantage that not only nullifies any potential height advantage of an opponent, but makes you dangerously unpredictable.

Left: Tense fist. Right: Relaxed but strong – the Wing Tsun 'Iron Fist'.

Staying Relaxed is the mental 'master key' to all these physical advantages. However, it provides so much more than physical prowess. When you start to master mental relaxation, your ability to change the outcome of a situation without the use of force is vastly increased.

This is only possible when you do not act out of fear. Fear, perceived or real, has very limited use for you in today's world, which is why Wing Tsun quickly teaches you to be able to defeat almost any attacker. When you know how to win on a physical level, the fear of getting physically hurt or intimidated subsides.

However, even without physically learning Wing Tsun, Staying Relaxed is a hugely powerful tool to incorporate into your life. With relaxation, fear melts away and you instead have concern and empathy for the other person. A sense of grievance is replaced by understanding the other person's tension. You don't have to make another person's bad day become your own. By becoming relaxed, you are given the option to escape that 'hijacked' feeling you experience when everything seems to be spiralling out of control.

The wisdom of Staying Relaxed teaches you about your own emotional response – the Wing Tsun concept here is 'respond, don't react'. Until this becomes instinctive for you, there will be a gap between your emotional response and your corresponding action. This slight pause is the difference between creating and dissolving conflict. Then, rather than making a decision based on fear and ego, you instead reflect and choose what is best in the situation. It's very rare that an immediate emotional response is going to be your best option – certainly not in the long term. Every action that 'triggers' you creates an emotional response and shows you that you need to go back to the first wisdom, Know Yourself. After all, it is you who is getting angry, and only you can understand why.

Wing Tsun shows you that what you focus on is what you create. Physically, you will come to this realization pretty quickly; if you worry about being punched then you will end up being punched. If you focus instead on the positive outcome, you might get hit, but you have a far greater chance of winning.

The same is true spiritually. This is the real meaning of *karma* (literally translated as 'action'). It's not a universal law of reward and punishment. It's a reflection of your own mentality. Simply put – how you think is how you act. How you act is how others respond to you. And this in turn determines what happens to you. If you can stay relaxed, you allow yourself to break out of this loop and create more positive situations and responses for yourself.

Relaxation allows you to heighten your sensitivity and your connection with the world. As we discussed in the first wisdom, Know Yourself, our ego, our self-identity and the associated judgements that come with this are a significant source of mental tension. You are unlikely to master ditching the ego immediately, but Staying Relaxed is a significant part of the process. There is a fundamental wisdom here: a life of tension is really not living at all. It removes you from the true essence of who you are, creating a disconnect between mind, body and spirit.

Wing Tsun gives you practical tools to relax immediately. The simple breathing exercises in Siu Nim Tao (the First Door) allow you to clear the mind, take control of your body consciously, and tune in mindfully to what's actually going on right now. It also gives you the ability to consciously calm down, slow your heart rate, to change between different parts of your physiology – from a fight/flight/freeze response (the sympathetic nervous system) to a 'rest and digest' dynamic (the parasympathetic nervous system). And, if you have the opportunity, the practising of Wing Tsun techniques, such as the punch, allows you to physically express negative emotions and feelings, and create a sense of movement and flow within your body.

Overall, Staying Relaxed has a multitude of positive health effects. From improving your mental health and the way your gut functions to releasing stress, the ability to stay relaxed is the key to longevity. With a focus on creating a balance in the body, Staying Relaxed teaches you how to master your mental and physical energy management.

In business, feeling tense is a good way to make bad decisions, and generate bad feelings and a stagnated culture. It creates more problems than solutions, and being tense will not make a problem go away or get any better. It just makes you suffer. By Staying Relaxed, you can escape to freedom at any point.

The wisdom of Staying Relaxed teaches you to be able to read situations and people quickly. Calmness spreads, and creates a powerful presence around you. You become far more influential, giving you much more gravitas when you speak. Just starting a meeting with a few simple breathing exercises can bring everyone together, creating a positive and connected energy in the room.

Finally, Staying Relaxed has a highly significant impact on decision-making and problem-solving. It allows you to have a greater sense of perspective and the options available, not just the challenge in front of you. It allows your creativity to flourish. By not allowing your own personal challenges to get caught up in what you're doing, you become the consummate modern professional, able to acknowledge and understand your emotions without having to act upon them. Similarly, this has a positive effect on negotiation. You gain a greater clarity about what you need to achieve, without allowing yourself to get sidetracked by emotive words or actions from the other party.

If you incorporate the wisdom of Staying Relaxed into your daily life, it prepares you for the Second Door, and enables you to connect more effectively with others.

Lessons of the Second Wisdom: Staying Relaxed

1. Staying Relaxed allows you to have immediate and sustained success.
2. It teaches you to 'respond not react' to situations you are faced with.
3. If you stay relaxed, you create clarity, calmness and positive options.
4. Relaxation is the foundation of health.

John

In Which Vida Has a Right Laugh

At our most recent 'this is our plan for the year' meeting, I put up the slide about 'responding not reacting' and 'staying relaxed' and Vida (who was then working with Julian on Leon well-being) laughed. It wasn't a small titter, it was a spit-your-drink-across-the-room kind of laugh. It conveyed a loving message: *Good luck, cos you're pretty crap at that, aren't you!!*

You will recall from the previous chapter that, with an Enneagram Eight character profile, I apply too much energy to most situations. It's quite tiring being a Challenger, you know. Sometimes I think it would be really nice to care less. And that, as it happens, is exactly what needs to happen.

Why Staying Relaxed is Important

Julian often uses me as a man-sized prop to demonstrate how to get out of an arm lock, or rather to prevent yourself from getting into one. The key is to stay relaxed, to respond and not react. You have three points of axis – your shoulder, elbow and wrist – and all three need to be controlled by your 'opponent' if you are to be held. But your opponent can only control two – normally your shoulder and wrist. By tensing (your body's unconscious response to reacting emotionally), you allow your elbow to be indirectly controlled and so create your own undoing. When you keep your arm loose – floppy, even – your opponents will be puzzled about why their arm lock doesn't work. Then you can either use your free arm to make the next move (to punch if necessary) or, if the dynamic allows, you can push the hand of the loose arm towards the floor and use your shoulder to invade their stance and send them across the room.

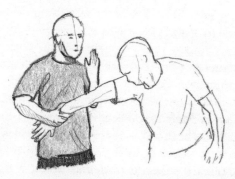

Arm lock – your opponent locks you through your own tension.

The first form, Siu Nim Tao, teaches you to be still, to punch in a fast and relaxed way, and to defend with a relaxed hand and arm without rushing. 'Go slow to be fast', as Julian explains, really works. This physical example of Staying Relaxed, and responding not reacting, is true of all Wing Tsun moves. In defence, we are taught to be like a ghost, and to move fluidly. It is always surprising to an opponent how the relaxed defence of, say, a round punch with the outside of your relaxed hand can hurt them so much, and deter them from trying again. And, as Julian has explained, your punch is so much faster and more powerful when you and your arm and shoulder are relaxed.

Siu Nim Tao also teaches you the mental and emotional aspects of Staying Relaxed, and these are just as fundamental.

They are key to not being drawn into conflict and key to sensing properly how to respond if you fail to avoid one.

You Get Angry, You Lose

I met British boxer Chris Eubank at a party once, and asked him if he needed to work himself up to be angry in order to win a fight.

'Oh no,' he said. 'Emotion is the last thing you need if you want to win. You get angry, you lose.'

In boxing, of course, you are meant to fight. The crowd would ask for their money back if you didn't. In Wing Tsun there is no one paying to see you fight. Much better not to.

What gets in the way, what causes you to fight, and what makes both a punch and a defence ineffective, is emotion. Ego. Fear.

Leon people do both physical and non-physical work – in the kitchens, at the counter or in the Borough office. For all these roles, being relaxed is key. It makes us faster, it makes us less prone to injury and it makes our decisions better. So when we talk about staying relaxed, and when we talk about responding not reacting, this applies to both our bodies and our minds. This is how we hit, or get close to our target of a 30-second transaction time – by being in flow, and staying relaxed.

Somewhere Up the Ladder

As discussed earlier, you have your own specific ladder (where Level 1 is the healthiest and Level 9 the least healthy) based on your Enneagram number. Climbing higher up the ladder is not a 'destination' or a long-term life goal. It is an emotional state to be enjoyed or endured in the present moment. But it is what we call 'winning' – being our most relaxed, true and fulfilled self now, while also protecting yourself and the world around you for the long term.

The lower levels of the ladder are reserved for people who are fighting. Unhealthy stress takes us down the ladder and results in us behaving in ways that neither we nor our friends, family and colleagues like to see or experience.

We have the binary choice to approach and respond to a situation with love not fear. We cannot come from both at once. We have to choose one or the other. Fear, conflict, ego: in Wing Tsun these are three bad musketeers, if not the equivalent of the unholy trinity. Seemingly separate, but ultimately one.

By choosing love, we disengage from fear and from conflict. And from our own ego. And we learn to stay relaxed. To react not emotionally, but through training your nervous system to sense the world exactly as it is.

The Danger of Ego in Business

When I was quite a new Labrador puppy at P&G, I went into a meeting with a top customer and the most senior person in our UK company. But it is not the meeting that sticks in my mind. It was what happened next. My boss turned to me and asked, openly, 'How did I do? What could I have done better?'

Here was the most senior person in the room asking for a quick review from one of the most junior. He put his ego aside, and he wasn't going to let fear of what I might say stop him from developing and improving.

This 'feedback culture' made P&G strong.

Ego is responsible for some of the worst deals. Acquisitions – or supposed mergers that are in reality acquisitions – should, in my experience, not be undertaken lightly. Some industries where manufacturing or R&D or distribution scale is key will naturally consolidate (for example, the civilian large-body airliner manufacturing business, where there are now just two players left – Boeing and Airbus). But not others. And many failed acquisitions are, at their root, the result of ego.

Ego creates problems when the CEO or CEOs, or boards, are – in the words of Sun Tzu – doing the deal 'to gratify their own spleen'. To feel powerful, to gain plaudits; to listen to greed, or fear of missing out. It seems from what is publicly known about the acquisition of ABN Amro by RBS, for example, and of NCR by AT&T, and of Daimler's merger with Chrysler, that they were driven more by ego than by commercial sense. This can lead to inaccurate estimates of the likely synergies, and to poor planning and overpayment. Worse than that, it can blind people to the potential for value destruction – including cultural differences or strategic misalignment, as was soon evident in the acquisition of Time Warner by AOL.

Ego can cause even theoretically good deals to go bad. The two CEOs or wider leadership teams – even if they have achieved the classic fudge of one becoming chairman while the other stays as CEO – can tear businesses apart.

One of the most active deal-doers in the last ten years is 3G. The three partners, Lemann, Sicupira and Telles, are known for their down-to-earth approach and lack of ego. When they turned up to lead their first operating business – Brazilian brewery Brahma – they arrived with rucksacks and in casual clothing. And they were humble in how they led the business. It was the hard-working cultural tone they set that allowed them to buy their Brazilian 'rival' Antarctica, and when Interbrew effectively bought their business, they were able to end up running the newly formed entity. Acquisitions of Anheuser-Busch and SABMiller followed. Over the last quarter of a century, articles have appeared lauding them – with others writing them off – and more recently they have faced challenges with their Kraft Heinz investment. But they keep going, putting aside ego as best anyone can as they go.

When we sold Whyte & Mackay to Vijay Mallya, my partner

and boss Vivian, the owner of the company, was magnanimous and egoless. 'We have taken the company as far as we can,' he said, 'and it is time for Vijay and his team to apply their skill and vision to take the business to where it deserves to be.' If you look at the price achieved on exit, I think you would conclude that this was a good example of Winning Not Fighting.

The 3G founders are good adverts for staying relaxed – the 2008 financial crisis hit just as they were completing their acquisition of Anheuser Busch. They were under immense pressure, or so one would think looking in from the outside. But people who were in attendance as they calmly set about rescuing the deal were witness to a leadership team staying extremely relaxed while under pressure. If you have chosen not to be driven by ego, and have been successful in doing so, you will find a route to doing the same.

How Many Restaurants Do You Have?

There is a famous story in Greek mythology about Odysseus and the Sirens. To get back home, Odysseus and his men had to sail past the coast where the Sirens lived. It was known to be an impossible task because, whenever they saw a ship, the Sirens would begin to sing. And the sound of their song was so irresistible that men would always steer towards it, to hear it better. Whereupon their ship would founder on the jagged rocks of the Sirens' island, and all would be lost.

So Odysseus ordered his men to block their ears. If they couldn't hear the song, they would be able to pass safely. However, he wanted to hear the song himself. So he ordered his men to lash him to the mast. On no account were they to set him free or to listen to his inevitable command to sail towards the rocks. Odysseus knew that he would be as fallible as every other man to their irresistible song. But his plan ensured that his curiosity didn't doom his ship and his crew.

131

Nice story, but what has this got to do with Leon? Well, the equivalent of the Sirens in the restaurant industry is attractive – well, seemingly attractive – properties. The ones in sexy locations that would delightfully feed the ego, but which ultimately prove to be financially destructive.

This is how the CEO of a growing restaurant chain falls into the trap. They will sit next to someone at a dinner party and, when they explain to their fellow guests that they are in the restaurant business, they will be asked 'How many restaurants do you have?' – as if that is the key metric of success. I cannot blame the people who ask the question, because how else do you break the ice? You cannot expect someone to ask what your return on capital employed is. For most people, this will not make for rich conversation. But it is the job of the CEO to not attach their self-worth to the metric of something like 'number of restaurants'.

In the same vein, in each year's budget there will probably be a target for how many restaurants the company will open. And if the investors are going for a quick return, or feel that unit growth will drive the valuation of the company, they are likely to put pressure on the CEO to open more restaurants.

A CEO of a growing restaurant business has to put aside both ego and fear to demonstrate the type of leadership that won't take the company off course. Or allow it to be slammed into the rocks. A lack of ego in order not to chase the pretty site. A lack of fear to be able to tell the board that you won't open the number of restaurants set in the budget, thereby avoiding openings that tick boxes but potentially burden the company with great losses.

Here I write from bitter experience. One of the biggest mistakes that we made was in acquiring three sites from a company that went into administration called Benjys. We identified three of their most high-profile sites – Cannon Street, Regent Street and Villiers Street – as ones we wanted to go after, and set about it. During the process, however, I remember a deep sense of inner conflict. At the time I was effectively wearing two hats.

The first as joint CEO with Henry. The second in my designated role as property director. I remember saying at a board meeting (effectively with the CEO hat on) that going after these three sites could be one of the worst decisions the company has ever made. But I also remember a deep desire to *win* these sites. To not let anyone else get them. To demonstrate that I had the nous and ability to make sure these ended up as Leon sites. ·

And I remember one of the board members phoning me up to say, 'The competition doesn't realize they have John Vincent going against them.' This gave me even more confidence, even more ego not to miss out. But no deal should ever be done in this frame of mind.

As a result, in the bidding process we ended up paying the administrators too much for the sites. On Cannon Street we inherited a site with far too high a rent. And on Villiers Street we ended up with a tiny unit that was very difficult to operate and make profitable. We ended up closing Villiers Street, and if I look back at the money spent on acquiring the sites and on converting them, the marginal profitability that we achieved from Regent Street and Cannon Street was not a good use of our precious money. To any Leon investor reading this, I would like to apologize.

Put Yourself Aside

Having taken time to know yourself, to stay relaxed you are going to have to start by putting yourself aside. This will not be easy to understand immediately, nor will it be easy to do – it is so contrary to how our modern culture has trained us to think. But it is possible with practice and it will come to you in two stages – you will 'get it' intellectually and intuitively, and then you will over time get better and better (with setbacks along the way) at doing it in reality.

To understand this more, let's begin by stepping outside our-selves and looking at that self we discovered when we walked through the First Door. In Wing Tsun, we think about that self as the sense of identity, both conscious and unconscious, that we have created for ourselves.

The 'self' that you understood using the Enneagram and the Insights Discovery tool is the character that you have created for yourself based on your experiences – or more importantly your perception and the stories you have told yourself about those experiences. It is the first layer of yourself that you need to understand before moving deeper into your shadow and then ultimately into your fundamental, innate self.

I set out in the previous chapter Jung's description of our collective unconscious. This is like the operating system that your smartphone comes with. This is the unconscious part of your brain that you inherit from your parents and which has been formed and then adapted by all the generations that have come before you, right back to when we were fish. We are born with a fear of heights, of loud bangs, and have certain constant archetypes – shared structures and beliefs in things like good and evil.

Then, slowly, we create a sense of identity that is not in-herited. To continue the phone analogy, we create apps (or new software) for ourselves. Some of this identity is unconscious, and some is conscious. It is the story – the wonderfully self-manufactured construct – that we convince ourselves is 'us'.

We begin our lives unconscious. And we feel entirely con-nected with the world around us. When we are in the cot, people lean over and make strange noises, some of which are grown-ups or our older siblings making *goo-goo* sounds, but we start to notice that certain noises keep cropping up. For example, 'John'. And we think to ourselves: *This is getting weird – what is this 'John'?*

And then the penny starts to drop. *Hold on, they think that I'm separate from them – how strange. Am I? Does that even make sense?*

They think that I'm separate from that thing that's hung above me and that my hands keep hitting. Slowly the notion of 'me' and 'I' becomes real to us.

Then, when we first go to school, the teacher (Miss Kirk in my case) calls out our name and we put our hand up or say 'Here!' when she says 'John Vincent'. And when we win a history prize or are told that we are good at football, all this reinforces the sense of self.

The fact is that the 'John Vincent' that I think I know is pretty much a flimsy and potentially fake piece of storytelling. As artfully curated as an Instagram feed.

Some events are fact. Most are semi-fact or even mostly fiction.

Everything that we experience is seen through a lens that has been created by previous events which have formed our warped sense of self-identity. Much of this identity has been created by the age of seven, though things that happen later can of course impact our self-identity too.

All of the things we do at Leon – the practices and the hacks to 'respond and not react' – are about being prepared not to overly attach ourselves to this character that we have created (and which is described in the Enneagram and in Jung's explanation of our learned bias towards thinking, feeling, sensing and intuition) but it is essential to understand it. While it becomes increasingly shaped and distorted by our experiences and our responses to them – and thus is not 'concrete' – it still has a great effect on us and on others, and understanding this layer of ourselves is of vital importance.

Whether you face someone who wants to be your opponent in a 'fight' (your task, of course, is for there to be no opponent and no fight), or you're about to make a big decision at work, or you are attacked verbally at work, or you're playing golf or chess, or disciplining your daughter or son, your response will be all the more powerful – and based on love – if you stop valuing or trying to protect this 'identity' that you have created. It is, after all, pretty much fake. Recognize its value, but don't create conflict to protect it. If another motorist swears at you and it wasn't your fault, apologize. You will see how quickly they calm down. If you are about to do a deal, not because it makes sense but because you have staked your reputation on getting it done, don't do the deal. If someone says that you have upset them at work, say, 'That's terrible, I'm so sorry. What did I do?' Bypass that self; don't protect it.

To be a good practitioner of Wing Tsun, and a good captain of your own life, you need to stay relaxed. Stay fluid. Don't entertain fear. Don't create conflict.

Love All

At Leon, we believe in exercise, in moving – of course we do. But we believe even more in the power of moving together. When we train with Marc, the Leon physical trainer, we do so as far as possible as one.

We all 'know' about the benefits of exercise on our physical and emotional well-being. But the advice to exercise often overlooks the fact that different types of exercise have very different outcomes. Popular culture loves to activate our inner chimpanzee by telling us we need to go harder, faster, stronger. But if you slam an already-tired body in the gym, you are going to burn out. If you stress about exercise and try to squeeze it into an already-packed schedule, when your stress hormones are high, it's going to make you feel worse and leave you inflamed. If you plug your headphones in and pound a treadmill for an hour in a windowless, strip-lit dungeon, you will not be feeding your spirit. This kind of high-octane, solo exercise ignores the emotional and spiritual connection we must feel in order for the exercise to benefit us mentally as well as physically.

A recent Danish study looked at how different sports affect

the life expectancy of their participants. From the 20,000 people taking part in the Copenhagen City Heart Study, researchers zeroed in on about 9,000 who had been involved from 1990 to 2017 and met a number of criteria for inclusion. Then they cross-referenced records with the national death registry to see when any of these people had passed away, and compared their exercise activity and lifespan.

The most obvious finding was that people who had reported almost never exercising were the most likely to have died early.

But the most surprising result – and anyone who is familiar with reading scientific papers will know that the word 'surprising' rarely gets past the editors unless it genuinely is so – was that spending more time exercising did not correlate with living longer. In fact, the group of people who spent the most time exercising were those who went to the gym, and they showed the smallest increase in longevity based on the average. Rather, it was certain types of exercise that yielded the greatest benefits, for example tennis (an extra 9.7 years), badminton (6.2 years) and football (5 years).

What do all these sports have in common? They are social sports. You play with other people, you are part of a club, you are outside. As the researchers explained, belonging to a group that meets regularly promotes a sense of support, trust and commonality. And this has been shown time and again to contribute to a sense of well-being and improved long-term health.

Another study – a very large one from Britain that took place the year before – came to the same conclusion: racquet sports have the greatest benefit in terms of all forms of illness and death.

Exercising your heart is important, but so too is opening it to others.

Role Play

There are two phrases in the workplace that people dread. One is 'You're fired!' and the other is 'We're going to do some role play.'

Despite people (or rather our ego) being perturbed by the idea, the process of simulating a real-life situation via role play has huge value in helping us to stay relaxed. It trains our nervous system in the same way that Wing Tsun drills do. And it makes sure that we are not overly reliant on our rational brain. When attacked, we do not want to react by thinking or feeling. We need to sense, to use another of Jung's concepts. To use our instincts that have been trained.

When we have a press interview, Faye, our head of press at Leon (amongst other roles), will first drill us using the most difficult questions we can imagine. I first saw this in action when we were launching the School Food Plan for the UK government, and Orla, the Head of Communications at the Department for Education, grilled Secretary of State Michael Gove ahead of an interview about the plan.

I think she enjoyed asking questions like 'Isn't this just another example of weak, rudderless flip-flopping from a Secretary of State who doesn't actually know what he wants?' (It can be surreal sometimes when the real interview is so similar in content and feel to the role play that preceded it.)

In practising Wing Tsun, we train the nervous system. The goal is that our response to situations is governed not by emotional reaction, and not by an inevitably slow, conscious thought process, but by a response that comes from our trained instincts – from intuition. If the brain needs to think, the moment for acting will be lost – and our defence, or our punch, will be far too slow in coming. And if our reaction is emotional, driven by fear or other such characteristics of the ego, we will not only be more likely to be drawn into a fight, we will be tense and slow as we physically respond. In Wing Tsun, the many hours of practising a defence – or in Leon, practising continued drills for emergency situations – get us closer to being able to respond instinctively. Practice trains our instincts so that we act intuitively without the mind overthinking or our emotion taking over.

How Many Lawyers Does it Take to Change a . . . ?

I was recently advised of an HR issue (actually outside the UK) involving someone who we believed to be innocent of an accusation that had been made against them. Our investigation concluded beyond reasonable doubt that the accusation was made without substance by someone trying to avoid being dismissed themselves. The manager of the accused also took legal advice. The recommendation was that the safest thing to do was to fire the accused.

'But we believe they're innocent?' I asked.

'Yes,' came the response.

So my colleague asked for a second opinion. This second lawyer made the same recommendation as the first. So I asked him to get a third opinion. Again the same recommendation was made – to protect Leon we should fire the accused.

'You know, you can give me a hundred lawyers' opinions that we should let them go and I would disagree with every one,' I said. 'We are not firing them.' The next day the accuser made another accusation and the police were called. But this time we had CCTV footage . . . that showed that the accused was entirely innocent.

These sorts of decisions need to be made calmly. The lawyers were all acting out of fear, and not from a point of view of what was right. I remember being very calm and relaxed about ignoring the advice.

Wing Tsun helps. Breathing helps. And the decision requires neither thought nor emotion. Intuition provides certainty.

The Shoe Game (and the Importance of Peripheral Vision)

The training of our nervous system in Wing Tsun – and the resulting ability of Staying Relaxed – is the reason that the student of Wing Tsun retains the ability to maintain peripheral vision.

In a state of fight-or-flight – in the event of an attack from a fearsome predator (or in more modern 'acute stress' states, when you are low on phone battery or have no Wi-Fi) – the body typically shuts down peripheral vision and creates tunnel vision to focus the mind on this single attacker. However, if your *default* state keeps you constantly in fight-or-flight, your peripheral vision is compromised and you will be less likely to see an oncoming attack. And, on the same basis, you are less likely to see opportunity.

It is only by staying relaxed as your ongoing base state that you maintain your peripheral vision. As you will discover in the chapter on Positivity (see p. 200), an essential part of Leon is having the ability to spot moments of truth for the customer and to do something wonderful with them. Without peripheral vision, Leon people will not be able to spot these moments.

We need to understand that if you are already in a chronic state of fight-or-flight or a chronic state of inflammation when an attack occurs (or, in business terms, a problem arises), you are in danger of overreacting and creating excessively tunnelled vision, meaning your peripheral vision is compromised.

When our fight-or-flight response initially evolved, we faced isolated attacks, most often from single predators. But today we face attacks from all sides. It is therefore even more important to stay relaxed and maintain our peripheral vision.

At Leon, we play games in training that are designed to help us relax – by bringing people together, by training the nervous system and by developing people's peripheral vision. Those of you who are into football (soccer, obviously) will know that some coaches, during training, blow their whistle and ask every player to close his or her eyes and explain where each one of their teammates is on the pitch. The best players can do this for their own team and for the opposition players too. By contrast, I know that when I used to play football it was like being extremely drunk – I could see about three feet around me, and everything else was a blur.

But one can practise this and get better. And you can do this with the shoe game. It is a game we first played when we opened our second restaurant in Ludgate Circus. Everyone takes off one shoe and puts it in the middle of the circle. The task is for everyone to grab a shoe. Then we throw the shoes around the people in the circle in unison until the right shoes are back with the right people. You have to throw, catch and keep an eye out for your shoe, all at the same time. Which requires a huge amount of peripheral vision.

Just a week after we opened that restaurant, I was sitting in the corner watching lunchtime service when a customer spilled a drink. What followed was as good as the Bolshoi Ballet. One team member, who was close by, went straight to attend the customer as the first responder (!), while at the same time another – who was on their way to give another guest a tray of food – grabbed a mop and handed it seamlessly to the first person, while a third team member, who had seen the incident, made a replacement drink and took it to the guest. It was a joyous orchestration, and a great example of peripheral vision and an instinctive response.

Staying relaxed keeps your peripheral vision open, while stopping you being stressed out or distracted by what you tangentially see as a result.

The Serious Downside of Taking Business Seriously

There is a myth that persists in most businesses and other similar organizations that getting results is synonymous with being serious, and that having fun or being childlike is not only embarrassing, but also a barrier for serious people to do serious, proper work. I do not believe this to be true.

The first ever low-cost airline, Southwest Airlines, has put fun at the heart of its business and at the heart of its success. Go online and you will find videos of stewards and stewardesses performing the safety briefings as raps or as songs. If this sort of approach was top-down 'enforced fun', it would not work. What Southwest Airlines has done is create a culture where all this sort of humour authentically and amusingly bubbles from the frontline teams. And it's no coincidence that they have (and I'm touching wood as I write this) one of the best safety records in the industry. I believe that a company that nurtures a fun atmosphere and maintains a childlike mindset enables people to speak up. It means that people feel confident to say when the engine is making a funny noise, and that the barriers are broken down between the engineers, flight crews and pilots, and, certainly, the chief executive of the company.

The airline industry has tried to undergo a complete transformation in culture because of the Southwest Airlines model. There were too many examples of hierarchy and overall ego and seriousness getting in the way of proper communication. There's the story of the KLM flight where the co-pilot attempted to stop the pilot from taking off in fog, but the pilot pulled rank in quite an egotistical way, resulting in an airline disaster. There's the example (the re-enactment of which you can find online) of the engineer and pilot ganging up on the co-pilot on a flight which crashed because it was going too fast, despite the co-pilot's protestations. In it, you hear the pilot saying how pleased he is that they're going to get in slightly early and have a good gate, and even time to have a meal, but the co-pilot timidly warns him that they're going in too fast.

The engineer then butts in, saying to the pilot, 'You know, John, what's the difference between a duck and a co-pilot? A duck can fly.' The pilot laughs and the co-pilot is embarrassed into silence, even though it turns out he was right. And should have been listened to. So whilst humour and fun can break down barriers if based on love, if humour is used to shame or control, you should know that there will be dangerous consequences.

This type of barrier is the result of ego. And it is crucial for this type of ego to go away.

It is critical in all sorts of work environments that relationships are strong and there is a mutual respect. This may come from fun or this may come from deep, emotional work that teams have done together.

At Leon, we look for every opportunity to break down barriers between people who might otherwise be seen as the 'senior team' and the people who *really* make a difference, serving the customers and making their food every day. For a start, I spent a year working every Monday in one of our restaurants as a team member. We also have the Winter and Summer Well-being sessions.

We think it's okay to laugh a lot, especially at ourselves. We don't make it an objective; we just find that this is what happens when we don't take ourselves seriously and when we stay relaxed.

And we laugh about our mistakes (as long as no one has been hurt). It keeps them in our consciousness and creates a kind of folklore that helps the next generation learn. Like when someone cancelled one of our biggest events, even though it wasn't her call to do so. Or 'Chilli-con-carne-gate', when we teamed up with a deal app and completely overwhelmed all the restaurants one lunchtime (experiencing our version of the famed and ill-fated Hoover promotion that almost sucked them dry).

Now and in the Long Term

In the Winning Not Fighting workshops we have held at Leon across the last year, we have invited people to take five minutes to write down the things they do or could do to become more relaxed both immediately and in the long term.

The things that appear most often on the 'immediate' list?

Laughing. Breathing deeply. Going for a walk. Having sex. Listening to music. Eating (a small amount of dark?) chocolate. Cooking some food and eating it slowly. Tidying up (!). Calling a good friend. Eating a Leon LOVe Burger.

And on the long-term list?

Getting to sleep before 10.30 p.m. Switching off devices by 8 p.m. Learning an instrument. Learning a new language. Building good relationships at work. Mending any difficult relationships. Removing yourself from negative relationships. Getting more sun. Doing something creative. Changing your attitude to everything. Eating more Leon (I added that one).

What is your list?

Psychobiotics

Leon has been at the forefront of understanding gut health, and the role that prebiotics (providing good bacteria with the right food, especially fibre), probiotics (the good bacteria themselves) and a relaxed mindset has on our mind–body well-being. We have worked with King's College researcher Megan Rossi (aka the Gut Health Doctor) to advise Leon guests on their gut health and also to develop new products to support it.

You are a (wo)man, not a mouse, but the research into the link between good gut health and mental health in mice is pretty promising, and is supported by research on depression in humans.

The experiments suggest strongly that there is a vicious or a virtuous cycle – or mutually reinforcing cause and effect – between mind health and gut health. Healthy mice were put under stress and, as a result, their gut bacteria profile deteriorated. The good bacteria were overtaken by the bad. The researchers then injected normal mice with the bacteria from the stressed mice, and this new group became stressed.

Loads more research on humans has now been done, and more will be done in the near future as this fascinating field of study expands (or rather, as it catches up with ancient wisdoms).

By staying relaxed, you will help your gut be happy, and in turn you will be happier. You will create a positive cycle. And if you want to give it more momentum, eat some fermented foods and take some mood-enhancing (psychobiotic) bacteria supplements.

Captain Patrick

A few months ago, I was sitting in a bar on the Ionian island of Meganisi, writing this chapter. It was 2 a.m. and I was drinking rum . . . and double espresso (use of natural stimulants is the ninth wisdom of Wing Tsun and not covered in this book). And sitting next to me was the skipper of a large sailing yacht called Patrick (the skipper, not the yacht). Who was also drinking rum.

He asked me what I was doing and I explained the thinking behind this chapter, which prompted a conversation in which he shared his experiences of how its lessons – the need for calm, the need to have no ego – are applicable to sailing.

He explained that, on any boat he skippers, he has a rule of no running and no shouting. (I then felt a little bad about an argument I'd had with a superyacht crew after they refused to move their anchor when it had crossed ours. I'd done a little shouting . . .)

And he talked about all the – usually male – people he had seen on sailing holidays shouting at their families as they tried to moor their boat, refusing to admit they had done things wrong and refusing to accept input from other people. Patrick also explained how, as skipper, he had to take responsibility for everything that happened on his boat.

'The other evening,' he said, 'one of my crew made a mistake as we came into harbour. I was initially frustrated with her, but then I remembered that it was *my* responsibility to train her better and instruct her better, or not give her that role to perform.'

We all need to be more like Patrick. Accept criticism, be like water and put yourself aside.

Learn to respond, not react.

The Second Door

Chum Kiu – Consciously Connect
By Julian

Chum Kiu means 'Seeking the Bridge'. If the *tao* of the first form symbolized your journey has begun, then *kiu* ('bridge') represents the connection to the next stage of your life. You are actively seeking (*chum*) progression, personal success and the best way forward. This door is where you step into your Yang energy, driving forward your passions and achievements with new focus, tactics and approaches. It's where you understand that the secret to life is to find what you enjoy and just get good at it.

Whereas the Siu Nim Tao is self-focused and reflective, and requires you to isolate yourself to create clarity, Chum Kiu is dynamic and expansive. Where Siu Nim Tao taught you inner stillness, Chum Kiu now teaches you external flow.

Physically, this progression is represented by the movement within the form. While in the First Door you stayed in one static position, only focusing on the arm techniques, in the Second Door you are constantly moving, fluidly covering 360 degrees. You now learn how to turn, step and kick to maximum effect. Just like the First Door taught you how to punch in a way that's almost impossible to see, the Second Door continues this with the legs, teaching you explosive kicks and footwork that is hard to read. In Wing Tsun, these are known as 'shadow kicks' – so named because your shadow hardly moves when you perform them.

The movements in this Second Door are not limited to the lower body, however. Building on the techniques from the first form, they put together the single techniques you learned to create potent hand combinations. You learn new strikes, and how to defend against more skilled opponents. Furthermore, as Wing Tsun is a progressive art, you learn how to defeat someone who has mastered the winning strategies from the First Door.

Shadow kick in Wing Tsun – the posture doesn't move.

Chum Kiu is where you start to develop real physical expertise; your foundations are now much stronger, and you have already gone through a number of powerful transformations. By the time you are ready to enter the Third Door, you'll have the prowess of a professional teacher.

To achieve this, the Second Door teaches you a new level of force. In Siu Nim Tao you learned to isolate the elbow to generate relaxed force (as opposed to using the shoulder like in other martial arts). In Chum Kiu you are now able to generate additional relaxed force through your joints – known as Chat Sing Lik (seven star force) – to significantly upgrade the amount of power and speed you have.

You then connect this force to the rest of the body, utilizing its

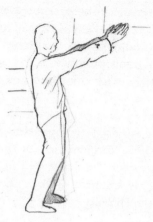

Seven Star Force – connecting the power of the body.

natural dynamics. You harness the force of turning and stepping so that all your weight and power is behind your strike – so no matter if you only weigh 40 kilograms, it still creates a huge force. A modern Wing Tsun saying explains this as 'the speed of a lightweight, but the power of a heavyweight'.

In Wing Tsun, we say 'movement creates flow'. This Second Door teaches what that means in practical terms. In combat, your

In Wing Tsun your force goes straight through the opponent.

flow of energy is essential. Your force needs to go through your opponent and not stop. That's why the old masters likened the strikes to an archer launching the punches. They are known as Zik Zin Choi, or arrow punches. Your body is the bow, and you fire out the strike with the speed and momentum of an arrow.

Mastering this flow of energy becomes a necessity in the Second Door, as you are also learning to deal with more than one attacker. You can't afford to spend time or energy using multiple hits on the same attacker. Your first shot must incapacitate the opponent immediately. In terms of force, the old masters called this principle 'first punch must kill'.

Redirecting the force of the opponent into a counter-attack.

Physical movement in turn creates more self-knowledge and heightened awareness. You have much more visibility of context, surroundings and relationships. There is greater clarity around the decisions and skills available to you. Whenever you have an unsolvable problem, the Second Door teaches you to start moving – whether this is just going for a simple walk or practising Wing Tsun – because staying in the same place will not help you find a solution. This principle is described by the saying 'If you stay, it is sure the opponent will hit you. If you move, it's only maybe.' Some of the biggest breakthroughs in the writing of this book happened while we were physically training.

Spiritually, the Second Door in Wing Tsun is known as the 'connecting door'. Thanks to your newfound inner awareness from Siu Nim Tao, you have started to develop a stronger sense of connection with yourself. And it's from this that you begin to bond with others. The connecting door has many openings, represented by the numerous motions in the form. As your skills develop, so does your sense of responsibility for all those around you.

Chum Kiu teaches you to search for the common and connecting points between you and others, rather than seeing the perceived differences. It also teaches you pattern recognition: how to see when something is being continually repeated in your life, and how to search out the reason why. Physically, this awareness prevents conflicts from being created. And in cases where conflict cannot be avoided, it enables you to know when – and how – to exploit your opponent's weak points should they attack you.

The development of this personal connection is seen by the concept of the Moon Pai – the Kung Fu 'family'. This sums up the beautiful dichotomy of the martial arts: we may be on our own path, but we all need support from others. In Wing Tsun, this is embodied by the Kwoon (meaning 'training hall'), which is the location where the teaching takes place. It is seen as a sacred space – not in a religious sense, but because it is safe.

This safe space is where all limits are challenged. A place of exploration and for physical, mental and spiritual transformation. You can be free to be you and to challenge your own boundaries, because the Kwoon is a fear-free place in which you can trust and be trusted.

You can see the nurturing relationships of the Kwoon reflected in the traditional titles. The master is known as Si-Fu, meaning

'Father-Teacher', and students more senior to yourself are known as Si-Hing/Si-Je, meaning 'Elder Brother/Sister Teacher'.

But the Kwoon is more than a physical space. The Second Door teaches you how to create this feeling of connection within you, so you can take it wherever you go. You become the embodiment of what the Kwoon stands for.

This feeling of flow comes with a sense of gentleness. You cannot connect to your body by force; it requires a natural process and understanding to develop. Similarly, you cannot connect with others by force; this requires a sense of harmony and a positive outlook.

The Second Door, therefore, is also about achieving balance. And not just in your movements, mindset and approach to life, but also in your self-care. Rather than only searching for a cure when there is an illness, you should constantly be working on prevention through awareness and understanding. Each aspect of your body affects and impacts others. For example, your gut being out of balance will affect your immune system, your energy levels and your brain. Similarly, a negative mindset will affect your gut bacteria, your immune system, your energy and your brain. The more you understand this interconnectedness, the healthier and more content you will become.

Finally, the Second Door illustrates the importance of physical motion to your health, gently reminding you to tap into our natural way of being as humans – which is to move. Even just moving every 20 to 40 minutes during the day will make a big difference to how you feel.

The third wisdom – Don't Force – teaches you the fallacy of force and control. The fourth wisdom – Positivity – teaches you how to motivate others and dynamically problem-solve. Both of them show you the power of honest, open and transparent conversations.

In business, the Second Door teaches you how to build

high-performance teams and a culture for success – creating a natural sense of movement and energy in your company and improving how you communicate with and relate to others.

Lessons of the Second Door

1. Search for what you are passionate about.
2. Search for the common and connecting points with others rather than perceived differences.
3. Movement creates flow – physically move whenever you are stuck trying to solve a problem or meet a challenge.
4. Connect powerfully with others by removing the need to control and replacing it with a positive, flowing approach.

5.

Don't Force
By John and Julian

Julian

The wisdom of Don't Force teaches you how to create healthy, empowered relationships. It illustrates both the fallacy and the illusion of attempting to use control when building and managing networks of people. It sets you up with the conditions for winning, and also maintaining this in the long term.

None of us likes to be forced. So why do we try and force others when it doesn't really work?

Forcing sets up a 'churn and burn' culture – when one person won't do something, you find someone else who will. There are, of course, varying degrees of this, but the result is the same: forcing creates repression. Repression creates resentment. Resentment creates conflict, both overt and covert. It becomes an endless, draining cycle.

The Chinese name for the wisdom of escaping this is Wu Wei. A Taoist term, it's often translated as 'non-action', but it's better understood as 'don't force' combined with the ability to use 'effortless action'.

Wu Wei is the Taoist notion that most profoundly influences

Wing Tsun. Taoists are deeply interested in harnessing natural energy forces and the flow of the universe, to connect to your own inner force. Its aim is to create harmony and longevity. Wing Tsun became the dynamic embodiment of this concept, creating a unique practical system to allow you to do this.

Wing Tsun first shows you the fallacy of attempting to use force when defending yourself. Forcing is based on physiological supremacy. It means that to beat someone you need to be stronger than them. A typical martial art 'block' is a great example of needing overriding force. It means that if you want to block a strike from someone who is more powerful than you, you will have a problem. Imagine a five-foot-tall woman trying to body-block a six-foot-five male bodybuilder who is running at her. It's possible, but unlikely. And extremely high-risk. This is why for many martial arts, the training in the Dojo is completely different to what they would actually do in a street-combat scenario, creating a potentially dangerous disconnect from reality.

And then there is the low level of actual effectiveness, even if you are powerful enough to block. For a block to be effective you need to know exactly what punch your opponent is throwing and which part of your body it is aimed at. The only way that this is possible is by relying on your eyes and the brain to process it. Unfortunately, as you saw in the chapter on Staying Relaxed, this is simply too slow. There are a great number of possible attacks, and you have to recognize them and respond perfectly in a split second. The only way that top masters of 'hard styles' manage to block is because they gain enough experience over the years to realize intuitively what will happen – before the strike has been launched. A non-telegraphic Wing Tsun punch, which gives no pre-warning as to when and where it will land, makes this method void.

One final issue with blocking is that, even if you are successful, you haven't actually solved the problem. All you've done is managed to stop one attack. The opponent is still free to continue with another strike – and with each attack your opponent is gaining more momentum and power. Sooner or later you will be hit.

So if you can't stop a person from attacking, what do you do? By using Wu Wei in Wing Tsun, the answer is simple – you just redirect the opponent's energy. By only using a small motion, you divert it to the outside of your body, where it is harmless to you. This relies on no strength from you, just a stable posture and good positioning, and it takes away all that mental and physical tension.

One example of this is the 'wedge theory', which takes away the opponent's force and directs your own straight through them. In almost the same moment as they punch, you counter-attack, using the mechanics generated by their attack.

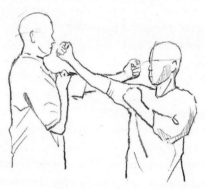

Defence and counter-attack using the punch as a wedge.

Combine this with using your own relaxed force – on the shortest line to the weakest parts of the opponent – and you have a powerful mechanism for winning. In Wing Tsun this is called the 'revolving door effect' – the harder you push one side of the door, the harder the other side of the door hits you. This is the practical example of karma for your opponent.

The combat wisdom of Don't Force tells you to do nothing unless there is a target to be hit. Fundamental to Wu Wei are the principles 'economy of motion', 'mini-max' (minimum effort for maximum effect) and 'less is more'. Physically, in a combat situation you only ever target a part of the opponent's body that will give an immediate win. That one strike should end the conflict immediately. Reflecting the dangerous reality of combat, this is known as 'first punch must kill' (not literally kill – rather rendering that person incapacitated), as you cannot afford for your stronger opponent to counter-attack.

Targets to win immediately in Wing Tsun.

Don't Force teaches you that if there is no target, then there is no strike – you never throw a punch for the sake of it. As your ability develops through the Second Door, you realize that there is always a target to be hit; it is simply a matter of timing and accuracy. No one can defend all parts of their body at the same time. And the more you train like this, the more this becomes instinctive – both physically and in terms of your perspective in life. This application of Don't Force is known as 'targetry' and 'spot the opportunity that presents itself'.

Finally, as you saw in Staying Relaxed, forcing creates tension and stops the flow of power from your body outwards. It makes you more likely to get injured, as you cannot feel or go with the force that comes into you. It also causes you danger via your own techniques – the lack of cohesion in your own movements can easily result in muscle tears or joint injuries.

Spiritually, Don't Force is linked to taking your judgement out of situations. In Wing Tsun, we talk about using discernment, not judgement, as a key step to personal harmony. Every time that you judge, you are attempting to force your own options, prejudices and upbringing onto a person or situation. Wing Tsun teaches you instead to take the personal aspect out and simply see if it is right for you right now. The end result is far quicker, with much less conflict and resentment created as a result. Letting go of the need to judge not only gives you the awareness to connect better with others, but also with yourself. It helps bring kindness to yourself; for when you are judging others you are really judging yourself too, through your own perception of what is flawed or wrong.

Don't Force is an easy wisdom to grasp. We get more from people when they are happy and want to do things. The use of force is similar to a battery power gauge. The more force you use, the quicker your life energy goes down. The less energy you have, the less you can achieve, the less you can do and the less satisfaction you derive from your life. Next time you think about forcing, take a pause and think if it's what you really need.

In business, Don't Force makes you far more effective, efficient and successful. It has a 'force multiplier' effect – it releases the energy spent trying to control, and focuses instead on achieving the best possible results. Similarly, if you can replace the idea of strong leadership linked with force to one linked with being calm, clear, focused and adaptable, then you have Wu Wei.

Don't Force also creates freedom – both for you and for those around you. (We will be exploring this further in the sixth wisdom, Freedom and Responsibility.) The opposite is true when you force – it creates an endless amount of complications and 'power play'. Relationships based on attempted control and fear are guaranteed to break down.

Furthermore, the longer you use force, the more it creates toxic codependent situations. Although this was understood nearly 2,000 years ago, it was more recently summed up in the Karpman drama triangle, which shows the switching roles in unhealthy relationships. Remove judgement and the attempt to control, and a lot of these situations go away. Don't Force is, therefore, about creating healthy relationships in the simplest, easiest way.

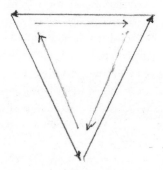

Karpman's Triangle.

The freedom and lightness you will feel from Don't Force allows you to tune into your natural adaptability and creativity. As you are no longer trying to force, it gives you the ability to see differently and create win–win situations. If you force, it masks your intentions. No matter how good these may be, it will be hard for others to see what they are. Wu Wei allows your intentions to be reflected in your behaviour, giving you a far greater chance of success. Don't Force allows you to create authentic relationships based on deeper connections, something that is an intrinsic need to us as human beings. Wu Wei, therefore, conveys a sense of naturalness and authenticity. Though, as we found out in Know Yourself, it can be scary to just be you, it is only by revealing your true self that you can actually create a lasting bridge with others.

For your own well-being, your ability not to force allows you to tune into your natural way of being. It allows you to understand your natural ergonomics – to feel how your body should best move, and to listen to it when it tells you to move. In particular, it's also about tuning into your biorhythms, and gradually matching your lifestyle to your innate circadian rhythms. The more you do this, the more energized you will feel. And, after all – as the Taoists realized two millennia ago – energy is the secret to living a great life . . .

Lessons of the Third Wisdom: Don't Force

1. Forcing creates resistance and conflict.
2. Forcing is ineffective and drains time and energy.
3. Don't Force allows you to have far deeper and longer-lasting relationships with others.
4. Don't Force allows you to have a creative, happy and motivated workforce.

John

Power Games

> Fierce winds do not blow all morning;
> a downpour of rain does not last the day.
> Who does this? Heaven and earth.
> But these are exaggerated, forced effects,
> and this is why they cannot be sustained.
> If heaven and earth cannot sustain a forced action,
> how much less is man able to do?
>
> Lao Tzu, *Tao Te Ching*

When one sees the world through the eyes of Wing Tsun, it's easy to forget that the way of Wing Tsun is so different from what is practised in our modern world.

When I meet other CEOs, many of whom have very big jobs, I find they believe that they have got to where they are by conquering, by fighting, by forcing. They often have a great intensity about them. They push hard, and then harder. Because no one gets anywhere without an aggressive plan, right?

One CEO and I were thinking of working together. Let's call them Alex. I actually like Alex very much. But Alex explained to me how they would fight to achieve outcomes at all costs. That they drove their teams hard. That they believed you need to constantly push harder. I explained my contrary views. And Alex concluded that's why we would make a good team: we were both very different.

'I'm not sure it quite works like that,' I said.

As it happens, Alex and I share a liking for the sea. But where I like a sailing boat, Alex likes powerboats. A sailing boat uses the wind and works with the tides. A motor yacht forces. And to what cost? A 70-foot motor yacht costs around £500 an hour in fuel, depending on how heavy it is and how fast you're going. Of course, over short distances, you'll get to your destination more quickly in a powerboat. Much like the way a CEO can power and force their way to short-term results. And then jump ship. Or grab an espresso martini at the yacht club. Or maybe have a swim in the pool and a club sandwich. But over the long term? To circumnavigate the globe, to go around the world in a complete, whole circle, the sailing boat will come back to where it started while the powerboat will have run out of fuel a long way from land. Probably somewhere in the Pacific, surrounded by lots of plastic.

As a society, we are choosing powerboats. And now these huge motor yachts have their own 'support vessels' to house the family's 'toys' – jet skis, helicopters, recreational submarines. It looked good in the 1980s, didn't it . . . But we cannot continue to bear the financial, human and environmental cost. Because, no matter how you look at it, a power that forces causes harm.

The First Follower

A good man called John Upton worked for Leon for a period, and in his interview he showed me a short film. Over two minutes or so long, it showed a real-life event that begins with one person dancing by himself to music on a hillside, while everyone else around him is sitting down. Then one other person decides to join him. This is the key moment where a lone leader is validated by the first follower – who is himself showing great leadership in doing so.

The role of this first follower is key. By dancing with the first man, he is saying, 'Hey, this guy is onto something – let's see where we can go with this.' The dancer is no longer the mad one, to be ridiculed. And it says to the others that it's okay to dance too. In the clip, a few others are inspired to join them, and they create a bit of a party. It becomes infectious. So more people join. Then more still. Then comes the tipping point – where the people who are not dancing suddenly feel like *they* are the odd ones out (perhaps you have been to the theatre when a standing ovation breaks out, and it goes from being strange to be standing to being strange to still be sitting down) and they join in the dancing. As the commentary on the film explains, the key moments include the decision of the first dancer to put himself out there and be prepared for people to think he is mad; the critical moment when the first follower validates him by dancing too; and the tipping point where it becomes the 'thing' to be dancing.

I was very struck by this film. And John's message was: *Let me come and be your first follower.* Now, there were other people in the previous 12 years who had been first followers in different guises, but I appreciated his point and the way he made it – so simply – very much.

The important point for this chapter – for the wisdom of not forcing – is that no one in the process depicted in the video had to force anyone to do anything. Each person played their part, like the runners in a relay, and the group dynamic was transformed in a way that reflects the fact that we are still at heart tribal beings. In us, we have the instinct to be like the pack of dogs who sense each other's minute movements and who move together. Or like the flock of birds who all change direction as one.

If you are the first dancer, just dance. That is all you have to do. And don't worry about what people think of you. You don't need to *make* anyone do anything. If you are the host at the party, you don't need to shout at everyone to 'start dancing'. It doesn't work. People will feel awkward, and unless they want to do you a real favour they will probably smile politely and say 'In a minute', or nervously mutter 'After this song . . .'

And if you are the first follower, it is not anything external that you need to control; it is your own inner confidence that enables you to stand shoulder to shoulder with the leader. This is its own special type of leadership. Jesus (the Lord of the Dance) had St Paul (though we can debate whether St Paul danced in quite the same way as Jesus). Del Boy had Rodney. Though maybe they did do a bit of forcing. Or was it fencing?

Nor did John Upton force anything in the interview with me. He quite simply showed me a short film. He didn't give me a hard sell on his 'plan' for Leon, or a PowerPoint presentation of his 'SWOT analysis' for the company, or tell me how his two biggest weaknesses are 'working too hard' or 'being a perfectionist'. And during his time at Leon he played a pivotal role in securing us some important franchise agreements, and in encouraging many other people both externally and internally to join the dance.

At Leon we are inspired by businesses that stand for something, that are trying to achieve something important beyond money. No business is perfect, but the early years of The Body Shop and the approach of adventure-clothing company Patagonia stand out as worthy of admiration. Both Anita Roddick and Yvon Chouinard had first followers who validated their 'madness' and who helped make sure others followed. Yes, they worked hard, but neither forced their businesses to succeed. Yvon Chouinard is very clear on what he does and doesn't do in the company, and he does not through ego try to pretend he is good at everything. It is rumoured that he says, 'If the factory burnt down I would not know what to do.' A friend of mine, who worked at The Body Shop as marketing director alongside Anita Roddick, explained that people he knows at Patagonia say that Chouinard (who was a pioneering mountaineer at a very young age) limits his role to something very simple – as did Arthur Stace, the man who repeatedly wrote the word 'Eternity' in chalk all over Sydney. Yvon tells his people which mountain to climb next and they climb it. And he spends a lot of time up an actual mountain, without a mobile phone. Occasionally he comes down to the office to answer a few questions, or occasionally his wife sends colleagues up to see him because she is mindful that he may be lonely.

The healer Jorge who attends our well-being events suggested at the last one that I would do well to spend every day at home and play the piano. In his rudimentary English he said, 'When John plays the piano, Leon will be well and grow.'

Before you laugh at this, reflect on whether there isn't actually some truth to it. When the leader is providing an environment where that is possible, they are inspiring the other thousand people that work for the company in ways that are far more powerful than coercion. (The only thing is, I can't really play the piano yet.)

By not overreaching, and by climbing mountains, Yvon Chouinard achieves more than he would if he were forcing everyone at Patagonia to 'go the extra mile'.

The Ego and Forcing

Your unconscious brain is, mostly, the boss of you. Or rather it *is* you. The bit of you that has conscious thoughts likes to think it's in charge, but in almost all respects it is not.

Imagine if you consciously had to think about breathing; if you had to remember to keep your heart beating or your stomach digesting. You probably wouldn't be able to think about anything else.

Fortunately, your unconscious brain takes care of everything without you having to consciously think about it. It monitors your peripheral vision and hearing, and constantly tests your gut reaction to situations. It has made many of the decisions that you believe you have taken rationally.

In an experiment that informed some of our thinking (or 'thinking') at Bain, people were left alone in a room and told to press a button whenever they decided they should. Their brains were monitored as they did so. The researchers discovered that the unconscious brain decided to press the button, and immediately after it had, the conscious brain fired up to rationalize the decision and convince itself that it had made it.

The unconscious brain allows the conscious brain, and the ego, to believe it is in control. There is a scene in the movie *My Big Fat Greek Wedding* where the female members of the family have an idea but agree that the only way to get it done is to get the father to 'have the idea'. So the women go and see the patriarch, and gently pose the problem in the hope that he will come up with the idea they have already formed. Slowly they wait for the penny to drop and for him to propose his breakthrough idea. The scene goes something like this: 'We can't work out what to do . . . we have two problems . . . we need someone to work in the travel agency. And completely separately, Elena needs a job.' There is a painful pause while they stare hopefully at him with raised, expectant eyebrows. Then, suddenly . . . 'Hold it! I have an idea!' he exclaims. 'What is it?' they say. 'Elena can work in the travel agency!!' he reveals. 'Oh my goodness, that's a genius idea,' they say, looking at each other in fake amazement that he has managed to come up with such a brilliant idea.

Your subconscious is the women of the family. And your conscious brain is the big fat dad. The conscious brain is not as clever, but likes to think it is in control. It wants to be in charge, to create (inadequate and misleading) maps of the world, and when fearful or angry it has a tendency to force. It places itself at the centre of the universe.

The desire we have to name and categorize and dissect and

define everything is part of our desire to control. As is the desire to be right and prove that others are wrong. We feel emotionally comfortable if we have subjected everything to our will in this way. Yet the words 'water' or 'rose' – nor all our scientific analysis of water or roses – can ever do justice to the complexity and awesomeness of what they truly are.

What you will learn in this chapter is to move from desiring to allowing. How to trust rather than seeking to control. How to give a little thought to – no, scrap that . . . Instead, let your unconscious reflect on Lao Tzu's suggestion that 'there is no way to happiness; happiness is the way'. By not trying to see the mystery of the universe, you are more likely to see it. To let the world unfold. I know from my home life and from running Leon that this works. Find the flow without forcing it and things will fall into place in ways that will at first surprise you. And, after a while, you will stop being surprised.

Jain's Guide

Jainism, like Buddhism, is an offshoot of Hinduism. Among other things, it advocates causing no harm to animals whatsoever. And in Jain temples in India, there are carvings that warn us to avoid five things: ego, jealousy, pride, greed and anger.

In Wing Tsun, we do not so much see these things as separate. We see them as faces of the same thing. Fear, anger, conflict, pride, jealousy, greed, separation – all can be used as synonyms for ego and desire. And yet humans also have a simultaneous yearning to love. To be whole. To not be consumed by a desire for things we do not have.

Ironically, in a bid not to desire, we find ourselves *desiring* not to desire. But not desiring does not come about as a result of forcing yourself not to desire. Forcing is an ally of desiring and of ego.

Don't Force teaches us to understand how love can calm the

ego, and that by practising not forcing, we can stop destroying the earth. But we had better do it quickly, before the planet shows us who's really in charge.

The task that faces us, then, is to choose love and wholeness over fear and ego and separation. Not forcing is a prerequisite for this. You cannot force yourself or anyone to choose love. Instead, you need to give up force altogether.

The trouble is, we are so conditioned to fight for everything that we are not even aware of the prevalence of this way of thinking. We have to 'fight for our rights', 'fight cancer', 'fight dementia'; we are taught to 'knock down doors' to be successful.

And so this idea of Wu Wei or 'not forcing' can seem extremely perplexing to people in the West who try to understand it for the first time – so contrary is it to the drip-drip-drip programming we have been given.

Growing from the Inside

Remember the tree? The seed has inside it a life force, an intent, that creates. It does what it does without forcing. It grows roots, and steadily, bit by bit, tiny step by tiny step, it does what it naturally knows how to do. It grows. From that seed, the tree becomes.

Occasionally, the concept of Wu Wei is described as 'allowing to grow'. And the strongest organizations are those which have grown rather than been constructed from the outside in.

This is how Innocent Drinks was built. Inside out, on powerful values, step by step. As soon as it became clear that they had created a profitable category of soft drinks, the big companies tried to beat them. PepsiCo, for example, spent lots of money to quickly launch a new Tropicana smoothie and juice range to compete. It didn't work, despite the fact that they are one of the most powerful consumer goods companies in the world. Or rather, *because* they are.

They could not replicate the organic layers, formed over ten years, that had made Innocent strong. The goodwill that had been built up with consumers and internally. PepsiCo could not force their way to success.

We have experienced the same at Leon. Many companies that are bigger than us have tried to get into the 'grab and go' and fast-food markets, including one leading British supermarket and a big casual dining chain. But money cannot buy culture. And many smaller- or medium-sized brands have been 'inspired' by our design, our food and our marketing. But all of this is trying to create something outside in. And it is a form of forcing.

Henry, my Leon co-founder, is always a rich source of fascinating insights and anecdotes. He was once shown a blueprint that a consulting arm of one of the major UK accountancy firms had created for a proposed Japanese mobile telecoms company that had no employees whatsoever and was some way off being launched. Yet the consulting firm had created a theoretical telco company down to the smallest detail. They had very detailed organograms, a plan for decision-making at every level of this theoretical organization (detailing who would be responsible for recommending, agreeing, inputting into and making decisions), salary details for everyone in the company, internal communication processes, marketing plans, theoretical locations of offices and depots – the works. All down to a rather reassuring but ultimately false level of detail. Calming for the ego; useless in reality. An organization created outside in, with no regard for the characters of the people who would work there, or for unknown and unpredictable future events or conditions.

The company did not succeed. Because success cannot be created outside-in like this. It must flow naturally from the inside out. Now I'm not saying don't have any forward planning. But concentrate on having the minimum required to know what to do next and to keep your options open as you flow down the mountain, like water, or grow like a tree.

Leon has been built inside out, and on natural rhythms and cycles of regeneration. In my mind, it has always been somewhere that reflects the seasons, the time of day, and that celebrates the summer and winter solstices, and so on. Unlike, for example, a Las Vegas casino designed to make sure you have no idea what time of day it is – or even what season of the year. By riding these natural rhythms, we do not have to force.

Dominating in Customer Service

When we were writing part of this book in the United States – out there for the launch of our first US restaurant, in Washington DC – we went to the supermarket. And, standing at the checkout, I spotted a giant noticeboard positioned by the exit for all to see. It featured a big photo of a proud employee, Matt, in his big green polo shirt. He had been recognized for his work. Under his photo it said: 'FOR DOMINATING IN CUSTOMER SERVICE'.

Let's just take a step back and ask ourselves what, actually, is customer service?

Being kind. Helping people. Solving their problems . . .

It's great that Matt's so good at it. But, of course, this supermarket had decided it was all a bit namby-pamby to put up a big photo of him in his big green polo shirt that says, 'WE LOVE MATT COS HE'S REALLY NICE AND GOOD AT HELPING'.

So instead, they've thought, *Because we're giving him an award for it, we're firing up the ego* – because that's what awards do – *so we'd better make it sound a bit more 'fighty'! So let's say DOMINATING in customer service, because then he'll have WON, and not just BEATEN everyone else in customer service but pretty much SMASHED EVERYONE ELSE INTO A PULP! BOOM!*

To help us not to force, we need to do away with the mirage of the fighting analogy. We need to replace it with something constructive, like the tree or garden metaphor. And we need to recognize that not forcing could also be interpreted as 'growing'. Or 'flowing'. Water flows without any real exertion.

We Need a More Aggressive Plan

The annual budget process – when most businesses ask their teams to commit to what they are going to produce next year in sales, profit and strategic goals – offers many opportunities to study human nature.

Imagine a projector screen with lots of data on it. To one side there stands someone whose turn it is to present their 'numbers'. The room is full of different types of people – poor sods who are about to do the same thing, or poor sods who've just done so; a silverback gorilla whose job it is to shout 'Higher, higher!'; and maybe the head of HR, whose job it is to make sure nobody cries, or to tend to the wounded if they do.

Typically, the presenter will forget the use of English. They'll jabber on about things they think are appropriate that have no bearing on real life, because this is something different – it's *business*.

At some stage, the presenter will be asked how they're going to achieve the 'numbers'. And they will reply, 'We're going to aggressively drive sales.' And people will nod, because that sounds like a very sensible thing to do. Plus it has some *grrrrr* in it, which will obviously make it work, and reassures everyone that there's a bit of obsession and grit in it.

Very rarely, however, someone will shyly put their hand up and ask, 'What does that mean?' And the presenter will stop, as if they've been asked a stupid question, and they'll look around the room for support.

Slowly, they'll realize there is none, because it doesn't actually mean *anything*.

And Leon is not immune to this. I sit in regional meetings (and board meetings too, with my excellent non-exec directors) and hear the phrase about driving sales. But imagine you are a restaurant manager and it's Monday morning. You say to your team, 'We have been asked to aggressively drive sales. So, hell, let's do it.'

People, out of loyalty to the manager and Leon, might say, 'Hell yeah, let's do it!' Maybe they'll high-five. But what then? How does one 'aggressively drive sales'? Stand outside and threaten people with physical harm if they don't come in? Drag them in by their hair?

At the time of writing, Leon has seven different sets of franchisees. This gives me an opportunity to compare how each operates and with what results. One of our principal franchisees focused for a few years on making money as the primary outcome, with little focus on customer or team. They made little money. Then a new leadership team focused on the customer and the culture and the well-being of their teams – and now they make a lot of money.

The real actions that are going to improve sales are actually these: make the food with genuine (not pre-packaged) love every time, give the guest a big warm welcome, serve them quickly, and thank them sincerely for coming.

No aggression. No shouting. Just knowing your food and your welcome will make them want to come back. And next time, they'll bring a friend.

So, don't aggressively drive sales. And don't force.

In the Shower, in the Bedroom – How Good Ideas Cannot be Forced

People do many things in the shower and the bath. A relaxing bath, so people tell me, can encourage one's mind into a state where ideas more easily flow. My personal experience is that the best time to imagine powerful ideas and to envision the future is in that precious, liminal place between sleep and waking (named the 'Theta state'). In this space, your conscious brain and your unconscious brain seem to be in dialogue. And often on a Saturday morning, when I'm supposed to be getting on with some household chore or other, my wife Katie might gently ask, 'Shouldn't you be getting up?' To which I often reply, 'Shh! I'm innovating.'

When I became responsible again for developing our food at Leon in 2013, I was frustrated that we didn't have a breakfast menu that truly reflected the promise of the brand. Then, on one of those Saturday mornings, the entire range appeared in my head. It was centred on three types of breakfast pots: poached egg pots (ham hock with truffle Gruyère; chorizo with our own baked beans; smoked salmon and avocado; and a full English egg pot with bacon, sausage, beans and mushrooms), live yoghurt pots, and porridge pots (Porridge of the Gods, blueberry and banana, etc.). For the next three years, we saw a 25 per cent growth in breakfast sales every year. And the egg pots and this range of breakfast dishes have inspired many brands on the high street with their breakfast menus.

Wu Wei teaches you not to strain the rational mind. Martin Luther rather insalubriously equated waiting for a good idea to come with relieving constipation. He said the key was to relax and not to force the idea to emerge. You have to trust that inspiration will come.

Keep your peripheral vision open – and your peripheral mind. Rather than laser-focusing on a problem, let your conscious brain send a gentle invitation to the real you underneath to come up with the solution. The *Tao Te Ching* tells us that if we stop trying to see the mystery, we will see it. Allow and trust, rather than desire. Relax and let go. Let the world unfold without you having to force it.

'Practice not-doing and everything will fall into place,' said

Lao Tzu. And: 'The master leads by emptying people's minds.' And, elsewhere: 'The best governor governs least.' How contrary to your upbringing is this? Or to how most businesses are run?

Recently, I made a list of some of the good things that have happened to Leon. None of them came about through forcing. Instead, they happened because we were clear in our intent and put ourselves in a position to spot and receive opportunities. We are, to use another metaphor, standing in our waders in the middle of a stream, fly-fishing, ready for a bite. Though spotting an opportunity is one thing; you then have to do something with it. Jim Collins calls this 'a return on luck'.

On my list: winning the *Observer Food Monthly* Best Newcomer Award (not the result of any PR effort, and thank you again to the judges); meeting an old colleague from Bain in the street who was working at investment firm Active, which subsequently became our first institutional investor; being approached by HMSHost, our first franchisee; being asked to create the School Food Plan by the government; being introduced to my business partner Brad Blum; being introduced to Fersen, who has become our biggest investor; meeting Steve Head (an important coach for all of us at Leon) at a conference; bidding for Julian at an auction; finding our US property agent by bumping into him on a visit to Chicago; and lastly – but not least(ly) – hiring many of our best people.

These are just a small proportion of the many things that I look back on as breakthroughs. And each time, I didn't do anything. I didn't push, I wasn't aggressive, I didn't force.

I'm not saying that you can just stay in bed, though it worked for John and Yoko. You still have to do Kung Fu – work hard without making it hard work. Focus on one thing, without overreaching, and maintain your peripheral vision.

Thinking is Overrated

Thinking has a role to play. As do words. But while they are a good servant they are a bad master. We must be aware of when thoughts and words are holding us back.

Our education system is based on rational structures. On essays, and on didactic argument. We live in a rational age, and while I don't want to dismiss the benefits that this has brought, we need to be more aware of the downsides.

Taoism invites us to be open to a special form of stupidity. And in doing so, we open ourselves up to our subconscious. To not look at a problem directly and with linear logic, but indirectly, keeping it in the corner of our eye, or tangentially in our thoughts. Without forcing.

The Chinese concept that we use in Wing Tsun, and which in turn helps us to not force, is Wu Shin ('no-mindedness'). Practise it. Just as a baby spends his waking hours unconscious, merging himself with his surroundings.

The *I Ching*, which predates the *Tao Te Ching* by a few centuries, offers us an even earlier insight into the notions of Taoist tradition. It is notable not so much for its specific content, but more for its description of the process of preparing for and practising divination. It includes ways to befuddle the rational mind so that it cannot get in the way of intuitive thought.

The *I Ching* describes the ritual of cracking a turtle shell and using the patterns created to help the person engaging in the process to glean new insight – one of the oldest recorded forms of divination.

It is similar to how people 'read' tea leaves. The turtle shell provides a reflection and a gateway into the subconscious and imagination. It is a way of scrambling or resting the rational mind – the equivalent of sticking it in the corner with a Disney movie while the grown-ups have a proper chat.

Describing the idea of no-mindedness, the philosopher Alan Watts wrote:

> The idea is not to reduce the human mind to a moronic vacuity, but to bring into play its innate and spontaneous intelligence by using it without forcing it. It is fundamental to both Taoist and Confucian thought that the natural man is to be trusted, and from their standpoint the Western mistrust of human nature – whether theological or technological – is a kind of schizophrenia.

We are encouraged by such an approach to let go. Imagine saying, 'Phew! I don't have to always think.' In fact, try it now. Breathe out and say 'Phew!' Especially if you're on a train or a plane. It will be funny. Make it loud. See if your ego is cool with it.

Move Your Body, Remove Your Mind

The fixation on academia and on rational thought has led us not only to ignore our unconscious; it has also led us to ignore our bodies. And, ironically, as our bodies and minds are linked, this has not helped our minds either. The academics that I know, on the whole, ignore their bodies, and often ignore their emotion and intuition too. (And they rarely move.)

By connecting our rational mind to our unconscious and our body, our ego and rational mind will learn to let go. It will learn not to force every situation. And it will stop thinking that it has to force and motivate us to act. We will remember what it was like to be moving as one tribe, trusting our natural instincts and not overthinking.

Procrastination is caused by overthinking. Stuff doesn't get done. Exercise and movement don't happen. To-do lists become longer. People put off asking someone on a date, fail to speak up at work or fail to go mountain-biking. The day remains unseized.

Mel Robbins's 5 Second Rule seeks to counter this. This is the story behind it . . .

Mel was very depressed. Each morning she hit the snooze button for hours on end. Then, one evening, she decided that the next morning, instead of prevaricating and sleeping in, she would count down – *five, four, three, two, one* – and get out of bed.

The next morning, for the first time in a long time, she found herself standing bolt upright as she reached 'one'. She was amazed. How could something so simple and potentially so cheesy have worked?

Because she had successfully disengaged thought and activated her body's innate desire to move.

Since then, not only has Mel used it to turn around her own life, she has successfully helped many others to do the same. Including me.

The message is that willpower and motivation are overrated. They often fail and they waste too much energy. And when they fail, you end up thinking you are not as good a person as all those motivated people.

So, instead – move. Count from five to one, be in flow, and act.

And if it's just getting up that's the problem, you can also move your alarm clock to the other side of the bedroom. You will instinctively cross the room to get it to stop the noise. You are not rationally deciding to do so; you are intuitively doing so.

You are not forcing yourself to act through willpower. Not forcing yourself to move. You are just acting on instinct and moving.

The next time you find yourself procrastinating, try it. It's time to show your rational brain it doesn't need to force.

Nature

There are two types of scientists. Those who wish to dominate, control and manipulate nature, and those who wish to work with it and learn from it.

It is not naturally possible for two women to work together to have a child in four and a half months. Nature cannot be forced, so maybe we should do ourselves a favour and stop trying.

The most experienced doctors – from paediatricians to A&E doctors – know that, most of the time, their job is to often leave the person well alone, to give the body a small helping hand, or take away the things that are getting in the way.

A doctor friend – an expert in intensive care – once said to me: 'We have to be careful not to fiddle too much out of an insecure need to intervene and prod. We have to let the body heal itself.'

Ayurvedic medicine, the oldest known system of understanding the body and mind – and how to nurture and heal them – is very aware of how we are attuned to the rhythms of nature. Our bodies change with the seasons, which are governed by the rotation of the earth around the sun. Female menstrual cycles and also male hormone cycles follow the monthly orbit of the moon around the earth; and the chemical, physical and energetic functions of the body and brain are defined by the cycle of the day as the earth rotates on its axis. By working with this flow, and not trying to force our bodies to do things that are not consistent with these rhythms, we allow ourselves to thrive.

In nature, of course, you cannot dig up the seed a month after sowing it and expect a proportion of the plant to be ready to eat. Julian's dad, when he left the army, farmed. 'You cannot force the earth,' he told Julian.

Businesses are the same. They have a natural growth rate that cannot be forced beyond what is healthy for the organization. At

Leon, we are limited by the speed at which we can grow talent, especially managers. And there is a natural limit to the speed at which managers can gain enough experience to be able to open or run a new restaurant. So we have to be patient. We believe we can probably grow our restaurant numbers by 25 per cent a year.

The same patience is required in turnarounds. In turning around Olive Garden, my friend Brad knew that he had to do things in stages. First, he had to reduce costs, and build a relationship with the key people he wanted to retain – people like his operations director Bob Mock. Then he had to hire a new team, improve the food (based on authentic Italian ingredients), clean up the restaurants, create a service culture, improve the PR and marketing of the brand, and finally – and this was only after five years – begin opening new Olive Garden restaurants. He knew, and made everyone aware, that the turnaround would take time.

However, we live in an age where investors, especially owners of public stocks, can be extremely impatient. So part of the job of a CEO is to explain the concept of not forcing to both board members and investors, and to be strong enough to hold out, knowing that the harvest will come – even though investors are staring at a bare field.

The mindful CEO has to have faith that the seed is going to flourish and bloom. You will sometimes hear in business – or in other areas of life – that 'it took us ten years to become an overnight success'. The public sees the moment of the crop bursting into life. They do not see the process of ploughing, planting and watering.

As a CEO, I see my role sometimes as a farmer, standing next to the field with my chin resting on the handle of the spade, chewing some grass, muttering phrases like 'Be patient, my friends . . .'

I am consistently repeating one message at Leon more than any other: nature looks complex, but when you break down each activity that nature performs, each one is remarkably simple. A human cell, for example, does what it needs to do simply and repeatedly.

As businesses and as human beings, we cut ourselves off from nature at our peril. The offices of big multinational companies – where big decisions are made that affect us all – are often devoid of nature. If a fly or insect gets in, people scream.

These are places where people try to force or outwit nature. They could do well to learn the lessons that nature offers. And they would do well to employ more farmers.

I am tickled by the definition of school that says it is somewhere you send your children to be brought up by other children.

Of course, the best – and worst – teachers can play an important role, but even without the actions of their teacher, children will grow, they will develop, they will get taller, they will learn, they will observe. They will discover how to relate to each other and they will understand how to interact with the world.

So there is a momentum, like a running river, with which teachers must deal. It is the job of the head teacher to make sure that the flow – this inexorable force of development – is nudged in the right direction. It is not the job of the teacher to interfere or direct constantly, or take away freedom or initiative from the student. It is the job of the teacher to inspire, to ask questions of the student, and to help the student come to their own conclusions. One of the best teachers that I ever had was a history teacher who never once made a statement, but instead imparted knowledge by constantly questioning the class. He never tried to force knowledge onto us. It meant that we were always alert and engaged, and continuously thinking and taking on new ideas by the way he embedded knowledge within the questions.

On my best days at Leon, I remember to be a teacher. On my worst, I want to shut the school and send all the pupils home.

But Wing Tsun has helped with this.

Be Like Water and the Mountain

The natural metaphors of the tree and the garden offer us an alternative model for how to think of 'growing' as opposed to forcing. But what of water?

When we launched our Leon water brand, we called it 'Be like' – as in 'Be like water . . .' We included a quote from Lao Tzu (and one by Margaret Atwood that we had to remove when her agent spotted it). It said: 'Nothing is softer or more flexible than water, yet nothing can resist it.'

Water appears throughout Chinese wisdom as something to be emulated. I have learned from studying water to try to be as low as the sea (i.e. have no ego), to go with the flow, and to approach a task, or run a company, the way that water gets from the top of the mountain to the sea.

Water does not over-plan – it sets its objective and begins. It fails, learns and adjusts. When its path might take it uphill (which it cannot do for long), it corrects. When it hits an obstacle, it goes round it.

For us at Leon, that means being clear about where we want to get to (to be the number-one brand in naturally fast food), and then trying lots of ways of doing so. We test out new products in one restaurant. We try out potential new hires before giving them full-time roles. We trial a new screen ordering system. Or a new way of doing online advertising. We fail, we learn, we re-route, and sometimes we succeed.

Jimmy Allen, one of the best business consultants I know, reminded me recently that every beer company in the world has an objective to 'win in China'. Most of them create steering groups and project teams, and have a global conference on the subject in Hawaii (or some other place that is convenient for all the global heads to get to, and which is not particularly close to China). And everyone leaves with a mug and a mouse mat that says #WinningInChina to remind them, when they're back at their desks, that this is a big priority. And they go away to develop lots of very clear plans and ideas and Gantt charts and timetables and they prepare their PowerPoint presentations for steering group meetings. And then, in the steering group meeting, they finally all agree after much discussion that there should be a *key next step* and that the best next step is to have another meeting – in three or four months – to 'keep up momentum'. And they start with some real action – well, real research. They commission competitor reports, do consumer research, have customer taste panels and write recommendation papers for the regional board that then get presented to the global board.

The best companies, and typically the ones that succeed, begin tomorrow or even today. The CEO gets on the phone and speaks to the local rep in Shanghai. They choose one bar in Shanghai, and speak to the owner. And not just the owner, but to the bar manager and the actual person working that night serving the customers. They partner them with a streetwise (typically young) sales and marketing person, and try to sell more beer. That night.

The next morning, the CEO calls the bartender and asks, 'How did it go?'

They encourage the people who work in the bar and the local marketing person to DO things – to fail, to learn, to try again. In parallel, they have a small team of people working out how the company will scale whatever has worked in that one bar across the whole of Shanghai, and then across the whole of China, once they have won in that bar.

They act, in short, like water – begin, fail, learn and flow.

Recently, I sat down with our Leon investor Fersen Lambranho from GP Investments to find out what he and his own mentors – 3G Capital's Jorge Lemann, Marcel Telles and Beto Sicupira – could teach me about how we can win. (We have already mentioned them, and will meet them again – because they are, to my mind, masters of business, and we need to talk about why.) What, I asked him, was their secret?

The answer was water. Sort of. He explained that they repeatedly ensure all their businesses have three things: a great team working within a meritocratic culture, a simple operating model, and a fluid management process where the management try, learn, check back and adapt.

If you want to win and not fight, don't force. Be clear on what you hope to achieve, and begin, knowing that you will adjust and self-correct in ways that you have no way of predicting when you start.

And when new opportunities arise, when new targets present themselves, be flexible and flowing enough to go for them.

Japan, Water, Perfectionism and the Tao of Total Quality

With its spirit of mastery – and in the very essence and teaching of the martial art itself – Wing Tsun is a safeguard against and antidote to perfectionism. Influenced as it is by both Taoism and Zen Buddhism, it offers (as far as it can) an egoless, fluid, flexible, not forcing, not rigid, soft approach to both the art and the learning of the art. Perfectionism is a twin of forcing – driven by the ego and a fear of making mistakes. And this insecurity for many people can lead to, as the saying goes, allowing perfection to be the enemy of good. The procrastination that comes from perfectionism has killed many a business idea, and stifled many a relationship and career.

Here's how we all got to this point . . .

After World War Two, the Americans were keen to help the Japanese rebuild their country and their economy. The Americans helped them instil systems to constantly improve their output based on a constant cycle of trying, failing, learning, reviewing, improving and succeeding. Much like water attempts to go down a hill, succeeds or fails, finds its way around a rock, readjusts quickly.

The Japanese used these principles of quickly trying and learning and adapting and being more flexible and applied them to their industries. The result was that Japanese industry blossomed.

Wind the clock forward to the 1970s, and American companies started to look at what was happening in Japan and compared it to their own performances. Japan was overtaking the West. So they went to Japan and asked, 'What's the secret?'

'What do you mean?' replied the Japanese. 'We're just doing what you told us to do. Be fluid, begin, try, fail, review and improve.'

America, having taught Japan these fundamental principles, had found itself stultified in a more top-down, militaristic, cumbersome, ego-driven corporate culture that loved a conglomerate.

It was then, in the 1980s, that the West – not Japan – created a term for the more fluid way of working: 'total quality management'. And in 1985, the US Navy explicitly used the term to describe its approach to improving the performance of its fleet.

Total quality management is, in my view, one of the most misunderstood ideas in business history. In the West, we looked at Japan and its manufacturing businesses and – to use the phrase from that book – saw that it was good. Or rather, saw that it was . . . perfect. *Shit*, we thought, *we'd better do everything totally perfectly too.*

'Everyone, gather round. I want you to make your fridges and cars perfectly, just like the Japanese. And I want all the documents you produce to be perfectly perfect, and the spreadsheets to be formatted perfectly perfectly. Don't present new product ideas to me until they're flawless. Capiche? Right, go.'

Our business and family friend Jane Melvin would later write a book about dance titled *What You See is Not What You Do*. In it, she explains that the moves you see a dancer make are the product of passion and practice. They dance like that because of what is coming from within. It cannot be replicated by observation from without.

We in the West made a mistake – we looked at the quality of products being manufactured by Japan and concluded that perfect products came from perfectionism. In fact, a perfectionist attitude slows down an organization, depletes innovation and does not inspire creativity and progress.

The quality we saw from Japanese industry was actually the result of countless failures and a commitment to constantly act, learn, check and readjust.

The Drawer of Wishes

Our second restaurant, Ludgate Circus, reminded me how to trust what comes without judging or fighting it. The night before we opened we needed furniture, so I went to an auction and took my daughter Natasha, who was then five. The inevitable happened, and Natasha put her hands up without thinking and we 'won' a rather chintzy tea set. It sat on the shelf at the back of the restaurant from then on, and it has become a treasured part of the place.

I also bought a chest of drawers that night that is still there in the restaurant. Spontaneously, people started putting wishes in it – 'I wish I was still with my boyfriend', 'I wish I could visit my mum in Brazil' . . . We don't know how it started, but it became like the Trevi Fountain in Rome where people throw coins, or the bridge in Paris where people attach padlocks. It filled up with wishes from people all over the world.

This is not something we 'engineered'. It happened and then grew spontaneously from the energy created by the place. We did not have a forced methodology for 'how to create a talking point' with a strict three-phase process of 'ideation, screening and priority setting'. It happened, and we were able to gently share it with anyone interested in the story, which was quite a few people. (You can see a photo of this 'drawer of wishes' and examples of some of the wishes in our second cookbook, *Naturally Fast Food*.)

One day, your PR company will come to you with an idea that is the equivalent of World Smile Day, which was created to promote toothpaste. It will be a terrible idea because it will have been forced. It will be fighting, not winning.

Taoism considers the universe – the Tao itself – to be unconscious of how it creates itself and grows from within. Unlike the monotheistic view of an all-knowing power who consciously created the world outside in.

I am not saying which is right – but what I am saying is that you would do well to live your life, and run your business, by being unconsciously in flow rather than fabricating events or ideas that are not from the way of the Tao.

When the Easy Thing's the Right Thing

My final major project at Bain was to advise a businessman called Vivian Imerman. At the start of 2003, Vivian had bought a 160-year-old business which had, for the previous 40 years, been what we call an 'orphan business' – it was passed between big global companies, conglomerates and entrepreneurs without ever having a stable home. When my Bain team and I completed the turnaround strategy for him, Vivian said to me, 'Would you be the CEO of Whyte & Mackay?' To which I replied, 'Thank you, Vivian, but I'm going to do my own sweet, pure little start-up.'

And he said, 'Well, why don't I fund your sweet little start-up so that we can then run Whyte & Mackay together?'

What followed was four years of extremely intense work.

As I reflect on it, the success of the Whyte & Mackay turnaround (Vivian bought it for £200 million and sold it for £595 million four years later) lay in the fact that we understood the need to not force. Throughout, Vivian was the clear boss. But I was responsible for leading the strategy on the branded side of the company, while he led both the manufacturing and the trading side (where we sold the whisky we made to other whisky companies so they could put our whisky in their bottles, and to supermarkets who could stick their own-brand label on it).

I set about turning around the company's major brands. In London, my friends Simon Baker and Adam Nice worked with me on the creative work, and Stewart Lawrie and Bob Brannan contributed commercial insight from the Glasgow office in their respective roles as UK MD and overall MD.

We focused on four brands: Whyte & Mackay itself, Jura single malt whisky, The Dalmore single malt whisky and Vladivar vodka.

In three cases we were successful, and in one we were not. Each case in which we were successful worked because we did what was most natural for the brand, given its history. The one that failed did so because we 'forced' a positioning onto the brand.

With Whyte & Mackay, Jura and The Dalmore, the branding of all three had become cheap – tacky, even. It lacked style and a core idea, and seemingly had nothing to do with what the founders would have had in mind at inception. To use language that I would be more familiar with today, I felt that these brands did not know themselves. In all three cases I went back and looked at the packaging and brand idea they had when they were first started over a hundred years ago.

We found a room at the Glasgow head office where one of the brands had all of the bottle styles it had ever made, displayed in chronological order. It was like watching the opposite of the evolution of humans – the regression of a brand. For the last hundred years, over a series of 10 to 12 generations, successive designers and brand teams had 'modernized' the brand. And like some terrible game of Chinese whispers, they had slowly stripped the brand and packaging of its original strength and identity.

With Jura, made on the beautiful island of the same name off the west coast of Scotland, there was so much ready material it was like owning a gold mine (I imagine). But not enough of this was coming across in the way the brand was being managed. Here was an island where there were more sheep than people; with amazing soil, water and air to feed the flavour of the malt whisky; featuring a whirlpool nearby, and a tombstone that seemed to suggest that someone had lived to 120 years old and their mother to the age of 200 (unlikely, but a nice story nevertheless); known as the country home of the Astors and the place where George Orwell wrote *Nineteen Eighty-Four*. There was even a lodge above the distillery that had been neglected.

The easy route (and, as it turns out, the right route) was to work with all of this rich material. The central organizing idea (and credit goes to Simon Baker and Adam Nice for developing and creating this) was 'Taste Island Life'. Since the island of Jura is warmed by the Gulf Stream, it doesn't look typically Scottish – and thus, as a whisky, the Jura brand challenged many of the stereotypes of Scotch. Its imagery is of white sandy beaches rather than the Highlands; its food is cooked crab not haggis; its 'kings' are the Astors not Robert the Bruce; its poet George Orwell not Robert Burns; it has warm blue sea not foggy valleys.

We decided to take the most obvious route, not just with branding but also with PR. Steve Coltrin is a good friend of mine and fantastic PR guy from New York. He rather amusingly does the PR for the Mormon Church, and it was he who – after *The Book of Mormon* came out – led the advertising campaign 'You've seen the play . . . now read the book'.

Steve explained to me that the way to do the PR for the Church was to never talk to the religious correspondents. Given Jura's dubious reputation (at the time) with whisky writers, Steve encouraged us to look for every opportunity to talk to other types of journalists. For example, we redecorated the lodge and contacted travel, design and style writers. We invited Alexander McCall Smith to become the writer in residence, which gave us the opportunity to talk to the literary press. We did not force. We went with what we had, and bypassed the whisky writers, not trying to get them to change their minds. Eventually, the whisky writers woke up and decided that they really needed to write a story about Jura.

When it came to The Dalmore, the brand teams in Scotland came to me and said, 'Right, now, let's do the same for The Dalmore. Let's build a lodge at The Dalmore and let's tell all the stories about where the whisky is made.' There was only one problem. The place where The Dalmore is made is not as picturesque as Jura. Rather than being different because of where it's made, The Dalmore is different because of all the associations of where and how it is drunk. Or, to be more precise, its role as a coveted luxury good.

So, rather than saying that The Dalmore competes in the whisky business, we were very clear that it should compete in the luxury goods business. We treated it as an alternative to Cohiba cigars and Purdey guns. And this informed how we talked about the brand, what imagery we used, where it was merchandised and how it was advertised. We positioned it as the ultimate gift and spent significant money upgrading the packaging, including the creation of a beautiful golden stag – and because the stag image had been bestowed upon the brand by a Scottish king, we called it the 'king of malts'. The single word that we used to describe this positioning was 'connoisseurship'.

When it came to Whyte & Mackay, we took time to explore the vision of the two founders, Mr Whyte and Mr Mackay, way back in 1844. We looked at the style of the original distillery, the copper stills, the dress sense of the two founders – coupled with the rugged masculinity of the pubs in which the brand is drunk today. We replaced something that had been tackily branded with something that was stylish and in keeping with the grittiness and strength of character, both of the original brand and of the places where it's consumed.

The brand with which we failed was Vladivar. Vladivar was launched in the 1980s on the relatively parochial, UK-specific tagline 'Vodka from Varrington', where (in case you didn't get it) the word 'Warrington' was given a V-sound by a Russian actor. The joke being that most vodka is from Russia, but this vodka was from the UK town of Warrington.

A brand idea that may have been amusing at the time of its launch was not strong enough to carry it in the twenty-first century, nor to carry it internationally. But we had very little to go on – well, nothing – in terms of reinvigorating the original concept. So the brand team created an idea of positive subversion.

I'm still intrigued as to whether it would have worked if executed properly. They wanted to own the cool, underground movement and youth culture, and help the brand leap into a new idea which had nothing to do with its original inception. The packaging was cool, the imagery was cool, the clubs, DJs and music events associated with the brand were cool, but the relaunch didn't work. I think there were some problems with executing the campaign – partly because the company had just employed a new marketing director at the time of the launch. However, it's interesting that the only brand of the four that failed was one for which we had no guiding principle that reflected the initial energy of the brand.

Where you can, go with the momentum and energy that exists. And don't bet on being able to force yourself to a new place.

Watch Out for Yellow Budgies

I was in the New York reception of BuzzFeed, waiting for the receptionist to contact the person we were meeting, when a young woman approached another receptionist and said, 'Hi there, I've sent my CV in online but wanted to drop off a hard copy too.'

'I'm sorry,' she was told. 'We don't do that.'

'I'll take it,' I said. 'I don't work here, but I do work at a company that likes to keep its eyes open for opportunities.'

A little surprised, but open to the offer, she gave me her CV.

Her name was Carlen, and she had recently graduated from the University of Miami. It turned out she had created her own online channel – based on positivity – and loved food. I suggested that, if she wanted to work with us, she should fly to London to find out who we are and what makes us tick. And she now works for Leon, making all of our US films for social media.

So not only did I go for the opportunity that presented itself, but Carlen did too. My experience – and my belief – tells me that the universe gives us these opportunities, and that our job is to keep our eyes open for them.

My friend Vivian Imerman, who owned Whyte & Mackay, calls this 'catching the yellow budgies'. I am not entirely sure where the phrase comes from, but his point is that everyone has yellow budgies (aka opportunities) flying past them. But few people have the vision and tenacity – and, above all, courage – to catch them.

Some people feel that life has not given them the opportunities that others have had. All I can say is that life probably gave them more opportunities than they realized. Keep your eyes open for the yellow budgies – whatever your own particular yellow budgies are.

Many of my key hires have been made by me being open to giving people a chance, and them going with the opportunity that has been given. Rebecca, who is now head of marketing, is at Leon because, after I received her CV, I offered her the chance to work on a consumer goods business plan as a trial. She agreed. And she blossomed.

Realize that spotting these opportunities is so much harder if you are forcing, are off balance, or you are trying too hard. Fear and forcing narrow your vision.

Business books are full of case studies that are structured something like 'here was the problem, so we took this action, and here was the result'. This paints business as if it is a struggle – a series of problems that require huge coordinated mobilization to solve. And in interviews, one is trained to recount the Herculean efforts one has made to transform the company or department – often ignoring the role that *chance* has played. People have more often than they like to admit been successful by allowing things to flow and grow, but they tell a story of how they have forced something or 'gone the extra mile' (which can be problematic, because it can take up to 45 minutes to get back to where you were supposed to be). I mean, who is brave enough in an interview to say, 'I imagined clearly what I wanted, put myself in the right place and waited for someone or something to come along, then grabbed the opportunity when it did'?

You, soon, hopefully.

If I look back on all the great things that have happened at Leon (and I use that phrase rather than 'the things we have achieved'), none of them have happened through forcing. They have occurred because we were clear on what we wanted to achieve, put ourselves in a position to attract and see opportunities, kept our eyes open, and grabbed the yellow budgies as they flew past.

When I was on *Newsnight* in 2012 talking about the economic impact of the Olympics, right in the middle of it I took the opportunity to use the fact that it was live TV and I launched a promotion. 'If anyone comes in tomorrow and says "I love your rings",' I said, 'I'll give them a free side.' We had quite good take-up.

You Can Only Force People for so Long

When I was in primary school, I used to have the odd fight with someone called Matthew Skordis. One lunchtime, we were in the classroom with no other kids around – and, for reasons I completely forget, we got into a tussle. This particular confrontation ended up with me holding him in a head lock. I remember thinking, *Well, what do I do now? I can't stay holding him like this for the next 45 minutes.* So I said that I would let him go on the understanding that the fight was over. He agreed. I released him. And he punched me right in the groin. It was a good shot.

You see, you can only force people to do things against their will for so long. At some stage, sooner or later, they will decide to rebel – or you will have to release them. Because when you are forcing someone or trying to control someone, you are only allowing yourself to be controlled.

At Leon, I make sure that only those who truly want to stay, stay. If someone says – and it happens – that Leon is not the place for them, I suggest that it would be a good time for them to leave. We are stronger when those on the bus want to be on the bus.

My job, then, is to create the space for them to do and achieve the things that they want to achieve. Which mostly means getting out of their way. Consider the advice from the *Tao Te Ching*: 'The good leader is someone about whom the people say, "We did it ourselves."'

> If you want to be a great leader,
> you must learn to follow the Tao.
> Stop trying to control.
> Let go of fixed plans and concepts,
> and the world will govern itself . . .
> How do I know this is so?

> Because in this world,
> the greater the restrictions and prohibitions,
> the more people are impoverished;
> the more advanced the weapons of state,
> the darker the nation;
> the more artful and crafty the plan,
> the stranger the outcome;
> the more laws that are posted
> the more thieves appear.
> Therefore the sage says:
> I take no action and people are reformed.
> I enjoy peace and people become honest.
> I do nothing and people become rich.
> If I keep from imposing on people,
> they become themselves.

Can you bring yourself to lead like this? You will need to put aside fear, and to relax your mind and your body. Let yourself go, but not in a 'he's really let himself go' way.

In fact, instead of being at work, trying to control, maybe do some gentle exercise or play the piano. It is just what my Mexican friend and shaman Jorge suggested I do: help Leon grow by staying at home and playing the piano.

Intention, and Coincidence

Kung Fu means 'working hard'. Wing Tsun believes that we must work hard without making it hard work. Which means putting in the hours, but not so many that you burn out. To practise, but in a way that you learn best, without forcing and obsessing. The obsessive, as we have explored (and will explore again), will 'win ugly' while at the same time seeking shortcuts.

My perception of my own experience (deluded or not) is that

if you ask the universe for help, it provides it. It is your job to picture exactly what you aspire to, and keep your eyes open.

Perhaps at a very ordinary level, we keep our eyes open for coincidence or patterns.

When we are clear on what we want, our brain is trained to spot patterns that help us achieve it. If we decide we want to buy a yellow Toyota, suddenly we see yellow Toyotas everywhere, or adverts for yellow Toyotas (although, these days, algorithms sell us yellow Toyotas because they know we've searched for them, or because we have a similar digital profile to existing buyers of yellow Toyotas).

I have also found that, by making a wish, the universe will respond by helping you out in ways that seem to go beyond co-incidence. People hold beliefs in private that they are not always prepared to voice in public, but I know quite a few interesting characters who believe we have an ability to create outcomes by clearly picturing them and then waiting for the 'universe' to deliver.

I will let you decide what you believe.

But here is an example . . .

I was in a meeting with Leon's managers explaining this con-cept to them, and had shared quite a few of my experiences. And they were kind and open-minded enough to listen without judg-ing. And then the next agenda item centred on the fact that our tables and chairs licence had been taken away for no good rea-son at our restaurant in London's Regent Street, even though the brands either side of us were able to keep theirs.

'I wish,' I said to the room, 'I could go on *Newsnight* and tell people how the government is screwing up the high street.'

Five minutes later, one of our colleagues, Beth, came into the room. 'I'm sorry to interrupt,' she said, 'but *Newsnight* have just called to ask if you'll go on tonight and talk about the future of the high street.'

I nodded, turned to the group – who were quite taken aback – and said, 'You see how this works now?'

A few hours later I was on the show, with a platform to explain how the high street will not prosper until rents are subject to proper market forces (they are one of the only asset classes that have upward-only prices) and the local authorities exercise the law on planning with more intelligence.

The sceptics argue that these things are always just coincidence, that we are programmed to spot patterns even where they don't really exist, and that you don't notice these coincidences when they don't happen. The rational part of me has some sympathy. But I also know that, for whatever reason, the less I force, the more opportunities and adventures arise. Am I more relaxed so I see them? Probably. Is there something weirder going on? Was Jung onto something when he started to investigate synchronicity? Dunno. What I do know is that you have to meet the universe halfway.

There is a joke about a man who prays to God to let him win the lottery. Three months later, he's still not won a penny. So he asks God why he has forsaken him. 'Meet me halfway,' says God. 'Buy a lottery ticket.'

The equivalent of buying the lottery ticket is deciding exactly what it is you want to create (fast food in heaven, in our case), practising hard without making it hard work, and staying relaxed enough to spot and catch the yellow budgies when they fly by.

6.

Positivity
By John and Julian

Julian

Positivity is a mainstay of Wing Tsun. It is about proactive action, rather than reactive behaviour. Whereas Staying Relaxed taught you about your internal response to a challenge, this wisdom now focuses on your engagement with the world. It shows you how to build meaningful connections, moving past a life of just surviving into one of thriving.

In Wing Tsun, the mind is not just an abstract or spiritual concept but a vital reality that makes the difference between your life and death. As any veteran of combat will tell you, mindset counts for far more than any training, talent or equipment.

Wing Tsun took a deep appreciation of combat psychology, along with the spiritual wisdoms of Zen, Buddhism and Taoism, and created a whole system based upon it. The key factor sticking it all together? A special wisdom known as Wing Tsun Positivity . . .

This wisdom is subtly different from what we understand to be positivity in the West – 'the practice of being or tendency to be positive or optimistic in attitude'. Instead, training in Wing Tsun Positivity is centred on creating trust in yourself in the present moment. This is a fundamental prerequisite for success, and one that is all too often ignored. Life is unpredictable, and this wisdom builds an unbreakable bond of personal self-belief and self-trust to enable you to deal with whatever you are faced with. The more you practise this, the more it transcends being just a mindset, and becomes intrinsic to your whole way of being.

As always, the physical teachings reflect the guidance for empowered living. So, physically, Wing Tsun teaches you this trust and belief in yourself from the first moment you move your arms. Fear can be positively channelled, and then dissipated, by our unique body language. Rather than lifting up your arms to create a guard to defend yourself (a negative state of mind), we instead go forward, ready to take positive action as and when it is needed. This is a significant contrast to other martial arts, which first start with the guard and then go to the attack. As you saw in Don't Force, attempting to try to block is a false pretence of safety. Wing Tsun acknowledges this from the beginning and creates a proactive strategy.

Wing Tsun hand position vs boxing guard.

Indeed, the Chinese name for the front-hand position tells you this intention. It's called Mun Sau, meaning 'inquisitive hand'. Even when this hand doesn't move, it isn't static. It contains an internal spring-force, where your energy is always flowing forward into an opponent, despite no visual cues. It's mastery of a Taoist principle called 'stillness in motion, motion in stillness'. Physically, this is like someone pushing your arms towards you while you push back, creating an inherent spring. By mastering this feeling, it allows you to move without any hesitation or delay.

Although it is proactive, Wing Tsun's hand position is not intrinsically aggressive. Unlike clenched fists, which clearly demonstrate that force is about to be used, Wing Tsun's hand position looks strange but assertive. It's also highly practical. By standing square to your opponent, both of your hands are able to effortlessly defend, as well as counter-attack.

In terms of physical action, Positivity is essential when you find yourself faced with a potentially dangerous combat situation.

By training in Wing Tsun, your instinct becomes no longer to flinch or block, but instead to nullify the attacker. The positive skills acquired when you go through the Second Door allow you to instantly go forward, closing the gap between you. This surprising motion gives you the immediate psychological initiative, allowing you to disarm the opponent by counter-attacking their weak points. At the same time, you intercept your opponent's attack, redirecting it away from you. Although this action is hard to communicate simply in words, this all happens as one simple instinctive response.

This method of positive engagement, rather than negative defence, has profound ramifications. The key teaching here is to 'start and then stop'. The alternative, which most martial arts rely on, is stop and then start. This means waiting for the brain to process what is happening. Unfortunately, this is too slow and leaves you vulnerable to fast, unexpected attacks. And, in combat, these are precisely the attacks you need to train for.

None of these actions should be forced. You are continually training yourself to go into a state of positive flow, which results in effortless motion at the right time.

Positive action is then combined with positive momentum – meaning that once you start your motion, you continue until the situation is over. This makes the most of the initial action, and ensures that no additional energy or time is required to go back to unresolved situations.

Positivity shows you that, from a negative action, it's very difficult to achieve a positive result. The more skilled the opponent, or more challenging the situation, the more integrated within you this Positivity needs to be if you want to win.

So begins the process of complete alignment of mind, body and spirit – ready for its fruition in the Third Door.

Your body, brain and actions also need to match your intention. It's a simple formula: if you want to win in life, your whole being needs to be aligned. As your intentions create the reality around you, every action, response and thought in Wing Tsun comes from a positive mental, physical and spiritual position.

Furthermore, Positivity is grounded in the present moment. It focuses on now – how to create a positive outcome regardless of what is happening to you. It gives you the ability to turn a negative situation into a positive one, stated in the fundamental principle 'whatever the person does is to your advantage'.

Wing Tsun further explains this as 'the power of positive pro-activity'. It allows you to see the gift in every moment, no matter how painful it may feel right now. It shows you that there is an opportunity for you to develop and for you to create a new reality for yourself.

Positivity is not easy. It requires overcoming a large amount of cultural and genetic programming. When we are in survival mode, we constantly (both consciously and unconsciously) scan the environment for perceived threats. Positivity cleverly changes this mental pattern so that we instead see opportunities to win. The thought process changes from the fear-based question 'What if this happens to me?' to the self-belief-orientated 'How can I succeed?' This brings you straight into the present moment immediately.

Influenced by the Buddhist concept of Kleshas – states of mind that create discontent – Wing Tsun Positivity developed from the study of optimum mindsets. In classic Winning Not Fighting style, Wing Tsun ignored trying to overcome the Buddhist 'three poisons' (ignorance, attachment and ill will), and focused instead on key aspects for development (wisdom, generosity and loving-kindness). Positivity makes you focus on the action, rather than trying to stop a non-action. Indeed, masters of Wing Tsun realized early on that the brain struggles with negatives – both in combat and from a communication perspective. Negatives often take longer to process mentally and create the need for more decisions, as they only focus on what you don't wish to do or happen – not what action should be substituted for it. Wing Tsun Positivity shows the power of simply reframing actions – from 'Don't do that' to 'Please do this'.

Like everything in Wing Tsun, this gradually becomes an instinctive part of your everyday actions and communication. The emotional part of this method should not be underestimated – negatives often elicit a feeling of fear, whereas a positive manner feels far more nurturing and loving. As we saw with the wisdom of Don't Force, this achieves a far greater compliance, buy-in and general contentment.

Positivity is also about letting go of past actions and thoughts that no longer serve you. And it addresses the idea of 'victim mentality'. This is an emotive topic, but – win or lose – feeling like a victim doesn't help you. Blame, while it may be legally and morally justified, doesn't get you anywhere positive. Instead, blame creates a never-ending cycle of conflict, prolonging the event and your suffering. By dropping blame, we are able to process and understand our own emotions. Our experience becomes one of positive inward reflection rather than a negative outward projection.

Wing Tsun Positivity shows you how to create psychological safety for others too. Continuing the learning from Don't Force, it teaches you to take a positive interest in others. This is one of the most powerful actions you can carry out – by being genuinely interested in someone else, and what they do, it creates a deep connection. It guides you to focus on the asking rather than the telling.

Similarly, it gives you the ability to see and get the best out of others. Accepting people for who they are makes an astonishing difference both to you and to those around you – even within seconds of meeting for the first time. As a leader and manager, you must remove fear and build up trust, belief and confidence. This simply can't happen if you're coming from a negative place.

Finally, Positivity fuels creativity and problem-solving. It shows you how to see the possibility, not just to focus on the challenge. Manage this, and you will have unlimited creativity, seeing unlimited possibility in the world.

Without realizing it, we are often so limited by our own conditioning that we take our narrow view for granted. But this is just another self-imposed prison, which Wing Tsun Positivity teaches you to remove.

The power of positive thinking can be used to great effect with your own body too. Many studies have shown that thinking positively has an astonishing impact on overcoming adverse health situations, even in cases that are seen as 'medically impossible'. Indeed, the largely unexplained phenomenon of the placebo effect is based on Positivity.

The more you apply Wing Tsun Positivity, the more you will realize the influence you have over your own life.

Lessons of the Fourth Wisdom: Positivity

1. Positivity teaches you how to harness the mind to create a thriving life.
2. Positivity builds trust and self-belief to enable you to deal with unexpected situations.
3. Search for the positive connections and attributes in others. Allow them to flourish.
4. Wing Tsun Positivity takes off the limits you place on your life, replacing it with a sense of possibility.

John

Whatever Happens is to Your Advantage

Leon is not a fairy-tale place where everyone is positive all the time and where fireworks shower twinkly sparks over the magical castle every evening. However, when someone meets or works with people from Leon, I hope that they will on the whole notice their attitude – and not only their positivity and possibility, but also their outlook and their sense that no matter what happens, it can work to their advantage.

This attitude requires people to be in the present and not living in the past, feeling guilt, or in the future, feeling worry. And it requires people to understand the difference between positivity and optimism. Optimism can feel very nice. But it is not the same as being positive. Optimism is conjecture, a judgement about the future. Positivity, in contrast, is a mindful decision which we make in the moment. It leads to action, or a deliberate decision to take no action, now.

While the future can be imagined, visualized and manifested, it cannot be controlled. The only choices that we can make are the choices for how we think and what we do now.

Optimism, like pessimism, is judgemental. And both are an unnecessary waste of time. When I was 18, I read Wayne Dyer's *Your Erroneous Zones*, and I was struck by the way he talked about guilt and worry as two wasted emotions. We spend a lot of our emotional reserves worrying about the future, which is simply a form of pessimism. And optimism is potentially just as distracting.

At the Leon head office, in London's Borough Market, we have painted on the wall the story of Choi, a tale told by Wing Tsun teachers to their students, to remind us to avoid being judgemental about events.

In the story, Choi is a poor man whose principal possession is his horse. One day, the horse runs away and is lost. Choi's neighbour (let's call him Bob) says to Choi, 'Oh no, that's so unlucky.' And Choi replies, 'Maybe.'

The next day the horse returns, and with it come two wild horses. Bob chips in to say, 'Well, that's lucky.' And Choi replies, 'Maybe.'

A day later, Choi's son breaks his leg trying to tame one of the wild horses. Bob, you won't be surprised to hear, has a view. 'Choi, that's so unlucky.' To which Choi replies, 'Maybe.'

A short time afterwards, the army comes to conscript his son. But, of course, they are unable to because his son is incapacitated. Bob (you've guessed it) says to Choi, 'Ooh, that's so lucky.' And of course Choi replies, 'Maybe.'

At each stage, Choi chooses not to apply judgement to the situation. He chooses neither pessimism nor optimism, instead he opts for positivity and calm.

I have also found Jim Collins's *Great by Choice* to be of immense value as a framework for thinking about Leon strategy. Two of its important concepts are 'productive paranoia' and 'return on luck'. The former shows that the leaders of successful businesses are not blindly optimistic – instead they know that something will go wrong even if they do not know what. So they proactively prepare for all sorts of potential scenarios.

Great leaders similarly deliver a high 'return on luck' by both spotting and making the most of lucky events.

I like both of these concepts, but neither includes the

lessons of Choi's story. Any event, if we are able to remain non-judgemental, can be turned into a good outcome – by choosing and applying the wisdom of Positivity.

Instead of thinking about productive paranoia, we need to think about positive preparation. Paranoia is an equally judge-mental idea that loads in too much emotion, too much fear and unnecessary negativity.

Positivity is not just for the good times. Partly because it is needed most when things are tough. And partly because, as Choi would tell you, the 'good' times and 'bad' times are not worth judging and labelling as such.

SO REMEMBER . . .

- Both pessimism and optimism need to be left alone . . .
- Do not entertain them . . .
- Not even with some nibbles and a glass of prosecco . . .
- Be more Choi.

Why We Know it Works

The reason I am able to talk about the nature – and power – of positivity is that it works. I have first-hand experience of it being a pivotal part of Leon's success.

For the first four years of Leon's growth, between 2004 and 2008, Henry and I were joint CEOs. For the subsequent four years, Henry took sole charge of Leon while I spent my time pre-dominantly working with one of Leon's original investors on consumer-based private equity transactions. Henry's years as sole CEO coincided with decreasing consumer confidence following the financial crisis of 2008, and during this period many in Leon experienced a corresponding decrease in internal confidence.

I became frustrated with not having my hands on the tiller. At the same time, Henry began to appreciate that there were merits in involving me in the business once again. So, in 2012, I took on responsibility for food. In line with the principles of Mastery (see p. 359) and focus, I took our menu back to how it felt in 2004 when we had first set out to create the notion of 'fast food in heaven'. I reintroduced our halloumi wrap, created a fish finger wrap reminiscent of the crunch-coated fish and tartare wrap from our early years, and launched a new range of chicken and chorizo club dishes across the menu.

While the improvements to our menu were important, I don't believe that they were the largest contributor to the company's transformation. A year after taking responsibility for food, Henry and I agreed that it made sense for me to lead the running of the restaurants.

It was here, of course, right in the core operations – where the culture touched our guests most – that the biggest change was required. And this cultural change was built entirely around the principle of Positivity.

The first step was to remind all of us of what we were doing and why. This meant being true to our original and defining purpose.

When I became responsible for leading the operations and culture within our restaurants, I brought in Steve Head to coach the team. Steve is a Geordie comedian-cum-motivational genius who captivates people from between 15 minutes and 10 hours, depending on how much time he has. People laugh a lot. And they have him in their heads for the rest of their lives. I know my life would not have been as rich or enjoyable if I hadn't met him. He applies common sense, and explains why it is far from common. And he leaves you able to laugh at yourself because, let's face it, you're a bit of an idiot.

I began by asking Steve to hold a session with all of our Mums and Dads, the titles we use to describe the general managers who run each of our restaurants.

I doubt if anyone who attended will ever forget that session. Steve introduced to us on that day philosophies, tools and vocabulary that would help centre our culture around positivity. We now talk about spotting what Steve calls Moments of Truth – the opportunities that arise to do something special for someone or for yourself.

In some restaurant companies, a spilled drink is viewed by the restaurant team with dismay. A complaint can be a reason to think about leaving the profession. But at Leon, we have conditioned ourselves to see each of these as opportunities to delight. Steve has taught us that the actions one takes in response to these Moments of Truth are to be recognized, celebrated and recorded.

In many organizations, customer complaints and staff errors are, by company policy, recorded. The good stuff rarely receives the same attention. A Moment of Truth can be any opportunity to delight. A customer with a quizzical look, a customer who has forgotten her purse, a customer's birthday, a colleague in distress. Thanks to Steve, the things that one does in response to Moments of Truth we call Glimpses of Brilliance.

There is a theory among some psychologists that we are programmed to remember the bad stuff because we need to remember it to stay safe. And that the good stuff, the positive experiences, we more readily discard. I would agree that we are sensitive to the things that make us fearful. But I am equally positive about the readiness that exists in people and organizations to notice and record and celebrate the positives.

People and organizations thrive when they can share and recall things that individuals and teams have done well. This breeds confidence, makes people feel happier at work, and makes it much more likely that more good things will happen.

If you would like to amuse yourself, go into a Leon restaurant and ask the team if you can see their GOB (Glimpses of Brilliance) book. They will look at you with slight surprise that you even know the expression, but in all likelihood they will find the time to show you and to talk you through some of the stories and successes which all the team have enjoyed.

A GOB might be an email or a letter from a customer. It might be a thank-you note written by a team member for a company accolade or a prize awarded at one of our company celebrations. Most importantly, team members are encouraged to write down achievements of their own that would otherwise have gone unrecognized. These books become one element by which the culture of positivity is continually and organically reinforced.

There are many stories that have been recorded since we began doing this in 2012. There's one of a manager who, when a tyre burst on a lone mother's stroller, found a bicycle shop, bought a repair kit and repaired the tyre himself. These actions are, I hope, the rule rather than the exception at Leon. I've even known team members replace a customer's meal if they have to pop to the restroom for long enough for their food to get a little cold.

I explain to my Leon family that I want customers to know that they can count on a Leon person to help them, even if they meet them outside a restaurant. I do not ask Leon people to put themselves in danger. I ask them to be kind, to take positive action and make positive decisions without ego, without unnecessary fear, in a way that responds to the situation rather than just reacting.

May I suggest you try spotting Moments of Truth yourself?

May I suggest you keep your own GOB book?

May I suggest you take positivity, not discouragement, from the fact that it is so easy, and so simple?

Four Minutes

Steve also taught me, and all of us at Leon, the Four Minute Rule. It goes like this: when you get home, you are only allowed to say positive things for the first four minutes.

You're going to need to walk over the shoes scattered in the hallway. You're not going to mention that the train was delayed again, or any other such commuting-related grumble. You're not going to ask why the washing-up still isn't done.

Instead you're going to exclaim how lovely the house smells. You're going to exclaim, 'I'm home! Are we all ready for the best Wednesday night ever? I *love* Wednesday nights.' (And then play the Flight of the Conchords' song 'Business Time' to prove it.)

We train our operations managers to follow the Four Minute Rule whenever they enter one of their restaurants. An ops manager looks after around eight restaurants, and it is their job to support each Mum or Dad in order to get the best customer, operational and financial performance from the restaurant they run.

I know from working as a team member in a restaurant that, having got up way before dawn and started work at 6.30 a.m., when an ops manager walks in at 11 a.m. and struts around 'cleverly' spotting the things that are wrong, your instinct is to be upset, or even angry. In your mind, you will be saying things like:

'What about the fact that we were here early dealing with the trash that someone had dumped on our doorstep . . . ?'

'Aren't you going to say well done for achieving a record breakfast?'

'Maybe if you were a bit less dim, you would realize that is the reason why the coffee machine is looking a bit untidy . . .'

If the ops managers follow the Four Minute Rule, these negative feelings can be avoided.

Trust Me

Trust is the glue that holds the best organizations together: the intangible, electrical energy that strengthens the bonds between people. And positivity is at its heart.

At Leon, we base our relationships on what we call 'presumed trust'. Everyone starts at the company with 10/10 on their forehead. When a problem arises, we blame the process, not the person. We talk about people as if they can hear us. This leads to a positive culture. It stops cliques developing, and it stops the corrosive mistrust that breaks teams and organizations.

Driven by ego, humans have a desire to spot faults in others. It makes us feel superior. So we can find it reassuring not only to look for the bad in people, but also to tell others about it. At Leon, we look for the good in people. We recognize that perfection does not exist.

Many businesses remind people of their failings constantly as a way of maintaining control over individuals. The reviewer is probably not even consciously aware they are doing it.

But Where's the Proof?

Moments of Truth, Glimpses of Brilliance, Four Minute Rules . . . What can this really do for a business aside from making us feel good? Can it actually fuel success? How can it pay the bills?

All I can tell you is, in the years since Steve and I began working together to implement this culture at Leon, our same-restaurant sales grew at a compounded 44 per cent. This is why our overall revenue went up four times, and the number of restaurants grew from 17 to 52. I cannot prove to you that the culture of positivity was the single biggest factor in this. But I believe it was.

If Leon were my only piece of evidence, you might have some grounds for scepticism. My second example is available as a matter of public record and centres on my work with Henry on the School Food Plan.

The government, and the Secretary of State for Education in particular, had found themselves at odds with Jamie Oliver, one of Britain's most popular celebrity chefs, over school food.

Jamie had conducted a very public campaign highlighting the inadequacies of school food provision, winning himself huge public respect and securing new laws and regulations governing both the quality of food and the quantity of micronutrients that need to be provided to each child each week.

However, the government was intent on simplifying and reducing the rules that had to be followed by academies – a form of publicly funded school the government had encouraged since it came to power in 2010. Among the many regulations that went were the rules on school food that Jamie Oliver had championed.

Once it was announced that we were now leading Jamie's project, we found ourselves – in the summer of 2012 – the subject of media scrutiny. As with all stories handed down from our ancestors, there needed to be a villain, victim and hero. We were the villain, the children were the victim and Jamie was the hero.

A Channel 4 programme set us to sinister music, and told the world that we were puppets of Michael Gove and not very good businesspeople. They narrowly stopped short of saying that we smelled.

We knew that, if we were going to be successful, we had to apply the same principles we used to run Leon. First and foremost, that of positivity. We said that we were not prepared to produce a report to be submitted and then replied to at a later date. We wanted to create an action plan that was agreed to before publication, built on consensus.

I was convinced that our plan had to be based on positivity. We were there, we explained, not to catch people out, or to sound clever and to criticize, but to find all the things that were working and to catch people doing things right. This was entirely consistent with the spirit with which Michael Gove wanted the review to be conducted.

There are 22,000 state-funded schools in the UK, and somewhere in these schools I believed we would find the answers. We found schools cooking great food, schools teaching cookery in inspiring ways, schools growing food, or engaging parents, or eating with the children, or overcoming the constraint of small dining rooms by bringing in portable kitchens, or engaging children by getting them involved in the school kitchen.

By refusing to throw stones or to criticize, we were able to encourage the support of the cooks, head teachers, industry bodies, caterers, unions, business managers and of media. It galvanized people behind a shared vision, and allowed us to collect and share GOBs in the same way we do at Leon.

Thanks to the School Food Plan, we were able to tackle the big problem that had made school meals uneconomic and of poor quality . . . the low, 43 per cent take-up of school food. The fixed costs were simply not shared among enough meals. The system had been caught in a financial and operational vicious cycle.

Under the plan, all infant pupils would be provided a nutritious school lunch at no charge; practical cooking would appear on the curriculum for the first time; and new, simpler regulations would ensure an improved understanding and application of what good food looked like. The culture change begun by Jamie Oliver accelerated, with head teachers at its heart.

By launch day, we had achieved the unthinkable: an action plan with not just the support of all the parties and the unions but also Alien and Predator (aka Michael Gove and Jamie Oliver).

And we had done it by applying the Wing Tsun principle of Positivity. I just didn't know it yet. It was to be another two years before I would take my first Wing Tsun lesson.

Scream if You Want to Go Faster

If you maintain a positive perspective, and practise the wisdom of Staying Relaxed as we've discussed, in both your personal life and in business you can respond to situations without being blinded by panic. When we had just the one restaurant on Carnaby Street, the landlord told us that they were going to redevelop the floors above our restaurant, and that the whole building was going to be obscured by scaffolding for some time. Many businesses have been brought to their knees by such scaffolding. And UK property law is such that you are not compensated by the landlord for any loss of trade.

In the spirit of responding and not reacting, we asked ourselves how we could turn this to our advantage. And we decided to cover the entire front of the building in a wooden facade painted like a fairground attraction. And, to emphasize the message of speed around our fast-food model, we wrote a sign in an appropriately fairground style saying, 'Scream if you want to go faster!' – a common phrase in the British fairground tradition.

It worked. Sales increased rather than decreased. And, as an added bonus, we were able to embed the idea of turning bad news into something significantly positive into the culture of the company.

As we write this book, the UK restaurant industry is having a tough time, and the prevailing sentiment within it is that business is bleak. Every cost, from wages to rent to ingredients, has increased dramatically, while the customer is showing no appetite for paying increased prices. At Leon, this is when we get most excited. We know that winners win in difficult times. To paraphrase Warren Buffett, it's only when the tide goes out that you see who isn't wearing swimming trunks.

Blue Zones (It is Not a Movie)

The United Nations designates so-called Blue Zones, pockets across the world where people live the longest, healthiest lives. In each one, the tight bonds between people stand out as a common factor.

Yes, some eat oily fish, and the Mediterranean diet helps, but the single biggest shared factor for longevity of life is the positive relationships these communities share.

They don't live longer because they wear Fitbits, or have advanced pharmaceutical interventions from constant blood, saliva and stool tests. In villages that the World Health Organization identify as having the most centenarians, people almost never go to the doctor.

The answers are staring us in the face. Yes, eat fewer carbohydrates and sugars, some good meat, a lot of veg and a whole lot of good fats. But laugh more, love more, and see your family and mates more often.

As we are about to explore in a teeny bit more detail, positive thinking helps heal the body. Or rather the mind and the body. (When Wing Tsun talks about Shin it is referring not to the mind as we define it in the West, but rather the totality of our mind, heart and gut, where our mind is in a state of positivity.) And good bacteria, essential for good overall health as well as gut health, flourish when the mind is happy.

As we explored in Staying Relaxed, the links between gut health and mental health are only now beginning to be understood by Western medicine, even though holistic practitioners have been onto this for years and it has been an important part of Eastern medicine for a long time (a couple of millennia). Rather than focusing on killing the body's bad bacteria, non-Western medicine focuses on promoting the good bacteria that colonize the gut and win against the bad. The more positive your 'mind', the happier your bacteria are and the happier you are. It is no coincidence that research has shown that cynicism is the trait most common in people with bad gut health.

Positivity, and Mind Over Medicine

Last year I bought each Leader of Leon a present. It was a book that Steve Head had spoken about on stage: *Mind Over Medicine* by Lissa Rankin.

Rankin – as well as Jo Marchant, in her book *Cure*, and friend-of-Leon Rangan Chatterjee in his book *The 4 Pillar Plan* – has provided us with up-to-date case studies and evidence that the mind, through relaxation and positive thinking and belief, can have a hugely beneficial impact on the body. And, in turn, a negative mindset can cause huge harm. Curses can work – probably because the victim believes in it and the mind kills the body.

In her book, Rankin explores some cases that are quite well known to doctors and sit apart from society's general conversation about medical treatment. Like this one, the peculiar story of Dr West and his patient Mr Wright:

> Dr West was treating Mr Wright, who had an advanced cancer called lymphosarcoma. All treatments had failed, and time was running out. Mr Wright's neck, chest, abdomen, armpits, and groin were filled with tumours the size of oranges, his spleen and liver were enlarged, and his cancer was causing his chest to fill up with two quarts of milky fluid every day, which had to be trained in order for him to breathe. Dr West didn't expect him to last a week.
>
> But Mr Wright desperately wanted to live, and he hung his hope on a promising new drug called Krebiozen. He begged his doctor to treat him with the new drug, but the drug was only being offered in clinical trials to people who were believed to have at least three months left to live. Mr Wright was too sick to qualify.
>
> Mr Wright didn't give up. Knowing the drug existed and believing the drug would be his miracle cure, he pestered his doc until Dr West reluctantly gave in and injected him with Krebiozen. Dr West performed the procedure on a Friday, but deep down, he didn't believe Mr Wright would last the weekend.
>
> To his utter shock, the following Monday, Dr West found his patient walking around out of bed. According to Dr Klopfer

[the author of this case study], Mr Wright's 'tumour masses had melted like snowballs on a hot stove' and were half their original size. Ten days after the first dose of Krebiozen, Mr Wright left the hospital, apparently cancer-free.

Mr Wright was rockin' and rollin', praising Krebiozen as a miracle drug for two months until the scientific literature began reporting that Krebiozen didn't seem to be effective. Mr Wright, who trusted what he read in the literature, fell into a deep depression, and his cancer came back.

This time, Dr West, who genuinely wanted to help save his patient, decided to get sneaky. He told Mr Wright that some of the initial supplies of the drug had deteriorated during shipping, making them less effective, but that he had scored a new batch of highly concentrated, ultra-pure Krebiozen, which he could give him. (Of course, this was a bald-faced lie.)

Dr West then injected Mr Wright with distilled water.

And a seemingly miraculous thing happened – *again*. The tumours melted away, the fluid in his chest disappeared, and Mr Wright was feeling great again for another two months.

Then the American Medical Association blew it by announcing that a nationwide study of Krebiozen proved that the drug was utterly worthless. This time, Mr Wright lost all faith in his treatment. His cancer came back, and he died two days later.

Positive thinking is powerful thinking. As is negative thinking. Dr Bernie Siegel has often cited a study where patients for a new chemotherapy drug were given nothing but saline, but were warned it could be chemotherapy. Thirty per cent lost their hair. In another study, hospitalized patients were given a sugar pill and told it would make them vomit. Eighty per cent of them threw up.

I have seen the power of positivity and what it does for others. The most positive person I know, my mum, is genuine in seeing the good in any situation or person. This may sound strange, but

I have never heard her moan about her life or about anyone or anything. A holiday where it rains is never a ruined holiday, it is always an opportunity to play more board games and spend more time together.

This is not to be confused with the denial of feelings that can sometimes occur, particularly in some parts of the Western world where difficult feelings are denied. This plastic, smiley, fake positivity is no good for the health of the individual or for those around them. Changing your mindset is very different from denying it.

Telomeres

Nobel Prize-winning molecular biologist Elizabeth Blackburn was part of a team that discovered how things called telomeres protect our chromosomes. And that they are themselves protected by positivity.

Telomeres are repetitive nucleotide sequences that cap the end of each chromosome. They don't contain any genetic information – their purpose is to protect the genetic material during cell replication. (They're a bit like the aglets on the end of your shoelaces that protect them from fraying.) However, each time a cell replicates, the telomeres at the end of each chromosome shorten, which is how we age.

Scientists have not only discovered that psychological stress in humans can shorten telomeres, they have also come to some astonishing conclusions about telomeres and positivity. In one giant study, researchers found that positive people had significantly longer telomeres than those who were less positive.

As Blackburn puts it in *The Telomere Effect*, 'Your cells are listening to your thoughts.' Which is why, of the approximately 65,000 thoughts our mind processes a day, it helps to be aware of the negative and positive styles of thought.

You, and your body, are your thoughts.

In buying Rankin's book for the managers and support team at Leon, we have placed this subject at the centre of our discussions as a team. And it influences how they in turn manage their own teams.

The main message? Do not think that your job as a colleague or mother or leader is to focus most on all the things that need fixing. Sure, if the engine is on fire, mention it to the pilot. But remember to keep a GOB book of your own. Positivity rocks. Choose it.

The Third Door

Biu Jee – Self-Realization
By Julian

Biu Jee, meaning 'flying fingers', is the third and final solo form in Wing Tsun. It represents the pinnacle of physical and personal prowess in the martial art. Known as the 'masters' form', it is typically taught after approximately eight to ten years of studying. Biu Jee's philosophical and practical focus is on freeing yourself from any constraints and enabling you to realize your innate power. For this reason, the Third Door is known as the 'free door'.

Biu Jee is a significant step up from the first two forms. The whole approach and methodology is of a distinctly different flavour. By the time you arrive at this level you are already approaching expert level, so it is now your turn to shine . . .

When you enter the Third Door, you are no longer focused on self-defence. Simple, direct techniques from Siu Nim Tao and Chum Kiu will suffice in 99 per cent of the combat situations you're faced with, so it's very rare that you need to resort to Biu Jee techniques. If you do, it means one of two things: the opponent you are facing is a highly skilled expert from another art; or they have developed Wing Tsun skills from the Second Door to a serious proficiency.

The first two Doors taught you effectiveness at defence, and understanding how to deflect and counter-strike. The Third Door takes the offensive, not waiting for the opponent's attack. It comes with the potential for significant risk if not done correctly.

Biu Jee teaches you to mitigate this risk by using your body to greater effect, obtaining crystal-clear mental lucidity and the development of an explosive new force. Furthermore, the skills are so subtle and nuanced that Biu Jee trains you to be able to defend attacks in a way that no other art does. This is known as 'the defence when there is no defence'.

The targetry in Biu Jee is highly lethal, intentionally aimed to leave your opponent critically injured or dead. Sadly, in high-stakes combat, there is little other choice. All the strikes target the weakest points with the maximum amount of force a human being can generate. This is delivered with pinpoint accuracy in a highly concentrated manner, for maximum penetration.

If this sort of skill makes you feel nervous, then you're not alone. The old masters stated it should only be taught to the most dedicated students, declaring: 'the Biu Jee never leaves the house'. My teacher made me promise the same. In reality, misuse is rarely an issue, as the learning process means that people who wish to use Biu Jee for less savoury purposes rarely have the patience to learn it.

So, where does this force come from?

It's from the realization that mental tension creates physical tension. That's it. You don't need to try to be faster or more powerful (which ironically will create more tension and make you slower). You instead need to let go of the thoughts, ideas, constructs, emotions and fears that are holding tension in your body. The skill of a teacher is to bring that out of a student. The skill of a master is to bring it out of him- or herself.

Biu Jee teaches you that self-realization is freeing yourself from this control of the mind (a control we are very attached to in the West). Instead, you are just you.

You started this journey with Siu Nim Tao, and your realization that what you thought is not who you are. In Chum Kiu you explored this further and started to embrace your strengths. Now, with Biu Jee, you finally put your ego aside.

By dropping your mental tensions and no longer being attached to the judgement of others, your personal power and influence is, ironically, also exponentially increased. In a world when most of us are pretending to be something we're not, this authenticity is captivating. You project confidence, belief and charisma.

Physically, these concepts are made reality by a special force called Chang Dong Lik ('vibration force'). Siu Nim Tao taught you how to isolate the elbow to create relaxed force. Chum Kiu showed you how to add the power of the body through 'seven star force', along with stepping and turning force. Biu Jee now combines these to create a flow of energy that releases all the energy in your body into a single, targeted strike.

The power from Biu Jee is not just physical. Harnessing the wisdom of Simplicity, it takes your mindset to a correspondingly high level. As your physical prowess grows, so does your mental resourcefulness. And Biu Jee helps create an unbreakable spirit, able to prevail regardless of what challenges you are faced with. This is known by the wisdom Expect to Be Punched.

The Chinese have long understood that if you take away your stress, you are more likely to live longer, and more happily. Today, in the West, stress is among the biggest killers. The final part of Biu Jee, Dai Cheun Leung Sau ('big wheeling arm'), takes this to its zenith, representing the Buddhist concept of escaping from the endless stressful cycle of life and achieving freedom. Escaping the wheel in turn sets you up perfectly for the fourth and final Door, and its own unique revelations.

Lessons of the Third Door

1. Attachment to thoughts, concepts and ideas separates you from your true self.
2. By putting aside this false concept of ego, you increase your personal power, presence and effectiveness.
3. Mental tension creates physical tension – by dropping this you create personal freedom.
4. Self-realization is fundamental to a stress-free and contented life.

7.

Simplicity
By John and Julian

Julian

Tzu Jan (Simplicity) teaches us that we only need the most basic elements to achieve great success, contentment and self-realization. Physically, Simplicity is the ability to use the lowest number of movements to achieve success. We quantify this with the 'and test'. This means that in any combat situation, there should only be one motion to any attack. Each movement you add before winning is an 'and'.

This is why Wing Tsun uses the principle of simultaneity – defending and counter-attacking in one response. The more movements you add in, the more likely it is that you will be unsuccessful. It takes too long, requires mental processing (as opposed to an instinctive response) and stops you adapting. If a martial art can successfully defend against a strong, very fast, straight attack, then it's on a good grounding. If it can't, then it is based on a fallacy. Simplicity becomes even more imperative when you are faced with more than one assailant. With a significant number of variables already, you cannot afford to add any more complications. In combat, failing to master Simplicity can have fatal results.

Wing Tsun one motion defence.

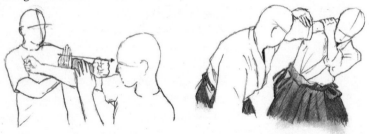

Aikido move, grab and twist defence.

Simplicity utilizes the best of stillness and motion, effortlessly combining them to great effect. It teaches you to never move until you have to, but never delay when you do move. In Wing Tsun, every movement has a purpose. While the Third Door can be pretty intricate, the more you look at it from the viewpoint of Simplicity, the more you see it is just movements from the previous two Doors, taken to a more refined level. When you look even closer, you see that the motions all originate in your basic movements, not advanced ones as you might initially have thought.

Door Three takes Simplicity in combat to its peak. It shows you the key targets you need to hit to win within two seconds. But as the threshold for Biu Jee is much higher than that of the other Doors, these are not techniques that you undertake lightly.

Simplicity also teaches you how to simplify the 'grey' of a potential combat situation into something more 'black and white'. It teaches that you only use force when you have no other option. The more danger you are in, the higher the level of force required to defend yourself. The Third Door specializes in the most dangerous attacks, training you to read and respond to them instinctively.

Furthermore, Simplicity teaches you to read the simple telltale signs that warn you a situation is developing. Self-defence situations rarely happen as fast as you think. There are often a lot of signs showing you where the situation is going before it physically occurs. Simplicity gives you options.

Simplicity is also the fundamental and most powerful aspect of decision-making. It allows you to distil complex problems, cutting through the chaos of the unknown to see the essence of the issue. And it allows you to make informed decisions, whereas complexity leaves you open to manipulation and control.

Simplicity shows you how to remove the pattern of conflict from your life. By stripping away all attachments to identities and belief patterns that you may have previously created in your mind, you step into your power. You no longer project the distorted view of the world those patterns cause.

Much interpersonal conflict occurs when one person's fears and trauma react to another's. The simplest solution is to remove your personal aspect. Do this, and suddenly a whole different way of being opens up in front of you.

In many ways, one of the biggest stresses of modern life is its complexity. We have more and more objects, and are increasingly dependent on these for our happiness. But we are mistaking our continual collecting of things for happiness. And it's easy to see where this leads – the more objects we have, the more there is to go wrong and the more they demand our time and energy. Technology, while having many benefits, rarely lives up to the promise of making our life simpler. When we look outside ourselves, today's solutions often become tomorrow's problems.

Spiritually, Simplicity is inherited from Zen and shows you that keeping things simple creates love, whereas complexity creates fear. By no longer grasping for objects, you will possess a clarity and insight that is rarely obtained.

Simplicity is by no means an easy choice. But by progressing through the first few Doors, you will have made it much more tangible. You now have the power to choose how much complexity you want in your life.

Finally, Wing Tsun shows you that it is possible to simplify your well-being into two essential parts – Yin and Yang. Yin deals with the internal, softer aspects. It's about getting in touch with your body and using the powerful silence of the meditation that Wing Tsun enables. Yang is about movement. It's the external, more dynamic aspect of our being. Humans are not designed just to sit still, and Wing Tsun teaches that 'with movement comes flow'. By mastering Simplicity, both of these become effortlessly integrated into your life.

Lessons of the Fifth Wisdom: Simplicity

1. Simplicity allows you to read telltale signs of situations before they happen.
2. Simplicity shows you the most effective way to approach problem-solving.
3. The continual desire for more objects creates stress. Simplicity shows you how to drop this from your life.
4. Well-being starts from a simple foundation – the internal and the external.

John

In Which John Talks About a Shell

At Leaders of Leon gatherings, I have repeatedly shown this image of a nautilus shell:

I do so to explain how, in order to grow big, to grow properly and to grow beautifully, Leon needs to be based on a very simple formula. The nautilus shell grows according to the Fibonacci sequence, where each number is the sum of the two numbers preceding it. This formula appears in many places in nature, including tropical or Atlantic storms, and it is my favourite example of how nature creates something wonderful from something so simple.

It has been said that 'God is a mathematician', because simple mathematical formulae create so much of what we see in the natural world. And in business, too, it pays to keep it simple.

Lao Tzu wrote: 'To attain knowledge, add things every day. To attain wisdom, remove things every day.' Keep this in mind as we go forward.

Why Simple and Focused Businesses Beat Complex Ones

In the summer of 2017, London restaurants suffered a perfect storm. Business rates (local property taxes) had suddenly increased, rents had reached historically high levels and the government had again increased the Living Wage – the pay defined as fair for a normal standard of living, and voluntarily paid by over 4,000 UK businesses. Worse still, the pound had weakened, meaning many of our ingredients now cost us more. Then two terrorist attacks in London discouraged domestic tourists from coming into town. And the customer, made to feel nervous about the Brexit vote, wasn't in the mood to accept higher prices.

The eagle-eyed among you will recognize that having all of our costs go up at once, with no opportunity to offset them with price increases, is not helpful. But these were all external events, and it was our job to navigate our way through these difficulties . . .

Instead, we made them worse.

We responded by introducing new items. Not only did we launch the new menu with 32 items, compared to the previous 28, many of them were more complex, with too many ingredients and too long a prep time, compared to those they replaced.

Suddenly, customers were overwhelmed by choice as they looked up at the menu boards. And our teams were overwhelmed too: our speed of service slowed as the kitchen teams lost their rhythm, and frustration set in. The rate at which people left Leon increased. Anger and concern over Brexit exacerbated the mood, but we could hardly blame that for this. We had complicated our process. We had scored an own goal.

Colleagues from across Leon pressed for a return to simplicity – in particular property director Adam Blaker and people director Marco Reick – so we *reduced* the number of items on the new menu from 32 to 25. Things quickly improved. Customers could see clearly now the pain had gone, and Leon teams returned to enjoying their jobs. It was a reminder of what we had always known – that simplicity needs to be at the heart of all we do.

And it is a fundamental irony faced by all growing companies: growth breeds complexity, and complexity kills growth. I am always alert to the danger of complexity and am keen to look for examples of businesses which have grown large while preserving their culture and protecting simplicity.

Whenever we open a new restaurant, we simplify something about how we run Leon. And there is a box on each new-site recommendation document where we specify what that simplification is. It is a discipline that goes some way to safeguarding us against the drag of complexity.

We remind ourselves that all problems and opportunities that seem complex can be broken down into a number of actions that are in themselves simple. At a biological and practical level, whether we are talking about cells in the body or tasks at Leon, at the lowest level each represents a very simple action or solution. Challenges that seem overwhelming can be broken down into manageable chunks.

When we were faced with needing to completely transform our training programme, someone produced a plan with 17 initiatives. Instead we decided to do only one thing and created a week of training that everyone who starts Leon attends.

The Sage of Alcoa

Remember the squirrel, the beaver and the goose? Back in Chapter 2, I introduced these furry and feathered friends as an alternative – and, I suggested, much more powerful – metaphor than the war metaphor. The single-minded focus of the squirrel is to find nuts; the beavers self-organize to get the task done; and the geese honk in constant support of the leader and each other. Simple.

I gave the example of my birthday in 2017, when for one day across all restaurants we focused (in what was a difficult time for the market) on achieving same restaurant sales growth versus the previous year – something that had been eluding us for weeks. By simplifying all of our potential targets and goals into one number to be achieved on one day, by whatever means the teams saw fit, we not only achieved that particular goal but also indirectly achieved a culture change, and we learned or remembered ways to grow sales and bring more customers into the restaurants.

As chair of the Council for Sustainable Business, I have the pleasure of working alongside the council's committed and inspirational members. They include leaders of some of the biggest companies and also the founders of dynamic start-ups. One such start-up is Bulb, a fast-growing renewable energy business led by Hayden Wood. In one of our council meetings we had discussed the question of whether carbon emissions should be the principal and perhaps only target adopted by businesses, or whether there should be a larger number of measurements that included biodiversity and water usage, for example. Hayden had been arguing for a single-minded focus on CO_2. And while it is for these purposes immaterial whether you agree or disagree with his specific point about CO_2, the story he shared with me is a very interesting illustration of how focusing on one goal can provide simultaneous effects in many other areas.

Hayden pointed me to the turnaround of the Aluminum Company of America – or Alcoa, as it is more commonly known. Alcoa in the late 1980s was a vast, bloated and inefficient corporate behemoth. It was also a dangerous place to work. Tragic accidents were simply accepted as part of life in the heavy aluminium industry.

Paul O'Neill was appointed as the new CEO in 1987. At his first analysts' meeting, he baffled and worried investors when he announced his new strategy and direction for the company. The people in the room were used to being told about capital returns and cash flow and asset utilization. Instead, O'Neill spoke without jargon of his intention to make Alcoa one of the safest companies to work for in the world. No mention of profit margins. No mention of new markets. No mention of competition. Profits, he said, didn't matter as much as worker safety. To understand how Alcoa was doing, you were going to have to look at workplace safety figures, he said.

The analysts were incredulous, and most ridiculed the newly appointed CEO. Many advised their clients to sell their shares. But within a year of his appointment, profits hit a record high. By the time he retired from the company in 2000, Alcoa's share price had quintupled, and, in addition, whatever money you had invested at the start of O'Neill's tenure you would have got back in dividends. The value of the company had in this period grown by $27 billion. And all this happened while Alcoa became one of the safest companies in the world.

O'Neill had turned this flabby, inefficient and dangerous company into a pinnacle of safety and a profit machine. By focusing on just one thing. How?

After hearing about this Alcoa story from Hayden, I read Charles Duhigg's excellent book *The Power of Habit*, which explores the science of habit formation and uses Alcoa as a case study. Duhigg believes that Alcoa's success is due to O'Neill attacking and changing one habit and watching the effects ripple through the organization. O'Neill targeted what Duhigg calls the company's 'keystone habit'.

New safety policies were written up at Alcoa. Safety railings at the factories were repainted bright yellow. Employees were encouraged to alert management of the need for machine maintenance. And O'Neill instigated a protocol that any injury must be reported to him by a factory manager within 24 hours. Previously isolated and slow chains of communication were, by necessity of the new safety rule, opened up and improved. Different areas of the factory were suddenly not just communicating about safety measures but about all aspects of production.

O'Neill even sent a note to every employee telling them to call him at home if their managers didn't comply with their safety suggestions. Workers started calling, but they didn't want to just talk about safety. They wanted to pitch their ideas for the company to its CEO directly. Previously ignored employees began suggesting brilliant ideas to streamline production and make the factories more efficient. By opening up the channel of communication on one issue – safety – O'Neill had empowered employees to share improvements for the company that would have otherwise gone unheard.

This triggered a chain reaction that electrified profits. Not only were the workers' suggestions helping to streamline the plants, but the workers felt empowered and valued and consequently began to work harder.

The implementation of better safety measures also lowered operating costs for the company. Molten aluminium was frequently spilling and injuring employees, and the improved system led to fewer injuries. But it also saved money, because Alcoa lost less raw material in spillages.

The aluminium itself produced by Alcoa improved. A major factor of subpar aluminium is faulty machinery. And if machinery is repaired to stop faulty gears trapping workers' arms, the likelihood of subpar aluminium being manufactured is reduced.

And because the people working at the company felt the company was looking after them, they in turn looked after the company. They worked harder, shared ideas, reduced waste and stayed with the company longer. And the quest for a breakthrough in safety removed hierarchical barriers that had stopped the flow of ideas and prevented communication generally. The fact that workers could call the CEO at home encouraged the people in the company to speak freely – and to share both challenges and solutions.

The example of Paul O'Neill and Alcoa is mirrored by the actions of my friend and Leon board member Brad Blum, who led the biggest turnaround in casual dining history with Olive Garden. The company was close to going under. But rather than spending money on advertising or kicking off a multitude of projects, Brad began with one aim – to clean up the restaurants. 'I decided that if we were going to go into the abyss, we would do so with the world's cleanest restaurants,' he says. This was not a decision motivated by ego – it was a recognition by Brad that he had to rebuild the company starting with the basics. And an understanding that focusing on this one thing – cleanliness – would have many powerful indirect (and perhaps even unknown) positive consequences for Olive Garden. He credits this simple focus, amid all of the countless other potential projects and manifest challenges, with beginning the turnaround of the company.

It reminds me of an aphorism that my friend and coach Ed Percival shared: 'How we do anything is how we do everything.' It is not, I believe, precisely true, in as much as there are some things that I do much more proficiently than other things, but it is true in so far as a lifting of standards and process in one area trains us to do the same in all we do. My friend Gabby was an international gymnast in her youth (her husband is the former international rugby player Kenny Logan – they are a formidable as well as a lovely couple). 'When I started to train as a gymnast, I became better and more confident in my subjects at school,' Gabby once explained to me. 'Even though I was focusing on that one thing, on the gymnastics, all sorts of other things started going well too.'

As I write this book, our number-one Leon priority for the year is to have the world's cleanest and safest restaurants. I have the support of my Leon team in making this our biggest focus – and just as critically, I have the absolute and unabashed support of the board to do so. Brad included, of course.

Fly Southwest

I hold Southwest Airlines in the highest esteem. And in this I am not alone. There are many reasons why this brilliant North American company has achieved such a consistent growth and won so many plaudits. And principal among them is their commitment to keeping things simple.

Early on, they made a decision to fly one model of aeroplane. To provide no food apart from a packet of nuts. To fly only point-to-point (avoiding a complex flight network). To issue no boarding passes, instead using a sales receipt to identify passengers. Not to codeshare or link up with other airlines. To sell tickets direct. To have one (low-cost) class of cabin. And to have no more than a ten-minute turnaround.

All of this helped to make them the lowest-cost airline in America – and one of the most valuable.

In the UK, almost 30 years after Southwest launched in 1967, their model was copied by EasyJet. If you compare Southwest and EasyJet to the full-service airlines in their respective countries, you will see how and why more complicated competitors such as American Airlines or British Airways came to be so bogged down.

British Airways flies many models of aeroplane, from the smallest propeller planes to A380s, which means that the pilots cannot easily switch between one type of aircraft and another. They offer three classes of travel – all with different catering requirements – operate many lounges, and have teams buying and providing everything from aftershave to toothbrushes.

Consistency of model and messaging *over time* is also an important aspect of simplicity. Southwest Airlines has changed its ways of doing things as little as possible since it started. In contrast, other businesses change their direction frequently – often annually – with a whole new 'idea' supported by a bold new theme or internal marketing concept.

At Leon, I expect (and indeed hope) we will have the same business model and idea every year. We aim to consistently produce naturally fast food with no more than 27 food items, with no more than five 'steps' to make each dish, where each dish can be assembled within 30 seconds, and where with every new restaurant we open, we make one new significant change that simplifies what we do.

One Idea

It takes a certain creative skill and emotional discipline to simplify seemingly complex ideas into one idea. One of our mentors and advisers, Jane Melvin, teaches companies and individuals about creativity using a model she calls the Five Faces of Genius.

She and her late business partner, Annette Moser-Wellman, identified five varying ways of being creative. These are the Seer, who sees the future as a complete snapshot in their mind; the Observer, who notices detail; the Alchemist, who takes ideas and transports them across countries, cultures and sectors; the Fool, who inverts ideas and turns weaknesses into strengths; and the Sage.

I find this last one the most interesting because it is the least obvious. It describes the person who is creative by taking complexity and transferring it to a simple idea or even a simple physical creation.

Nick Park, the Oscar-winning animator, is a great example. His pitch for his film *Chicken Run* to the big Hollywood studio DreamWorks inspired me to have an equally clear touchstone for Leon.

Park, as he tells it, was flown to Los Angeles on the DreamWorks private jet to present his idea. There, he faced a huge board table, around which sat all of the executives of the business. The meeting went something like this . . .

'So, Nick, what's the pitch?' they said.

'Well, it's like *The Great Escape* . . . but with chickens.'

'Carry on,' they said.

'No, that's it.'

They looked at each other, and the chairman said, 'Okay, Nick, we'll take it.'

It is the search for such simplicity that brought us to the idea of 'if God did fast food'. And that's it.

Thanks, Nick.

Companies and Countries

When I ask people at Leon, 'What brands do you admire or like?', it is rare that the group does not mention Apple. It has simple products, simple operating systems and, ever since the rainbow stripes went, the simplest of logos. (Even though the product design is not as modern or original as you might think – type 'Apple vs Braun' in your search box to find out more.)

Contrast this with Microsoft, who hyperactively add as many messages on their boxes as they can. There is an amusing animation online of what Microsoft would do to Apple packaging if Microsoft owned and branded the iPod.

The Apple brand – the company – owns its simplicity.

And what is true of companies is equally true of countries, but often with much larger implications. Compare and contrast the

Constitution of the United States with the rules and regulations of the former Soviet Union, and you will find a few clues as to why the Americans won the Cold War.

The United States Constitution has remained reassuringly simple. It is like a short pamphlet. The more simple the set of principles, the more likely it is for a country or company to be sustained. (Southwest doesn't even write its values down.)

Countries struggle with branding too, often overcomplicating their self-image. In the middle of a design agency's pitch to us recently, they showed me some work they did for the UK Foreign and Commonwealth Office.

'Look,' the FCO had said to the agency, 'we're using all sorts of different logos at our embassies.' And indeed they were. There were lions on red and white backgrounds, flaming torches in red, white and blue, and many more. It was a mess.

The agency settled on a solution, and presented their idea: the Union flag.

The Foreign Office laughed and agreed.

How People with Simple Lives are Often More Contented

When we named the business, I was taken by the name 'Leon' not just because it was my dad's name, but also because I was a bit intrigued by the film of the same name. (It's called *The Professional* in some countries.) It's about a hitman who ends up, frustratingly for himself, helping a young girl (played by Natalie Portman) avoid capture by a group of rogue cops.

Léon's only possession, apart from his clothes and his guns, is a small pot plant, which he takes from one cheap, basic hotel room to the next. His is a very simple life. Or so I thought. Many people who watch the film have a small pang of envy. What must it be like to be so free? So free from the burden of clutter and responsibility? But they misunderstand. Léon lives not a simple life but a rootless one. We know this from the film's final scene, in which Mathilda – the girl he's rescued – replants his pot plant in a large garden. At last, he is free.

The point here is that simplicity requires one to be rooted, just as we are when we take up our first stance in Wing Tsun.

My friend David Spencer-Percival is very calm under pressure. He is wise, extremely fun, and he has built two £100m businesses in his career. It is possibly not a coincidence that he has practised Wing Tsun. I admire him enormously. He finishes work at 6 p.m., and spends his evenings with his wife Bonita. He exudes the energy of a master. Of someone who has worked out what is important in his life.

Two years ago, he started a third business after reading an article about Acciaroli, a village in Italy's Campania region, where one in ten live to the age of 100 because of the high amount of rosemary they eat. Scientists concluded the herb was providing anti-inflammatory and antioxidant benefits. This inspired David to launch No. 1 Rosemary Water, one of the coolest brands I have seen emerge in the last few years. And it is built on one of the simplest business models.

David buys the rosemary extract, and markets the brand. He works from a small office just off Chelsea's King's Road in London, or from his house in Gloucestershire or from his farm in Ibiza. David outsources everything else. A botanical extracts business produces the rosemary ingredients, which are sent to a third-party bottler to be produced. All of the design is done by a small design company and the advertising managed by a freelance ad man. Third-party agencies make sure that the product looks good in-store. He has one finance person in-house, four salespeople and somebody who liaises with the factory. And that's it.

This simple business model mirrors the simplicity of the Coca-Cola operating model. Warren Buffett, the famed investor and a shareholder in Coca-Cola, says that he believes the business could be run by just 200 people. And I believe him.

Coca-Cola provides the syrup, sends it to third-party bottling companies, and globally manages the brand identity and major global sponsorships. Everything else is outsourced to bottlers in any country. In many ways, No. 1 Rosemary Water is the Coca-Cola of the twenty-first century.

David's understanding of the need for simplicity extends to his private life too. David left school at 16. And in building two recruitment businesses to £100m turnovers, David experienced the sometimes negative impact which new financial wealth can bring.

Of course, in our complex society, where money is required to travel to work, to pay for heating, for food and for housing, having no money is a unique and major source of stress. If you are in that position, you may have little sympathy for this problem. You might think, *I should be so lucky*. And he would agree with you. But that doesn't mean that the problem doesn't exist for many people who experience financial success, or financial luck.

'As I made more money,' David told me, 'my life became more complicated. Soon I had cleaners, gardeners, bankers, accountants, and lots of people who did things for me. And it made me increasingly unhappy.'

David was experiencing what Julian's dad calls 'the tyranny of servants'. The more people you have responsibility for, the less freedom you have. Suddenly, you can find yourself keeping afloat a complex system of people, and they are reliant on you for their livelihoods.

Fortunately, David realized this before it was too late. 'Everything became more and more complicated. I discovered that the more money you have, the likelihood is that your life becomes less and less possible to manage. I ended up shedding as many of those complications as I could. It was incredibly cathartic. I sold the cars, I reduced the number of staff and advisers I had. It felt like a balloon had been untied and I felt young again. Be careful what you wish for.'

Caterpillar, Sandstone, Wave

In 2018, my dad died. A few months before that, he went into hospital for an operation and ended up in a windowless, basement intensive care unit. He suffered from claustrophobia, and the mask constantly covering his face was making him even more panicked. I felt so helpless.

One morning, our home phone rang. He had apparently been begging the nurse all night to call us, and at dawn they finally relented. Dad was quite full of drugs but making enough sense for me to realize that he was extremely distressed. He beseeched me to get him out of the hospital. He explained, and I remember it quite well, that he was completely cut off from the world and had not seen 'a caterpillar, a sandstone or a wave'. Despite being quite delirious he was very clear. Very clear that these simple things are the important things in life. Very clear that a caterpillar and a sandstone and a wave is what he would do anything to see. I was struck by his instinctive choice of words, and it made me even more desperate to help him.

Let's all remember that these simple things that nature offers us are 'it'. Pick up a luxury goods magazine that you will find in the clubs and offices of Mayfair or the City, and you will see many mega yachts and private jets and expensive watches, but find me one thing that can compete with a caterpillar or a sandstone or a wave for value. Wakey wakey, us.

The Universe Has a Sense of Humour

Most of the things that make our lives complicated are born from a desire to achieve simplicity. As I sit here trying to write this, the doorbell has rung three times. Each has stopped me being able to get much work done. Once was for the supermarket delivery man, and I helped him unload his baskets. Then to let in the dishwasher repair man, who it turns out likes his coffee a certain way. And again for a parcel delivery. Supermarkets, dishwashers, Internet shopping: they are all created for convenience. Yet are our lives simpler than they were a hundred years ago? Are we humans fundamentally more fulfilled than we were then?

I'm not saying don't embrace these things. I'm just saying don't expect to get anywhere. The universe will make sure that things stay balanced. It has a sense of humour – 'You think that you can create simplicity through machines? WRONG! Try looking within.'

And you know what? I think the universe is right.

Simple answers are available to us without spending too much money. Sometimes I ponder with wry amusement that, while Western charities raise money to build schools across Africa so that children there can sit in rows in front of a blackboard, progressive Western families are spending fortunes to send their children to forest schools. And Internet and tech billionaires who've made fortunes from apps ban their kids from using screens and encourage them to play outside.

Somewhere, somehow, we're getting something very wrong.

Song and Dance

My friend Ed once visited the young shaman of a tribe in Brazil. The shaman had quite the routine – a whole to-do with rattles and fire and dancing around. There was also chanting.

Then, a few days later, Ed saw a second shaman. This was a much older man. And Ed thought to himself, *Well, what do we have in store here? If the young shaman did all that, what song and dance will we see from one who has practised for much longer?*

To his surprise, the old man simply sat with him, and gently and calmly put his hands over his head.

'Excuse me,' said Ed. 'I hope you don't mind me asking, but why is there such a difference between you and the younger shaman with all the bells and whistles?'

The old man looked at him and said, 'He is a great man . . . but he hasn't learned yet.' Part of learning is not adding skills, moves and complexity – it is learning to simplify.

In the same way, those who practise mastery learn to use plain language. When people go to university or are starting out in their careers, they will equate using complicated and impenetrable language with being clever. (A friend used to joke that, if you could get the words 'hegemony', 'dichotomy' and 'juxtaposition' into an undergraduate essay – or anything prefixed by 'meta' – you'd get a top mark.) In contrast, John Maynard Keynes, one of the most notable and influential economists of the twentieth century, deliberately chose to write his books in the simplest possible English, and to include no graphs.

When we wrote the School Food Plan, we did our best to write every sentence in the simplest possible way, being very clear about what we wanted each line to say. And we said to ourselves: 'If our mum or best friend can't understand what we're saying, we won't write it.'

The master chooses simple English, and does not create barriers to hide behind.

It Extends to How We Manage Our Time

I've known my friend Dave McClements since our P&G days. He now runs a training and development company. And he once told me that time management is more of an emotional than a practical consideration. It wasn't until I started to practise Wing Tsun that I understood what he meant.

To manage time, we need to be present and we need to recognize that the present is the only time in which anything can be achieved. We need to stop being perfectionists, stop feeling the fear of missing out, and instead make the choice to prioritize one thing, now, and to focus on it with love and intent.

Multitasking, Wing Tsun believes, is an impossible dream. Our conscious brain can only entertain a small number of thoughts at once. And when it comes to doing things, we can only really do one thing with focus at once.

When we plan our diary, we need to plan a series of present moments, and recognize, emotionally, that we can only ever be doing one thing in those present moments. Be present, focus, and bring love to what you are doing. It is the thing that you have chosen to do, now, above all else. And it is the thing that deserves your attention.

Brad, whom I have mentioned before, was once given some wise life advice by his dad: 'Don't try to drive and make out with a girl at the same time – you might not do either justice.' Seems like a fair shout. It is this advice, plus his own business and life experience, that helps Brad to advise me regularly: 'John, you can do anything . . . but you can't do *everything*.'

While you can make the one action achieve multiple things, like a simultaneous defence and attack in Wing Tsun, you cannot carry out multiple actions at once.

I encourage people at Leon to slow down and choose just one major task to accomplish each day. And I do my best to show them the way in this. Recent examples from my diary include working with a Leon colleague to redesign the drinks range, agreeing a new franchise partnership, and finalizing a contract for a new Leon consumer goods company. But, occasionally, 'having a haircut' is the most that I feel I can achieve, so I keep my day's aspirations modest!

All of this is designed to help us avoid procrastination, which stems from the fear that we might be doing the wrong thing – or, worse, the fear that it won't be good enough, let alone 'perfect'.

Miles Ahead

A young man called Jack has recently joined us. He likes jazz, and he plays the jazz guitar. We have travelled together to see the opening of the Leon in Washington DC, and he has politely endured my music then put his music on when he can take no more. He likes Nubya Garcia, Kamasi Washington and, of course, Miles Davis.

Miles first changed the course of music in the late 1940s when, together with Charlie 'Bird' Parker and Dizzy Gillespie, he was one of the inventors of bebop. The style features astonishingly fast chord changes and blistering solos. And yet Miles never lost his understanding of simplicity's place amid this complexity.

My colleague Michael tells me that a good friend of his befriended Miles, and had the privilege of sitting with him during the playback of a new recording. There was a short pause as the song ended. And then Miles took a breath and said, 'Shit. I didn't leave out enough notes.'

Simplicity, here, is the place where the music gets to breathe.

I suspect this stemmed from the late 1950s, when Miles was growing increasingly unhappy with bebop's pyrotechnics. 'The music has gotten thick,' he said. 'Guys give me tunes and they're full of chords.' It was time to change the course of music once again, and so Miles went in the opposite direction, towards simplicity, encouraging his band – an extraordinarily talented sextet featuring Cannonball Adderly, John Coltrane and Bill Evans among them, all of whom would become jazz legends in their own right – to improvise and create rather than push the limits of their technical mastery. And over two sessions in March and April 1959, they performed and recorded *Kind of Blue*.

When the band assembled, they had no idea what they would be playing. Davis had given them only sketches of the melodies, and he had abandoned the complex chord structures of bebop in favour of modal scales.

'No chords,' Davis said in an interview the year before, 'gives you a lot more freedom and space to hear things . . . You don't have to worry about the changes and you can do more with the [melody] line. It becomes a challenge to see how melodically innovative you can be.'

By dumping chords in favour of modes, Davis was forcing his band to listen more closely to each other; and, by not telling them what to do, he released their incredible potential.

Working with such a loose script (or without a script) forces everyone to listen, to ensure that their collaboration is contextually relevant to what the band as a whole is doing in the moment. And it worked so well that it is rumoured that each track was recorded in its own single take, though in fact only one, 'Flamenco Sketches', really was.

At one point, on the song 'Freddie Freeloader', Davis comes in a bar early. The other musicians adjust to his mistake so seamlessly that very few people notice it. And Davis clearly liked this subtle glitch enough to leave it in.

This is the power of collective improvisation. Everybody listens to everyone else, and modifies what they're doing.

The results of Davis's methods were phenomenal. *Kind of Blue* remains the best-selling jazz album of all time, and one that many critics point to as one of the most influential ever made.

In a Q&A with jazz drummer and founder of JazzCode Carl Størmer, which can be found on the Harvard Business School Working Knowledge website, HBS professor Robert Austin uses this album as an analogy for business (which is not a war, remember?):

One of the big problems in innovation is how to free yourself from preconceptions, to get outside your expectations and normal tendencies, so that you can create something really new . . . Get really good people and put them in situations they can handle, but also circumstances that challenge them and their preconceptions.

He goes on to say:

> Simplify the task down to its essential elements, put your smartest people on it, and force them to listen – to each other, to the interaction between the company and its customers, and to the market.

For Miles Davis on *Kind of Blue*, those essential elements were modes and melody. Everything else was unnecessary.

Deep Work

I explained the distractions and interruptions that I have endured while I've been writing this morning. Each time, it has taken me a good while to get back into the right mindset. But at least I'm working from home today.

At the time of writing, our Borough Market office is located in a cramped building where we all rub along well, but which is not so productive. People meet in the corridors and stairwell. Even the toilet is used as a place to convene. And there is a handset on the wall next to the lift that buzzes throughout the day – and throughout the office – whenever someone rings the doorbell on the street downstairs. People look around – as if to say 'Bloody hell, whose turn is it?' – and then someone gives in and gets up and walks over to answer it.

It does not make a gentle buzz. It screams a nerve-jerking *NG$X€HG&HH*HGGYYGH#GRHG* (this is not the official spelling of the noise, you understand). I don't know how people get any work done. I have been known to forget the wisdom of Staying Relaxed, and to see if I can use the handset part to 'disable' the base. Despite my efforts, it never works. The buzz is still there, just as loud, but now you can't really hear the voice of the visitor. So someone could be saying, 'We have come to steal all of your computers and set fire to the office', and the Leon person who had got up to answer it would still say, 'Hi, great, come on up!'

The importance of tackling one big issue without distraction is well described by Cal Newport in his book *Deep Work*. It is now required reading for all new joiners at Leon.

Newport proposes that most of how we conduct our personal and business affairs is ineffective, because we make the process of work excessively fragmented and complex. We convince ourselves at the end of the working day that we have achieved a lot. Perhaps we have deleted a lot of emails, which in reality does not significantly move us forward. We may have done a lot of filing, or sat in a series of meetings, which probably resulted in little positive action.

He argues that productivity has not greatly increased despite the advent of computers and the Internet. The new technical tools and the speeding up of communication has actually confounded us and made us less efficient and less effective. We have more distractions, there is more confusion, and it has actually led to a whole bunch of what he calls 'shallow work'. And he encourages us to focus on what he calls 'deep work'.

When we are distracted by an email or message or tweet that pings up on our phone, iPad or computer, or a CNN news announcement appears on a device or on the TV, our concentration is broken. It takes many minutes to get back up to full concentration again. And we have so many distractions that, for most of the day, our focus is severely compromised.

We need to rediscover the ability to clear our desks and our minds in order to do deep work, one piece at a time – to immerse ourselves properly in a problem, to apply our brains properly to that one problem and to follow through sufficiently to achieve a solution.

The subconscious and the spirit have so many answers for us. If we face a challenge that requires us to tap into them, we need the clarity and simplicity of focus in order for our relatively unpowerful rational brains to listen to our more powerful sub-conscious brains.

This cannot be done by overloading the rational brain with tasks. And if it is a rational problem that needs solving, like a mathematical equation, we need singular focus.

This is simplicity in action.

There is a verse in the *Tao Te Ching* that talks about the importance of space – of the vital role of emptiness. A vase is only a vase because of the space of its interior. A room requires space between the walls, floor and ceiling to be a room. Otherwise it would be a pile of bricks.

Music requires space between the notes to allow the notes to be. My wife Katie is a presenter on BBC Radio 3, the classical music station, where they joke that you are most likely to tune in and hear silence – for example between movements in a concerto. Every musician aspires to the perfect silence at the end of a performance before the applause begins.

If we are always filling every moment, we leave no room for ourselves to simply be.

Simplicity is – and Requires – Love

We hold workshops at Leon on all elements of Winning Not Fighting, and when it comes to the wisdom of Simplicity I ask two questions:

Do humans aspire to have simple lives, or enjoy their lives more when they live simply?

The answer is: 'Yes, absolutely.'

Why do we mostly fail to do so?

The responses can be grouped as follows:

First, that humans have a natural desire to always do more things and achieve more things.

Second, the 'paradox of invention' – many of the things that make our life complicated are driven by the desire for simplicity. (The dishwasher, the lawnmower, the trouser press, and all the depreciating equipment that clutters up most Western garages.)

And third, we have – especially in middle life – many responsibilities (jobs, children, ageing parents) that make complexity inevitable.

So let's explore each of these, beginning with the role of desire.

In Wing Tsun, the tension of desire is reconciled by an understanding of its destructive influence and our need to replace it with a contentment for the present moment. Ego seeks to protect itself through the accumulation of possessions and certificates and status.

When we are desiring these new things, we are off balance. We are grasping. We are not in the present moment. And doing many things provides an excuse for failure. *I've been so busy, I've had so much to do, it's been such a busy time, that's why I haven't finished . . .*

The driver of desire is fear. Specifically, the fear of missing out (or FOMO). Or being lonely, or not being respected. We seek more successes, more accolades, more money, more security, more praise – and, in the case of the mega-rich, more homes, and more and bigger boats.

The ego breeds complexity. Complexity becomes addictive as we continually Elastoplast over our unhappiness with the search for more things and even more complexity. And it confounds contentment.

We come back, once again, to one of this book's central themes – that we are at any one time driven by either fear or love, and never both at once. So the antidote to FOMO is to replace fear with love. Wing Tsun seeks to keep us in such a place of love. Because love defuses conflict.

Wing Tsun teaches us to be both physically and mentally balanced and grounded. The footwork, the way we punch or kick, is intended to keep us rooted to the floor and to make it difficult for the opponent to knock us off balance. Someone who is grasping is off balance. They are, to use another term, over-reaching, and are taking themselves out of the present moment.

When you picture someone grasping, what do you see? Perhaps someone who is happy to compromise relationships to get what they want. Or someone who takes shortcuts to achieve their goal. Or maybe someone who has some unattractive personality traits.

Replacing Fear with Love

All of the wisdoms in Wing Tsun, when practised together, combine to make it possible to replace fear with love. Knowing yourself, putting that self aside, positivity, not forcing (and the others) create a virtuous cycle where love wins over fear.

A first step to beating FOMO is to notice and value what you do have – not what you don't have. Both counsellors and now doctors encourage their patients to write down all of the things that they are grateful for. Some call it a 'gratitude journal'.

I have done it. And I have found how many things there are to be grateful for. Literally thousands. It is incredible.

The important thing about the wisdom of Simplicity is that it brings people right into the present. And it teaches us to value what we have, not to seek what we do not have. This is fundamental to moving from fear to love. From being off balance and living in the future to living now. When you realize that you have access to all the riches of nature right now, you can live simply and with great contentment.

If you lost all the people and goodness in your life tomorrow, you would do anything to get them back. So be grateful for the life you have now.

Love Grows When We Live Simply

If simplicity requires love, then in turn, I have concluded, love grows when we live simply. There is a virtuous and positively reinforcing cycle between love and simplicity. When we are too busy, when our lives are complicated, we find it more difficult to empathize and engage with others. Context impacts our behaviours as much as – or maybe more than – our values.

In his book *Blink*, Malcolm Gladwell recalls an experiment that compared two groups of theology students. The first group was told to prepare a talk about the story of the Good Samaritan, and the second was given another, unrelated subject. At the end of their preparation time, some from each group were told that they were late to go give their talk – and others were told that they had plenty of time.

The experimenters had deliberately placed an obviously distressed man, slumped down in an alley, between their classroom and the students' next destination. You would think that those who had just been preparing to talk about the Good Samaritan parable would have been the ones to stop – but it wasn't this factor that made the difference. Instead, it was how much time the students had (or thought they had). Of those who were in a rush, only 10 per cent stopped to help. Of those who believed they had some time, about two-thirds did.

The lesson? Context matters more than values. I know from my own experience that when I'm busy, I make less time for friends, write fewer thank-you letters, remember fewer birthdays, spend less time helping my daughters with their homework, and I am more brusque and arguably less loving to my family, colleagues and friends.

When my dad died, so many people wrote the most amazing cards and letters. I only hope that I would do the same. But I know that when my life is complex, I am taken out of the present moment. And I tell myself, 'I'll do better when I'm less busy.' There has been no change in my values as I define them to myself. But, thanks to my actions, people probably think there has been.

The simpler your life, the more space there will be for love. And, looking at it in reverse, complexity depletes empathy.

The digital age, while providing some technological solutions, for the most part makes our lives more complex. I went to my next-door neighbour's house to collect my daughter recently, and three teenage girls, my daughter among them, were lounging on the sofa. In the 1970s, they would have been talking or maybe watching TV. Here, while they did have the TV on and were watching it, they were also on their laptops, while also being on their phones . . . all at once. No one thing was getting their proper attention. And they were not talking to one another.

In 2008, a US study concluded that 16-year-olds were 40 per cent less empathetic than people of the same age 10 years earlier. They were less used to reading faces and body language, less likely to be connected to others, less likely to be engaged in the present, and more likely to have their heads lost in a digital world. I fear that, today, the data would show a continued decline.

Being content with simplicity is like being comfortable with silence. Silence requires you to put aside ego in order for you to be comfortable within it. In my first proper job, as a salesperson at P&G, our sales training taught us, among many other things, to use silence as a 'weapon'. Julian was taught the same when he trained as a barrister.

In sales training, we were taught how to get the other person to open up – to start with a 'general lead' ('How are you?') and then to . . . keep quiet. Even after the person gave a first response – 'I'm fine' – the trick was to say nothing. The other person would, 99 per cent of the time, fill the silence and tell you how they really were . . . 'Well, actually, I've been pretty busy because my dad's not been well' – more silence – '. . . and that's really affected my sleep and my work.'

Silence can become so painful – even excruciating. The ego becomes uncomfortable, and as a result most people will fill the silence with words. The ability to cope with silence requires self-esteem, and to be loving and not fearful.

What has this got to do with simplicity?

For the same emotional and spiritual reasons, we do the same with the spaces in our lives – both the physical and the emotional spaces. To hide discontent, we buy things. And we fill our diaries. We leave no time for meditation and no physical space for calm.

For most of us, the realization that simplicity is required for contentment, and thus for fulfilment and success, will come too late. When asked their regrets on their death beds, no one says they wish that they'd spent more time in the office. They regret not spending time with the people who were the most important to them. They regret that they allowed their lives to become so confused with things that took them away from the present.

As you master Wing Tsun's principles, you will become comfortable with silence, comfortable in yourself and comfortable with simplicity.

Die Every Day

We create complexity when we have a fear of death. Keeping our lives full means we don't have time to contemplate dying. (The Seven in Enneagram terms, the Enthusiast, is a character who is . . . *enthusiastic* about many things, but who is actually avoiding emotion and fear in doing so.) And in our minds, we are in a race to do many things before we croak, a desire that is not eased by books called *100 Places to Visit Before You Die* or *50 Bands to See Before You Die*, and many, many more. The pressure is on . . .

As an antidote to this, the *Tao Te Ching* invites us to die every day – to go back to the Tao, which is effectively the eternal nothingness that exists before we are manifested in a particular point in space and time. The Samurai had a similar approach, taken from Chinese teachings, of acting as if you were already dead.

Remind yourself of how to 'put yourself aside'. Remember your insignificance and impermanence, and make this a source of comfort not concern.

As we discussed previously, nature may look complex, but it is made up of cells and particles that each have a primary, simple job. At a biological level, each cell has one job. And at a physical level, each atom comprises subatomic particles that are formed from repeated and simple vibrations and waves of energy.

I am always amused by the reflections of Alan Watts on the reality of life in its raw simplicity: that we are really just a series of tubes (blood vessels, lymphatic system, intestines, and so on) with a brain that sits on top.

And, despite its complexity, the brain has pretty simple needs. Most human activity, Watts suggests, comes down to the fact that the brain likes to vibrate and jiggle. By which I mean it likes making, hearing and moving in time with nice noises (singing and dancing). It likes connecting to sound and light. The brain enjoys classical concerts, or pop concerts with energizing sound and light, or listening to Spotify, or chanting at a sports match. When we speak to each other, the words themselves are often much less important than the energy and intent within them. When we engage in small talk, we are finding indirect ways to share energy and, ultimately, love.

Watts also reminds us that our idea of heaven is quite simple too – people sitting around looking at God and making strange noises and vibrations and being bathed in beautiful light for eternity as we think, *God is really cool, isn't he?* Simple, really.

Watts talks about Nirvana being *Phew!* Realizing that we are 'it' or 'that' or 'tut' (the noise that a baby naturally makes as it points towards things for the first time) – the true essence of a thing or person that 'is', before it is adulterated or limited by the inevitable use of words to describe it. Zen Buddhism encourages us to experience the world as it is, and not to create constructs and rules and ideas and paradigms that one might find in more organized religions. One is encouraged to employ what Jung would call our 'sensing' capability. Not to judge, but simply to experience. Not to provide commentary, but simply to be immersed.

8.

Freedom and Responsibility
By John and Julian

Julian

Freedom and Responsibility is perhaps one of the greatest dichotomies of Wing Tsun. Its overriding teaching is simple – that by allowing people freedom, they take on the greatest amount of responsibility. In Wing Tsun, this is taught through the sixth wisdom of Lat Sau, meaning 'free hand'.

This wisdom goes to the heart of what makes a 'martial art' – the expertise and discipline required to be successful in combat, combined with the artistic freedom to develop continually and be yourself. Centuries of enlightened but pragmatic masters realized that this was an essential combination for worldly and spiritual success. The perfect synergy between the 'martial' and 'art' elements is a healthy creative tension that keeps harmony but allows the best progression. This balance is most famously symbolized by the Taoist Yin Yang sign.

Physically, Lat Sau is the ability to free up your techniques so they can be applied without any sequence, thought or preplanning. You could call this 'sparring', which it does contain, but that would do a disservice to the depth of this training.

Yin Yang symbol.

Lat Sau is the third aspect of the training triad of Wing Tsun: the forms, which teach you the fundamentals in a simple format; Chi Sau (meaning 'sticky hands'), where through movements of the forms you learn to feel and use the attacks of an opponent; and Lat Sau, where you apply both of these aspects to unexpected attacks from others.

That Freedom and Responsibility is necessary for success in life is hard to argue with. The question, however, is how do you achieve this? The development of Lat Sau is graduated, beginning back at the First Door and led by an experienced teacher. It starts by practising individual techniques against set applications. These are done with both hands so you don't depend on a dominant hand. You then practise combinations that are mixed up, so as not to be predictable. This is further followed by training cycles with variations for speed, timing and dexterity. By the time you reach the Second Door you begin to freely apply all your hand techniques against a training opponent. Finally, by the time you reach the Third Door, you no longer need a teacher to guide you. You incorporate kicks, elbows, throws and strikes in a fluid, unrestrained manner. Adapting as necessary, you are now able to apply your knowledge, skills and wisdom freely, to any situation you are faced with.

This practical graduation of Lat Sau is essential for a number of reasons. First, it's for safety, due to the potential for great harm to both the practitioner and the training partner. Second, it helps you to achieve the best results in the fastest time, utilizing the Wing Tsun principle of 'go slow to go fast'. One of the biggest challenges in creating personal freedom is removing fear. If you start Lat Sau training too aggressively, or too early on, you create a fear response and a flinch reaction that has a highly negative effect on your development. It becomes deeply ingrained in the mind and the body, taking many years to remove. On the flip side, by starting gently you can increase the pressure, speed and power in an appropriate manner, and within just days you can achieve astonishing results.

Finally, this incremental method helps you achieve a different perspective. You will innately learn Responsibility through Freedom, as you understand all too well the consequences of your actions. By the time you reach the Third Door, with the power and skills of the Biu Jee form, you are all too aware of what happens if you use it: death or serious injury. There is no such thing as a 'friendly fight' – that is left to the movies. So as you progress through Wing Tsun with Lat Sau, you develop a serious degree of controlled skill. You learn how to hit and then stop as required. You gain complete control over how and when you want to send out your energy. This allows you to have a positive instinctive reflex that bypasses the slowness of having to think first, while avoiding the double crucial errors of poor training: to hit someone when you don't mean it, or not hit them when you mean to.

Wing Tsun is fundamentally about creating an environment that is free from conflict. However, this has to start with us. The old masters knew that it was impossible to have widespread peace on a societal level if we cannot first have it on a personal level. By recognizing that we are responsible for creating much of the conflict we experience, and are free to act in a way that prevents this, we are doing a great service to ourselves and to others.

Wing Tsun teaches you about the connected nature of the world and to take responsibility for it. War is, in many ways, an emanation of personal conflict. So for us to be able to achieve peace we must truly understand the horrific nature of war and also learn to have peace as our natural way of life. Freedom and Responsibility, therefore, teaches you to see the true nature of the reality of combat, fighting and war, without making it a way of life for yourself. And it is here that we move far beyond Sun Tzu and *The Art of War.*

Practically, Lat Sau teaches you to prepare yourself for reality. With it, you avoid learning skills that work in the training hall but are otherwise ineffective. It gives you the skills, trust, mindset, belief and wisdom to succeed, but tells you that you cannot simulate reality. You can train to prepare yourself, but combat reality has no rules, gives no warning and cannot be controlled. There is no such thing as true 'no holds barred' fighting without a significant risk to your short- and long-term health. No matter how tough a competition is, and how few rules are imposed, even full-contact competitions do not allow spine, eye or throat strikes due to their potential lethality.

In Wing Tsun, freedom is not the same as anarchy, which implies a negative disharmonious chaos with no boundaries or guidelines. Freedom and Responsibility teaches you the importance and drawbacks of structure. No structure means it's impossible to achieve optimum skills and development; yet too much structure creates a rigid prison for yourself, strangling your natural flow and creativity. Wing Tsun, in a typical Buddhist sense, teaches you the 'middle way'. It teaches you that the structure is only there to create freedom. And, like the Buddhist concept of a Yana (or raft), when you have safely arrived on the other side of the river you leave that structure behind. There is no need to carry it with you for the rest of your life.

Wing Tsun took on the key essences of military reality without needing the structures, uniforms, language and management that together make conflict inevitable. It seamlessly integrated practical skills with spiritual harmony. But discipline is a fundamental part of freedom. Western schooling and subsequent workplace language (like attending a 'disciplinary') have eroded away this key feature of discipline. It's been made to be a form of punishment or about the highest productivity, rather than being a form of personal empowerment.

Freedom and Responsibility creates the greatest amount of good for the greatest number of people, but only if you approach from an empowered personal viewpoint. You cannot create discipline in anyone who does not want to change, no matter how much you try. The more extreme your efforts, the more you create co-dependency and fear, and both of these will lead to poor outcomes.

This is one of the challenges facing the modern military, in terms of recruitment and training as well as mental health. However, viewed correctly, discipline is extremely positive. It simply enables you to have a better way of enjoying what you are doing. It allows you to harness the best of your time and energy so that you have the most enjoyment in the moment, and also longevity in your results.

Similarly, Freedom and Responsibility doesn't mean that there aren't standards, thresholds or boundaries. There are – perhaps even more so. But the way they are approached is different. They are enacted in a supportive way, where you are much more a mentor and coach than a figure of authority. Authority creates rebellion and reaction, whether manifested internally or externally; whereas support creates love and adoption. Even when you are being directive, it comes from a place of love rather than force. This is possible when you apply the wisdoms of the First Door (Know Yourself and Staying Relaxed) with the ability to 'consciously connect' (Don't Force and Positivity) from the Second Door.

Freedom and Responsibility works not just on a personal level but on an organizational level. At its peak, the Shaolin Temple had thousands of monks studying there, so having a sophisticated way of organizing them – while ensuring the cultural and spiritual essence of the monastery was maintained – was vital. They did this by having an individual focus, which was then spread to the collective.

The monks understood that freedom is personal and has to start with you. If the leader of the community cannot feel free, there is very little hope that others within it will feel free. However, once the leader achieves this feeling, freedom is beautifully contagious. It's what makes you smile, makes you feel so light you could fly, and gives you limitless energy, drive and passion.

Freedom creates trust, and trust creates more freedom. This interlinked wisdom explains the root from which you create true loyalty.

Finally, in Wing Tsun we act as if we are responsible for everything that happens to us. That doesn't mean that we take on additional blame, guilt or legal responsibility. It simply means that we don't externalize what happens to us. Instead, we look to see how we can change our intentions, methods, actions and behaviours to achieve a different result and way of life.

Just this small shift of focus creates a significant sense of relief and relaxation, rather than the tension caused by trying to control the outside world.

Spiritually, therefore, Lat Sau is the process of letting go of the structures, supports and ideas that you have learned. They have got you to this point, but they are no longer needed. Instead, you go into a state of being – rather than thinking about being. Life has no real structure or support that the human mind can understand. It simply is.

Perhaps, then, the most important teaching of Freedom and Responsibility is that the greatest freedom is to be yourself. No one else can tell you who this is, and only you can take responsibility and make this happen. Do this, and your winning will have neared its zenith.

Lessons of the Sixth Wisdom: Freedom and Responsibility

1. The more you create an atmosphere of freedom, the more responsibility people will undertake.
2. Structure and discipline should create freedom, not imprisonment.
3. Societal freedom and peace starts with you.
4. The greatest freedom – and the essence of winning – is to simply be yourself.

John

You Can Change Your Stars

In his book *Great by Choice*, Jim Collins takes pairs of companies who were at one point in time in very similar circumstances, and explains how and why one of them failed while the other one prospered. This is the business equivalent of a 'twin study', in which scientists such as Tim Spector, professor of genetic epidemiology at King's College, London, track the lives of identical twins to look at the impact of environmental factors separate from the impact of genetics. And it allows Jim to isolate management and leadership decisions from the otherwise identical contexts, structures and strategic situations of these 'twinned' companies.

The unmistakable conclusion is that leaders and the choices they make matter far more than any strategic context. More than any good or bad luck. This should give leaders great hope. It means they cannot blame or bemoan the hand they have been dealt. But when a chief executive wakes up and realizes this, it can give not only great freedom but potentially lead to great anxiety. *What if I cannot blame my strategic position or others for what happens to my company?* A good CEO must accept that, whatever the context, it is their job to ensure that their company and their teams prosper.

This is Freedom and Responsibility. And everyone in business, in all positions, needs to wake up to it.

The ability to take full responsibility, unabashed, for your own happiness, well-being and performance is the single biggest differentiator between those who thrive at Leon and those who leave.

In this book, I talk about ideas of wholeness and love. To avoid confusion, I do not as a result seek to create a culture based on unconditional employment for all. Love does not guarantee employment.

I believe in the saying that you can take a horse to water but you cannot make it drink. So I see my job as creating an environment where everyone has an opportunity to know themselves and become conscious, to connect with others, to free themselves, and to remember their right relationship with themselves, with each other and with the planet.

Sounds hippy? Or conversely too harsh? Zany? Unrealistic? Whatever you might want to call it, it works. And if people take responsibility for their lives at Leon, we will support them. If they blame others for what has happened to them, they need to find their personal path outside Leon. Anyone willing to progress through the stages of Wing Tsun and of Leon will need to understand the critical wisdoms of this Third Door.

Our UK managing director, Shereen Ritchie, has lived her life determined to change her stars. Shereen had what can only be described as a difficult childhood. On her eighth birthday (and this is a typical example), Shereen's dad presented such a physical danger to her mum that she had to pass a note over the fence to a neighbour to tell them to call the police.

Shereen spent a large portion of her childhood in care homes. And when she wasn't, she found herself having to care for her mum, and her stars seemed set. But her mother's greatest gift was to tell her that her future was in her own hands. Or as Shereen puts it: 'My mum always said to me – Shereen, you can change your stars.'

There are many people who have endured situations like Shereen's, but it was her decisions and her sense of self-responsibility that have allowed her to flourish. She could easily have chosen to bemoan her life and to spend her life as a victim. But thanks to her deep-seated belief, gifted to her by her mum, that she *could* change her stars, she has been able to build a fantastic career and grow into a wonderful person who people want to be led by.

You will know many people who would rather criticize others than take responsibility for their own actions. I have never known Shereen to blame others for anything that has happened to her. She tells her team, 'It's our job to be a little bit better tomorrow than we were today.' If something goes wrong, she says, 'We'll fix this, JV,' or 'We've got this' – and does not allow her team to blame 'Leon' or 'Head Office' for their results.

Hers is a can-do attitude. When I was about to go to Oslo for the launch of our first Norwegian restaurant, I discovered, at the last minute, that my passport was locked in the Borough office in London. No one could figure out how to get it to me. No one but Shereen. She found someone with the keys to the office and organized for someone else to race my passport to Gatwick. I call this Shereen's ability to 'get the dinghy'.

Let me explain . . .

Go Get the Dinghy

In October 2017, faced with a very difficult market situation, we decided to take the senior team sailing on my very small boat in Greece. We had moored in one of the bays at Kioni, on the Ionian island of Ithaca, and decided to have dinner at a taverna on shore. Once everyone had made their way up to the taverna, Antony (Leon's CFO) and I dragged the dinghy up onto the beach and made a rather half-hearted attempt to tie the painter to the rocks. When we returned a few hours later, there was no dinghy.

Suddenly, a classic outward-bound management exercise became reality – how would we return to the boat? – and incredibly, fascinatingly, everyone reverted to type.

Nellie, the food director, who as well as being a great innovator is skilled at spotting what might go wrong, concluded that the boys she had seen messing around on the beach earlier must have taken the dinghy. Nellie concluded that, even worse, they would have taken our passports and money from the boat, and we would now be stranded in Greece unable to return to the UK. (At Leon we have many reasons to be thankful for Nellie's ability to see and prevent problems – including the hiring of Anca, the Leon food safety manager.)

Kirsty, the very strategic and smart brand and marketing director, who had previously been head of strategy at an advertising agency, decided that we needed to go to a high vantage point to scout the whole bay and formulate a plan. Meantime, Shereen had stripped down to her swimming costume, dived into the water and started swimming round the corner of the bay.

I couldn't let her go by herself. So, rolling my eyes, I dived in to follow her as Nellie muttered, 'She won't find it.' Which was followed a few moments later by Shereen's deep, unmistakably Essex voice shouting, 'I've found it!'

Sure enough, as I swam around the bay, there was Shereen riding the dinghy like Boadicea, paddling an oar on alternate sides towards me.

'See! I got the dinghy. And we didn't even have to have a meeting about it.'

I was glad that Shereen got the dinghy and amused that we didn't even have to have a meeting about it. More than anything, though, I am pleased that Shereen has, in so many situations, continued to go get the dinghy.

Lao Tzu vs Confucius

The writer of the *Tao Te Ching*, one of the principal texts that underpins the religion and philosophy of Taoism, wrote his 81-verse treatise around 500 BCE. Perhaps its most famous line is: 'A journey of a thousand miles begins with a single step.' But even though it is the most remembered, it is probably not the most profound.

Taoism specifically introduces elements like the need to put aside ego, the need to be flexible, to be like water, to lead without forcing, and to recognize the role of emptiness and stillness. Wing Tsun draws a lot of wisdom from the *Tao Te Ching*, but not only adds Zen Buddhist thinking but also links it to the deeply practical elements of the martial art.

At the same time as Lao Tzu was writing the *Tao Te Ching*, Confucius, who has ended up more famous than Lao Tzu, was creating an entirely different type of thinking. Confucianism is based very much on rules and etiquette – while the *Tao Te Ching* celebrates fluidity and freedom.

Confucius met Lao Tzu, and credited him with being one of the most spiritually aware people he'd ever met. But Confucius nevertheless ploughed on with his rules- and etiquette-based thinking and teachings.

The British-American philosopher Alan Watts stands out as one of the major figures who have explained and popularized Zen thinking in the Western world. In a lecture he gave in the late 1960s, he explained the idea that Taoism is typically something one picks up around or after middle age. It is then that its message begins to become attractive to those looking to free their minds, who are perhaps better able to understand the power of ego. He then suggests that Confucianism is something that is more suited to the world of work.

At that time, the world of work was extremely hierarchically organized, and the big, flourishing American corporations of the time were pursuing relatively militaristic, top-down structures. But I believe that, in the world of work today – and certainly in businesses like Leon – we should experiment with introducing Taoism.

In applying Wing Tsun to Leon, we are attempting to introduce the ideas and wisdoms embedded within it. Wing Tsun does not shun Confucianism – and in fact some of the master–student etiquette is influenced by Confucius. Wing Tsun, especially in the First Door, relies on structure and discipline to create space for fluidity and increasing self-discipline. However, as one progresses through the Four Doors, one learns through a graduated process to replace externally imposed rules with freedom and internally driven responsibility. Likewise at Leon, as soon as people are ready and as soon as it is possible, we seek to give them great responsibility, to not force, and to have more 'servant leadership' rather than top-down control. We want them to be flexible and trusting, to focus on strengths and positives rather than on weaknesses, and to be prepared to have fun at the heart of work. Rather than waiting until *later* life to engage with Taoist principles, we want to see if we can embed Taoism into working life *now*.

In so doing, we must be mindful of Alan Watts's reminder that 'Taoism is a means of liberation, which never comes by means of revolution.' To see work, business, capitalism and humanity in a healthier way does not require violent revolution. Every such revolution just creates an equally strong reaction.

If enough people are like you and change from within, and then change the organizations you work with and for from within, we will see a change in how governments act and communicate, and how newspapers and consumer products sell us ideas. And in how we and the companies we buy from and work for treat the planet.

In rereading Jung, I was struck by his belief that people, certainly from the age of 20 upwards, are in danger of becoming so rational and so technocratic that they do not access, understand or reap the benefits of their more mystical subconscious. That they close off the power of their irrational mind.

I contend that there is a certain joy and childishness inherent in the young, which is also inherent in retired or more senior citizens. And society and business can shut off this joy during our working life.

At one point, I started a brand called Flat Planet. In it, I talked about wanting to bottle the gap-year spirit. A gap year is, certainly in the UK, a year people take off between school and university where you set out to see the world for what it is. You meet and connect with lots of different people you would otherwise never meet. You try to discover and understand yourself (very much like the precepts of Wing Tsun). And then you come back down to earth with a bump, and you join an accounting firm because you think that's real life. Before you know it, you find yourself wearing a security pass, dressing in clothes you'd never have worn before, getting up at hours that are not natural or healthy. You're probably more shut off from your friends and family than you were before, because of how hard you're working. You suddenly find yourself having to adopt the rules of this institution you're working for. And you feel stifled.

Today, many businesses are recognizing that they are potentially losing their best people because they're putting the institution ahead of the individual – ahead of the human.

I believe that over the next 20 years we will see a dramatic shift in business. Companies will become more flexible with their people and will at last understand that the power of the organization lies in the power of the individual. You often hear people say, 'I have a gap to fill in my business.' I think this is the wrong approach. At Leon, I explain to people that Leon can only be as big as all of the people in it put together.

By this, I mean that I don't want to squeeze people into any 'gaps' I may perceive in the company; I want to help people fulfil their potential, to become as big and wonderful as they can be. And thus the gaps will fill themselves. The bigger and stronger people grow, the bigger the organization will be without you having to hire anyone else. Or before you have to hire anyone else.

To free yourself from convention is not to reject it in its entirety. But it does mean not being fooled or constrained by it.

Fundamentally, my job as CEO is to create an environment in which people can flourish. And in my experience, applying the principles of the Tao (75 per cent) and the principles of Confucius (25 per cent) – i.e. 75 per cent flexibility, fun, joy, not forcing and lack of ego, and 25 per cent rules, processes and boundaries – we create a healthier balance than the 1960s-style top-down, hierarchical structure that still exists in many Western businesses.

Chairman Tao

It's amazing what you can accomplish if you do not care who gets the credit.

Harry S. Truman

There's that line in the *Tao Te Ching* which says a great leader is someone where people at the end of the day say, 'We did it ourselves.' In business, this requires the leader to have no ego and to be comfortable with the fact that, even though they may have made a key difference to the success of the company, no one may ever acknowledge that.

Alan Watts's assertion that Taoism is something that one understands later in life (and by reading the *Tao Te Ching* itself) has led me to think about the role of the chairperson in businesses. In particular, how they have to learn a special skill or role in not forcing and allowing the chief executive sufficient freedom and responsibility.

Often, the chair of a business has also been the chief executive of a business, and it must be very difficult to find themselves in a situation where they are not playing the executional, everyday decision-making role of CEO.

The best chairpersons follow the *Tao Te Ching*, even if they don't realize it. They make sure that they have chosen the right CEO. They help that CEO create an environment in which the organization can thrive. And then they leave them alone. This means not forcing, not being overbearing, but instead giving the CEO support and positivity and offering gentle guidance where necessary – without trying to do the job of the CEO.

At Leon I have a chairman called Tim Smalley, who creates conditions in which my fellow executives and I can prosper. And my largest investor, Fersen Lambranho, says to me: 'You are in charge, we are here to support whatever you want to do. All I ask is that I am able to share with you the mistakes that I myself have made in case they are useful for you.' This act of not forcing takes a lack of fear and ego on his part. And it creates great energy and a sense of purpose and accountability in me.

I've been honoured to be chair of an organization called the Council for Sustainable Business (CSB), which I was asked by the UK government to set up. There have been times when I've wondered if I've taken on too much. However, I have attempted to implement the principles of the *Tao Te Ching* and Winning Not Fighting in the way I have approached the role: to not create too much work, to not take on too much direct responsibility myself, to create a positive environment in which people want to work and can flourish, to make the meetings fun and human even though, or rather because, we are dealing with serious issues.

I like to think that the results we have achieved so far on plastics – effectively implementing a UK tax on virgin plastics and making sure any new industrial project or residential property development has a positive environmental impact – are, in addition to the very hard work of the teams involved, in some small part the result of my ability to deploy the lessons of the *Tao Te Ching* and Winning Not Fighting.

Any success to date has been based on an early decision to populate the council with change-makers who have demonstrated the character, leadership and proactivity required to make dramatic improvements in how we respect our environment.

The Third Man

I declared my love for Jung in the chapter on Know Yourself. Both he and Freud provide explanations that help us understand who we are. Or, to clarify, who we have become. Or think we have become, and here's the rub . . .

It has taken four years to write this book. Julian and I have spent days, weekends and evenings together in the Kwoon, in the woods, in small barns, or in mates' flats by the sea. And we have sat at my desk as we both type, converse, challenge and ponder.

One such exchange led to a discussion about how we can reconcile the teachings of Jung with the Biu Jee principles of freeing yourself, and with the view shared by so many – like Steve Peters in *The Chimp Paradox* – that much of our character is set by the age of seven.

'I think we're going to have to recognize that, in saying that one can free oneself from one's past, we are in contradiction with the big teachers of psychology,' I said to Julian.

'Fair enough,' he replied. 'It's just that based on my experience of Wing Tsun, I don't believe they're right.'

I was a little taken aback. Julian is a confident man, but also measured. So I was quizzical – amused, even – that he was sticking his neck out on this issue. I then spent a few weeks reflecting on this point, and revisited the works of Jung and Freud. With the help of my friend Vanessa, then in training to be a Jungian therapist and very patient with my layman's questioning, I uncovered more layers to what Jung calls 'individuation'.

Individuation provides tools for freeing us from past dysfunctional patterns so each of us can become more conscious of our true self. But it still didn't quite get to where Wing Tsun does. It loosens the shackles of our past – lets us out at weekends, even – but does not break them.

Inspiration came from a surprising source. As part of my role as chair of the Council for Sustainable Business, I attended a meeting with Michael Gove, then the Secretary of State at the Department for Environment, Farming and Rural Affairs, to discuss plastics. And I raised my conundrum. (He had rattled through my questions with his usual clarity and intelligence, so we had some time to spare.) As with most meetings with ministers, there was a member of his team in attendance, this time his Private Secretary, Caz.

'Ah,' said Michael, 'you need to take a look at Adler.'

Adler?

'Not as remembered as Jung or Freud, but an interesting man,' he told me. 'While Freud thought that we are pretty much conditioned by our past, Adler believed we can break away from it. And that our view of the future and our aspirations shape our behaviours much more.'

Caz stepped in to remind Michael that we only had five minutes left, and he left me with two things – a clear direction on what we were going to do with plastics, and a potential solution to my conundrum.

Here is what I have discovered . . .

Firstly, Adler could have done with Sun Tzu's PR manager. The medical historian Henri Ellenberger wrote in *The Discovery of the Unconscious*: 'It would not be easy to find another author from which so much has been borrowed from all sides without acknowledgment than Alfred Adler.'

Alfred Adler was a long-serving member of the Vienna Psychoanalytic Society, alongside Freud, before he left to establish his own school. Accounts vary on how the two men got along, but Adler maintained enough respect for Freud's thinking to stay on speaking terms even though their schools of thought took different paths. Adler's work was deeply practical, and he used real-world experience and case studies to work out ways to help people change their behaviour in order to live more flourishing lives.

He loved a coffee and a discussion. He hung out a lot in the coffee shops of Vienna and, because there was no Wi-Fi, he passed the time engaging with all sorts of people – debating, exploring and discussing psychology, and dealing with specific cases.

I have subsequently explored the world of Adler. And while I'm not sure AdlerWorld is going to be built in Orlando any time soon (even though he does have a street and buildings named after him in Vienna), the psychological rides in the real world of Adler are fun, pretty feel-good, and some of them are about circuses.

We will come to that.

Leon is a place that invites people to go as far as they would like to in understanding who they are. And I hope that people at Leon would say that it is equally generous in how it offers opportunities for people to free themselves. Most find that the process of discovery and release dramatically changes their mind and physiology. Inevitably, others find the process highlights an irreconcilable difference between their current situation and the company's culture, energy and dynamic. They leave, or are left.

What I can assure you is that everyone I share these experiences with has my full attention and my full intention. They are not 'human resources'. They are people who are part of a clan, a tribe, a family, whose needs come before anything. Money, profit, 'shareholder returns' – they are all essential to keep the family fed. To help the family flourish.

While I recognize that my investors have a responsibility to give *their* investors a decent return, it would be impossible for me to hold workshops on well-being or psychology if I were doing so with the primary aim of financial gain. ('Hello, my name is John, and my purpose is to make money, and in order to do that I'm going to try to help you with some psychology stuff.') I've just finished a two-day well-being event at my house, where I overheard people saying, 'John really cares about our well-being.' Well, of course I do. Who wouldn't? Who doesn't?

Many leaders, alas, feel that they cannot sincerely care to the same degree when they see their people as 'human resources' to provide the company with the means to achieve a financial outcome.

The conversations about Adler are some of the most powerful and revealing discussions I have had in Leon. They revolve around what he called our 'self-ideal', which is an imagined sense of who we want to be – a picture we paint for ourselves of the ideal 'us'. It has been formed since childhood, influenced by parents, movies, comic books, fairy tales, Disney, teachers and formative romantic relationships – and from all the snatched images we have seen and the stories we have been told.

It is made up. And it is like an iceberg – some of it may be sitting above the water of our conscious brain, but much of it we are unaware of as it lies in our unconscious.

We have, too, an equally fabricated and distorted image of where and who we are now. And the gap between the two creates feelings of what Adler called 'inferiority'. This is not a sense of being less good than others – it merely describes the fact that we have to elevate ourselves from where we perceive we are to where we perceive we want to be.

I ask the Leon participants in these discussions how they respond to, or deal with, this gap. Their responses – encouraged through group discussions, individual work and intimate conversations in pairs – confirm the conclusions that Adler came to 80 years ago:

- 'I tell myself it's because I'm too busy.'
- 'I get frustrated and blame my boss.'
- 'I resent the people who I think are standing in my way.'

These are examples of one type of response – they project fault away from the individual. *Life is tough, and other people get in the way of my dreams.*

Then there is a second group of responses, which are not

about blaming others but are instead about how we can deliberately create distractions that sidetrack us:

- 'I create smokescreens.'
- 'I focus on fun things like birthday parties.'
- 'I put things off until after Christmas or after the
  summer holidays.'
- 'I clear all the unimportant emails and don't touch the
  most important and difficult ones.'

Both blaming others and creating sideshows are what Adler
called 'safeguarding behaviours'. Based on his observations, he
said that we often blame others or we create what he termed
'sideshows' (Adler loved a circus analogy) or maybe 'trivial
pursuits' (my phrase, not his). He believed that we all rely on safeguarding behaviours at some stage, but problems arise if they
go on for too long. Brace yourself for this next bit: he saw
those who rely on safeguarding behaviours as 'pitiful individual[s]
who made use of transparent tricks in order to escape . . . life's
duties'.

We see through them, and so do others. Eventually they
become obvious excuses. And our sense of inferiority com-
pounds and our self-esteem plummets.

Adler frequently referred to the concept of the 'life-lie'. He
argued that we create excuses or fabrications for ourselves that
do not live up to scrutiny. For example, you may say 'I have a
horrible boss so I can't get any work done' when in fact you have
created the idea of a horrible boss because you don't *want* to get
work done.

Before you reject this, consider the following: Adler said that
we convince ourselves that our lack of action is not down to us.
Someone who is afraid of writing a novel will say 'I never have
time to write' when they are in fact driven by a fear of failure.
They can be comforted by the feeling – or life-lie – that says, 'I
could be a great writer if I had the time.'

We have, however, an alternative choice. And this choice does not have to be based on our past, Adler says; it is a decision we can make right now. We can choose courage, and what Adler called 'coping behaviours'.

A coping behaviour can either be problem-solving (if you lose your job you look for another; if your skills are inadequate you improve them) or compensation (you choose to be good at something else in order to compensate, for example if you become deaf you learn to read lips).

Adler believed that we have the ability to stand up to our challenges, and that the primary concern of therapy should be to help people adopt a more courageous attitude towards life.

'Courage is not an ability one either possesses or lacks,' he wrote. 'Courage is the willingness to engage in a risk-taking behaviour regardless of whether the consequences are unknown or possibly adverse. We are capable of courageous behaviour provided we are willing to engage in it.'

In the most recent Leon workshop, we examined the role of the self-ideal and how we can develop a healthier response to the 'inferiority' gap. One of the managers, from London, worked out that her self-ideal was based on a desire to not be her mum and instead to be her dad. A product developer concluded that she was blaming someone unfairly for things that were her own doing. Two other people told the group that they were using food as a distraction, as a trivial pursuit. And someone who has recovered from addiction described the role of his drug abuse in creating sideshows, and how he had made the decision to change.

One of our longest-serving managers, Tom (he has given me permission to use his name), discovered a few weeks ago that he had not been successful in his interview for a new role inside the company. He is a great person, who has shown great character throughout his time with us. His immediate response to not getting promoted was to blame others. He had been given some feedback about what he needed to do differently next time, and he wanted to sit down with me to discuss it.

He was, in his own words, 'disappointed, shocked, stressed and overwhelmed'. And when we met he was not taking responsibility for what he needed to do to change. He said, 'I tried being positive and taking responsibility, but that clearly didn't work, did it, because I didn't get the role.' When I suggested he would help himself if he were to dress in a slightly tidier way, he said, 'But Robin doesn't dress very well and he's an ops manager.'

I know and love Tom enough that I was able to tell him very directly: 'Mate, you need to take responsibility for yourself right now. Stop blaming others or using others for comparison.' And I told him a little about Adler and held a figurative mirror up to his safeguarding behaviours.

The next day, he texted me to say that our conversation had had a profound effect. And I began to hear from his manager that he had seen an almost-instant turnaround in Tom's attitude and approach to the situation. And the email from Tom that I just received? One full of responsibility and courage:

> I have had time to have some good reflection on the feedback and myself . . . the feedback made such good sense and the process of understanding it has shown me I wasn't being true to myself but I just couldn't see this . . . I have the biggest pleasure in being able to help and support the new people in LEON and showing them the opportunities they can have in being part of something special . . . so I would like to apply for the Training Manager role, using all of my knowledge and experience from being at LEON for so many years.

This is a coping behaviour. We'll have to see what happens, but whatever the outcome, I know that taking responsibility makes you happy now and more successful in the long term. However you choose to define that.

Tom explained further when I called him just now:

It was like I have lost two stone – though I haven't actually lost two stone because I have still got a little bit of a paunch. When I wasn't taking responsibility for what happened, or didn't happen, it was like my mind was going round and round on itself. But looking back I think you almost have to go through that process of frustration. I am so glad I took the decision to come out the other side. It's so valuable that I have that journey under my belt. And I don't know whether if I had got the Ops Managers job I would have been happy because it wasn't deep down what I really wanted. I know that a training role is exactly what I am made for. I was going for the Ops job because I thought that is what one is supposed to do. I am just so happy now. I have such clarity. And if I don't get the role this time, I will keep trying.

In this one short example, what lessons are contained?

Yes, Freedom and Responsibility, but also Know Yourself and Expect to Be Punched. And validation that the process and journey of Wing Tsun works. Choi would be happy with Tom, wouldn't he?

At Leon, we now have many flip charts full of examples of people's safeguarding and coping behaviours, and the terms have become part of our vocabulary.

But Adler offered us another route to freedom: the opportunity to adjust and reimagine our self-ideal, and to realize that the self-ideal we have developed is unhelpful to us. Parental expectations, images we've consumed via all sorts of media, unrealistic or fabricated role models, airbrushed photography – all these are mostly fictional stories and 'pictures' that have in turn created an equally fictional self-ideal.

In the workshop, Andre, the manager of one of our most important airport restaurants, summarized it like this: 'Until today, I was not aware of the power of my own sense of who I should and want to be. I totally have this vision in my mind of how I should act and what I should achieve. I have to tell you that it is totally unrealistic and I have only just admitted it to myself.'

Andre is happier today than he was yesterday. And if the experience of other Leon people who have done this is what happens with Andre, he will be a better leader, and so his team will be happier too.

These ideas and constructs have a funny magic spell. And we can break the spell or burst the bubble with one pinprick. Change doesn't always happen in an instant, but it can.

Of course, I am not immune to the spell.

I remember writing down the heading 'SUPERMAN' on a piece of paper. I had decided I had to be physically fit, full of knowledge, kind, good at languages, academically smart, and so on. Surely it should have registered that Superman is a fictional character? But we get our self-ideal from many sources.

Up until four years ago, each year I wrote the most unrealistic plan of what I needed to become and achieve in the 365 days to come – all of it unachievable, and all of it with a psychological price to pay for being unachieved. But I have been helped by Adler's ironically reassuring reminders that we are, quite frankly, not very special. And Wing Tsun and the soft teachings of Taoism and Zen Buddhism have helped me loosen the grip of an unhelpful self-ideal, and given me reminders of how ordinary and insignificant we all really are.

In the later chapter on Mastery we will go one step further and provide you with the opportunity to escape completely from such constructs. Right now, you are in Biu Jee, a Door that offers you freedom from the patterns of past behaviour and which enables you to take a courageous and healthy approach to moving forwards. Biu Jee provides you with a chance to win the game. But it is based on the assumption that there *is* a game in the first place.

Let's maintain this assumption for now.

Adler is Biu Jee's best friend. He offers positive coping mechanisms. He challenges how wedded we are to trauma. And he believes that our own feelings and decisions should not be influenced by what others think of us. His views can feel challenging, and even controversial. He acknowledges the presence of trauma, but is far more bullish about our ability to choose our response to it. He doesn't believe we truly suffer because of our experiences, but instead make out of them whatever suits our purposes.

If you think this sounds a little bit of a stretch, you might try a more modern version in the work of neuroscientist Lisa Feldman Barrett and her book *How Emotions Are Made*. Barrett concludes that emotions are not so much responses to the environment, but rather are constructed by the brain to shape our understanding of our surroundings. Adler believes we have much power over these thoughts. This is a hairy topic, and one which has sparked debate and will likely continue to do so.

To grasp the whole of Adler's thinking, one must understand that he also offers insight that reinforces the principles of the first two Doors. His practice focused squarely on the need to know ourselves, and showed how we can do so. And his belief that other people should not be a source of negative emotion for us should not be interpreted as a recipe for heartless or sociopathic behaviour. Someone who is comfortable with being disliked should, at the same time, be kind to others and seek to create a feeling of community, even if no one else seems to be of the same community-driven mindset.

'Other people might not be cooperative, but that is not connected to you,' Adler once said. 'My advice is this: you should start. With no regard to whether others are co-operative or not.' He was not just an advocate of emotional and psychological freedom. He knew that this came with the responsibility of good citizenship and care for others.

Our daughter Eleanor, who was 13 at the time, came with me to see the team training for the first ever Leon restaurant in America. Afterwards, we went to dinner with some of the management and support team, which includes a number of twenty-something women who attended high school in the States. I asked them if they would share one nugget of wisdom with Eleanor. In different ways, all of them said the same thing: don't give a shit what people think about you, but show compassion if those people are being hard on themselves.

Steph, who managed marketing in Leon America, summarized it like this: 'At school, I felt like everyone was looking at me. Now I realize they were just looking at themselves in the mirror. I was the only one worried about what I looked like.'

Adler offers a more hopeful, more adaptable view of the human mind than many psychologists hold. More plastic, less rigid, more bendy, more flexible – and squarely rooted in the principle of Freedom and Responsibility.

I believe that our ability to continue to grow sales and open new restaurants in a difficult climate (and I am paying the appropriate homage to the gods of karma and hubris as I type this) is because the leaders running our restaurants know that they are not only responsible for the results in their restaurants, they are also responsible for their own lives and, to a large degree, for their feelings. Anyone who chooses the courage to adopt positive coping behaviours or a more helpful self-ideal is encouraged and applauded (in the spirit of the Gift of the Goose).

And, in Adler, I have found there *is* a Western psychotherapist who provides a 'scientific' backing to the principles of Wing Tsun.

Not that Julian ever felt we needed one.

But I did.

The Beautiful Marriage of Freedom and Responsibility

Inherent in Wing Tsun, and therefore in this book, is the knowledge that to understand love you have to understand hate.

There is a verse in the *Tao Te Ching* which says that 'up' can only be understood if we understand 'down'. Or 'out' if we understand 'in'. To comprehend any concept, we must inherently understand its opposite, because one cannot exist without the other. Taoism also offers a challenge to the separation of good and evil, God and Devil. They are like the two Janus faces that make up a whole. Two sides of a coin.

For us to understand freedom, therefore, we must understand that it comes with a conjoined twin of responsibility, although they are not strictly opposites, and this brings some inevitable constraints.

Be the Gravity and the Riverbank

Water can provide us with a lesson here.

We discussed before how water seeks the sea. It begins, it goes the right way then the wrong way, it learns and adjusts while keeping its goal in mind – to be as low as the sea. Or rather, to become the sea.

Now we must consider the riverbank, which constrains and directs the water. While water flows freely in a river, it is the riverbanks themselves that give it structure and direction. They are essential to creating the flow.

Retaining the final decision on who we hire to join our Borough support team (aka head office) is one such example of me taking on the role of the riverbank. At one point, we had reached a stage where there were people working at Borough that I did not know, who I hadn't recruited, and who possibly or openly didn't represent all of the values of Leon.

Fersen, our brilliant Brazilian investor, encouraged me to rethink my policy, and to make sure I interviewed everyone who joined the Borough team. The first time I did so, I had been told the candidate coming in was great for the role. It turned out that they couldn't answer any of my questions. They had never eaten Leon food and had no point of view on it. They had no opinions on some of the challenges facing the world or the things that were important to their generation. I was shocked – actually actively shocked – by their low cultural fit with our company.

Later, I sat down and explained to all of the management team how important it is that we hire the sort of people who, if someone met them at a dinner party, would be an ambassador for everything that Leon is. Anyone – absolutely anyone – at Leon needs to be a person that we could send as a delegate to any organization to represent who we are.

This is one area where I've chosen to provide some structure and discipline, and to be the riverbanks between which people can freely flow.

Acupuncturist Ged talked about some advice he was given about not using ruled paper. 'I was having real trouble getting some ideas on paper. I had writer's block. And a friend from Canada told me to stop using ruled (lined) paper. So I found a blank sheet of paper and things just flowed. There are boundaries – it's still an A4 piece of paper with bits I can't go outside, but it somehow freed my thinking.'

And there it is: the need for freedom but with, at the margins (literally), some constraints. It's like a game of football: white lines show the boundaries of the pitch; it has goals to give it purpose; there are a few rules about not using your hands or being offside (a long story), but a player has full freedom to produce creative play within these rules.

And so, to be *in flow*, my team at Leon need to understand that there are constraints. It is therefore important that, in accepting freedoms, one is prepared to assume self-responsibility.

There is in Wing Tsun a belief that the student gains more and more freedom as they move through each Door – the objective being close to 100 per cent freedom from outside control. But it is a graduated process, and freedom must be earned. It requires self-imposed discipline, and anyone working alone must impose constraints and discipline upon themselves.

For those of us in positions of authority, we must lead and manage people in a way that recognizes what freedoms people are ready to be granted. Discipline and responsibility are the necessary flatmates of freedom.

There is a pattern that repeats itself over and over again in the music industry. An amazingly creative band appears on the scene. Their first album is full of lyrics about teenage angst, sexual tension, the challenges of relationships, the challenges of living without too much money. And the creative expression that comes from this concoction of experiences often produces edgy and extremely engaging music. Their sound is unique and deeply original. People love it and the band explodes onto the scene.

Then, off the back of this popularity, the record company decides that they are going to deploy a huge budget with the second album. The band, who potentially wrote their first album while working in a bar or at another job that provided them some poetic and musical inspiration, suddenly find themselves given anything they could ask for. Where the first album may have been written on an old guitar with a broken peg, now the band suddenly find themselves with an expensive recording studio in an expensive house in the countryside with a cook, drivers, limos, their own fast cars, and as much time as they need to write the new record.

These new excessive freedoms rarely produce the desired creative outcome.

It is typical for a band's second album to not only be musically boring but spiritually boring, written about problems that everyday folk cannot relate to. The problems of missing their family because they are always on tour. The problems of press intrusion because of their fame. Or the rather first-world problem of not knowing what to spend their money on. And the musical spirit with which they are composed and recorded never matches the creative genius of the first album.

What is required in this situation is for the band to recognize this, and to apply restrictions within their new-found freedoms. Which may go so far as refusing the expensive studios, country houses and fast cars, and maybe even recreating the basement conditions in which they wrote their first record.

The same is true of the creative process at Leon. To create new dishes, we are best when we set ourselves a deadline. We are best when we limit the number of people involved and the amount of resources we allocate, where the brief comes back to the need to create food that is flavourful, fun, functional and fast. (By *functional*, we mean that it ticks all of the boxes from a health perspective, a price perspective and a sustainability perspective.)

The tighter we make the brief, the more we unleash the creative freedom of the team. The creation of the vegan LOVe Burger or the meatless meatballs or the original fish finger wrap was helped by the tightness of the brief and the sense of constraint that we put upon ourselves. Operational tension creates the alchemy.

Wizards of Westminster

A few years back, the newly appointed Archbishop of Canterbury made a maiden speech in which he encouraged people not to expect the government to make their lives better. Some people took his counsel to mean that we can't rely on the current government because they're useless. I think what he was actually saying was that no government – or any third-party authority – should be relied on to make us happy, or happy and well. Or happy and well and wealthy. Or anything else for that matter.

The government are the last people you should blame for your failures. But they are often the first people we blame.

I remember talking to a former Chancellor of the Exchequer, who said, 'I keep looking round expecting that I'm going to find the people who are really running the country. I keep thinking that I'm going to open a door in Number 10 or Number 11 Downing Street and behind it will be the grown-ups.' Such is the power of constructs like 'the Government'.

It is spiritually dangerous to pass notional responsibility for our lives onto someone else. And, practically, the government is really like the Wizard of Oz. It may pretend to have immense powers. But behind the curtain, there is just a man – or rather a few men and women – trying to pull a few levers and probably not knowing which to pull or how to pull them.

During our work on the School Food Plan, Henry and I went to the Cabinet Office. By their own admission, they were trying to solve too many problems with too few human and financial resources. 'People think that the Cabinet Office is full of well-funded people who are going to somehow solve the country's problems. People would be better served to know that they have much more control over their own destiny than we ever will,' we were told.

When friends of mine have found themselves in difficult situations financially, it is interesting to see the response. Three people in particular (one a chef, one a businessman, one a cleaner) have stood out for me because of their refusal to blame others. 'Whatever is happening to me is down to me,' one said when caught up in a very bad financial situation to do with a mortgage on his house. 'No one made me sign the piece of paper.' This attitude, although he was tied in financially, had given himself emotional freedom. Three years later, having worked his socks off, he made a little bit of money and was able to free himself. This is real responsibility, and with it comes the freedom.

There are 1,500 people in Leon, 66 million people in the UK and nearly 8 billion people in the world. Imagine if all of them assumed the responsibility that they currently pass onto organizations that cannot do anything with it.

Eight billion mindful leaders could make things a whole lot better.

The World as a Brazilian Tribe

Capitalism is not a self-correcting, self-managing system. It needs human agency. We are part of it, not observers of it. (We could talk about the role of consciousness here, but let's wait.) It is like a knife that can be used to cut cake or to kill.

When Henry and I were kindly given an award for sustainable capitalism, the UK business secretary said, 'The purpose of capitalism and business is to make money. But we had better make it sustainable.'

When I was invited to speak at the ceremony, I abandoned what I was going to say on my way to the stage (it's an ADHD thing, I think) and instead responded, 'I wonder whether the purpose of business *is* to make money. If all the world were living like a responsible Brazilian tribe – living in harmony with our surroundings – we would not act as we currently are. A leader of such a tribe does not wake up in the morning and say, "Gather round, everyone, our goal is to make money." They do not chop down all the trees, catch and sell all the fish, poison the rivers, decimate the wildlife, and then go to a charity ball and "give back" by buying a signed Wayne Rooney football shirt.'

The purpose of business must be to sustain life. To do some good. And then we need to make money to make this sustainable.

We have been looking down the wrong end of the telescope.

A Brazilian Reasons to Be Responsible

We've concluded that, while it's a good idea to give your customers things that they love in a way that they love, if our future plans were only led by their feedback and current opinions, we would, ironically, end up doing them a disservice.

Companies that wait for 'demand' for positive corporate

behaviour to drive their actions will find themselves behind the curve, and they will have damaged the environment for longer than was necessary or healthy. At Leon, if we had waited until the public and press had become anxious about high sugar levels in food, we would not have been years ahead of the issue. And on sustainability, we've been determined to lead not by what the public thinks right now, but by looking at the science and reality of the problem – irrespective of whether it is yet in the public consciousness.

In 2016, two years before David Attenborough presented the famous *Blue Planet II* episode that shocked the world into action on plastics, we sat down with a number of scientists and environmentalists, including the chief executive of Greenpeace, and identified three big areas of focus.

One, going from oil-based energy to renewable energy. Two, accelerating our move from red meat to plants. And three, getting rid of as many plastics as possible.

So because we had been working on a solution for the plastic lining of cups, and for the cutlery and other plastic consumables, for two years prior to that show, by the time public opinion had shifted to 'no more disposable plastic' we were already implementing initiatives to reduce and remove plastics.

A similar thing happened with veganism. Two years before the real acceleration of vegan diets, we had in place a major project called 'The Power of Plants'. This was both customer-facing and menu-based, and set out to significantly increase the number of vegan dishes. We went from 25 per cent to 50 per cent of our menu being completely plant-based.

And we also shifted all of our restaurants to ensure that we buy our energy from entirely renewable sources.

Organizations that are led by public opinion will often get to challenges or solutions too late. Take responsibility and do the right thing – the added bonus is that the customer will get there at some stage, sooner or later.

I Run Nothing

About a year before I became full-time CEO of Leon, I took over the 'responsibility' for the operations – the running of the restaurants.

However, thinking I was actually running the restaurants would have been the biggest mistake I could make. Responsibility and freedom to exercise authority must not only be twinned, they must be placed where they belong. If you were to drop Leon on the floor by mistake, it would break into pieces that are restaurant-sized.

To put it another way, each restaurant is its own business run by a CEO – a manager (aka Mum or Dad) who has full responsibility for this business, which by itself could be worth £1–3 million. This is a big job. Managers are often in their late twenties or thirties and have responsibility for the working lives of around 20 people. They are responsible for their team's safety and welfare, and that of the guests. They also have responsibility for all of the things that make the restaurant profitable (or not).

Confusion over who is in charge will at some stage, in my experience, lead to failure, and it will often be catastrophic failure. And the more people involved, the greater the risk becomes. Big senior teams in any business act similarly if there is not constant clarification and re-clarification of who exactly is responsible for what.

There is the terrible – and now infamous – story of Kitty Genovese, who was stabbed to death outside the apartment block where she lived. According to the *New York Times*, 38 people saw or heard the attack, and not one of them called the police. This, despite her screaming, 'Oh my God, he stabbed me! Help me!' Apart from one neighbour, who shouted 'Let that girl alone!', each witness assumed someone else would take action.

They believed they were just onlookers – emotionally involved but morally separate from the situation.

The first thing I did in taking over the restaurants was to get the managers together. I explained to them that they, and only they, were responsible for the success of their restaurants and their own livelihood. I encouraged them to see me and the others in the support team as people providing them with a service. I implored them to have a strong point of view about the menu, rather than roll their eyes if they were offered a new menu launch that didn't serve their needs. I encouraged each of them to actively contribute towards the discussion about menus and to challenge us if we were not giving them what they needed for them and their business to be successful.

I told them it was their responsibility to question the way that we were managing the Leon culture or recruiting new Leon people, and to challenge and also help out with the way we were depicting the food or talking about the food through PR and the press. And I explained to them that it was not my job to run their restaurants but to create the conditions in which they could perform well – through smarter support from the 'brand' teams and by helping them be well. (It was at this point that, internally and more formally, we introduced well-being as a major part of our culture.) While you're thinking about running your restaurants, I explained to the managers, I will be thinking about how I can help you eat, sleep, move and relax.

Soon I had a group of people who were leaning forward rather than leaning back, and no longer breaking off into cliques to criticize. I explained to them how much more important they were in the running of their restaurants than I was. We made sure, too, that we explained to *everyone* in Leon that the managers were the most important people in the company. While this ruffled the feathers of some people in the Borough support team, most people recognized what I was saying and were happy to acknowledge the truth of it.

It's important that anyone from a head office or support team in such an organization does not go into restaurants and make the managers feel as if head office is in any way more important than – or more responsible for – what the manager and the team are doing. Because it is quite clear that the opposite is true. There is no one in head office – no one in the support team – who knows as much as the people who are serving the customers and leading the running of the restaurants.

We have always made sure that we ask a manager's permission before going into their kitchen, and it's always been critical that the people from head office visiting the restaurants do so with humility and without any sense of superiority.

I believe that the more freedom we give the managers, the better job they do and the more they will take responsibility. We have made sure that they cannot blame 'Leon' for what's going wrong. They can, in Adlerian terms, tell themselves no life-lies. And they have been a lot happier as a result. They have taken on the responsibility for their own destiny.

My job is to celebrate and applaud when they use discretion. If a guest has lost their wallet or purse and cannot pay, the team member must use discretion and their freedom to give the meal to the guest for free.

And this doesn't just apply to them using discretion in a way that I approve of. The important thing is to praise them for using discretion even when I would have done something different.

I was sitting in our Southwark Street restaurant when a team member said to a guest, 'They've taken that off the menu.'

We hadn't met, so when I was leaving I introduced myself. She was very cheery.

'When did you join Leon?' I asked.

'Four weeks ago,' she said.

'Do you think you're ready to say "we" and not "they" when you talk about Leon?' I asked.

'Oh yes, yes. I see. Yes, definitely. I'll do that. Of course.'

If you have an organization where the team talk about the company as 'they', without taking the responsibility inherent in 'we', then there's a problem brewing.

As I mentioned earlier, we encourage Leon people to look out for Moments of Truth. Opportunities to do something special for a guest or a fellow team member. These are things that they *choose* to do. They are not from a head office manual of 'nice things that you must do'.

We do this because organizations can sometimes get to the point where people start blaming 'the company' for their lot. They break off into smaller conspiratorial groups, criticizing the company for what it is doing or bemoaning a lack of opportunity, as opposed to proactively volunteering to help the company fix the issues. When I took over operations, we had got to this point. I can guarantee that if you ever find yourself in the pub or in a bar throwing stones at 'the management' of your company, you should leave the pub immediately and phone the CEO and tell them instead. The CEO will be pleased you did. And if they are not, then it's time to find a company with a CEO who is.

Values Engineering

I talked at the start of this book about Wing Tsun being the best framework I know for personal and organizational development. With it being a framework, and not a set of rules, I hope that it will provide you with a structure to grow your own thinking around it.

I know some people who become slaves to these sorts of books and believe that they should be used as an operating manual. Anxiety grips them, and the book becomes an impediment not an aid. It helps to remember that anyone who writes these books is as flawed as everyone else, and that if and when I meet you, you will be able to teach me so much about many things and I will be grateful to learn them.

The Four Doors of Wing Tsun provide a framework that acts like a trellis – a wooden garden frame on which plants and flowers grow. Around the concept of Winning Not Fighting, we can hang and grow our own existing ideas as well as the new insights we glean as we learn and develop.

The same is true of our values at Leon. I aim to provide a trellis around which the values grow and bloom. And you won't be surprised to learn that the framework we use is the Four Doors of Wing Tsun and Winning Not Fighting. We seek to avoid our values being something to beat each other up with or as a means to control others.

My friend Richard has long inspired me with his insight 'You can either tell someone you're funny . . . or you can make them laugh.' The person at work who says, 'I'm mad, me,' probably isn't. I'm always amused by the memory of my history teacher pointing out (as many do?) that the Holy Roman Empire was not holy, was not Roman and was not an empire.

We are surrounded by so much 'doublespeak', to quote Orwell, that it is not always easy to spot. When you go into most global headquarters today, you will see in reception or in the staff canteen big posters outlining their 'values'. Their vision, even. Probably their mission too. These things can play a role to bind an organization together, but I would like to suggest that culture is not created by diktat. People are not held together by rule books. The one 'value' that you will find on most walls of offices, behind the fern plant and just to the left of the regulation Health and Safety at Work poster, and just beneath the poster on Respect, is *Trust*.

Businesses are right to see this as the essential glue that holds companies together. But they often fail to realize that it is not built by putting the word on a wall. Companies tend to put up on the wall things that they want to be, but are NOT. (We do this as individuals with New Year's resolutions.) And these posters become depressing reminders to the people who work there about the gap between hope and reality.

The Bible is used by some to hold power over others. Official company values are used much the same way in companies. But a king who orders his subjects to 'respect me' probably won't get any further than the guillotine. Respect is not commanded, it is given.

So a leader is left to work out how to build a culture implicitly. To build it through actions not words. Through who it hires, who it promotes, how it trains people, how the leaders actually act, how people are forgiven and praised, where money is spent, what things are celebrated, what people are (not) chastised for. Southwest Airlines (yes, I love them) do not publish their values. There is no list on the wall for people to beat each other up with. In Leon we DO write down some of the behaviours that we notice make us strong. And yes, trust is a theme that unites some of them. But we do not produce a top-down list of what to do and not do. Instead, we ask Leon people, 'What do you notice that we do that makes us strong as a Leon family?' We have done this right from the start, and we have collected lots of tangible examples of actual behaviour that create a strong set of stories that bind us. My favourite is: 'We talk about people as if they can hear us.' We record these, but they come from the bottom up. They are the things that people notice already make us strong, not a list of things that we wish we did but don't.

It has been extremely important to me that our values are recorded, not prescribed. And it is the 75/25 per cent principle at work.

So the conversation we have about our values is organic. It is alive. They are not 'exhaustive' or 'comprehensive' – there will be many other things that make us strong as a Leon family, and we encourage our people to notice those and maybe even write them down and share them.

Then there will be all the things that all of us do unconsciously that we may not realize. We will probably never know what those are, but that's okay.

Breaking Free

At the time Buddha was preaching, Hinduism was in need of a bit of a clean-up. The priests had become as interested in how to fund their own livelihoods as they were in the religion. Rules and rituals had come to obscure the true essence of the teachings. So said Buddha. He offered a simpler way of thinking that quickly resonated. It freed people from the complexities and control of what Hinduism had become.

Mark Twain said that history does not repeat itself, but it does rhyme. And we see the pattern repeat itself in many religions and other movements and organizations.

Five hundred years or so later, Jesus challenged Judaism in the same way. Fifteen hundred years later, Martin Luther opposed the Catholic Church. Each offered a religious idea that questioned the need for a professionalized and controlling class of priests.

What is just as telling is how Hinduism responded. It could be called a carrot-and-stick approach (reminiscent of Eddie Izzard's 'Cake or Death'). The stick: persecution. The carrot: to claim Buddha as an avatar of the god Vishnu. In so doing, Hinduism countered the threat. It invited followers of Buddha back into the Hindu temples. And it cleaned up its act – at least cosmetically. It adopted Buddha's ideas into its creed. Buddhism in India today, as a separate religion, is a fraction of the size of Hinduism. While Buddhism never really took over from Hinduism, it retained enough momentum to prosper.

Businesses and other organizations are like religions. They have an innate tendency to become more rule-based over time, and few can remember why the rules were created. They tend to destroy freedoms rather than respect them, and they create a rigid culture. Businesses that started out small, nimble and pure can end up bureaucratic.

The corrupt priesthoods of the past (and the present, perhaps) find their modern equivalents in all sorts of institutions. In business, Warren Buffett bemoans the rise of the professional management class, who end up serving their own needs ahead of the needs of the company and its shareholders. Buffett talks eloquently of the 'institutional imperative', where decisions are made on behalf of the professional management class as if they are somehow a separate (and ultimately preferred) set of stakeholders.

The same is true of religion, where the clergy become professionalized. This is particularly true in Hinduism, where the four castes have been traditionally determined by familial rite and tradition: Brahmins (priests, scholars and teachers), Kshatriyas (rulers, warriors and administrators), Vaishyas (agriculturalists and merchants) and Shudras (labourers and service providers). By making priests a professionalized caste rather than a vocational role based on a calling, there is a risk that money becomes the goal.

The same is true of business. As one company becomes 'professionalized', or perhaps Confucian, or perhaps like the navy, the likelihood is that it will be challenged by others seeking to question the complexities and controlling culture of the incumbent. They seek a culture of freedom, where actions are based on a cause not on rules. They are less Confucian, and more Taoist. Less like the navy and more like pirates. (Something we will come to later on.)

To illustrate, let me tell you a story about McDonald's. I believe that, when we started Leon, McDonald's had lost its way. It had become too complicated. A lot of the franchisees were not engaged with their own businesses and had become members of a professional management class and were disconnected from their franchises. The book *Fast Food Nation* and the film *Supersize Me* had highlighted the environmental mistakes being made by the company and the impact that their approach to food was having on human health. It was the right time for Leon to come along.

Interestingly, since we started, McDonald's has to some degree (and not in its entirety) reacted to the creation of businesses like ours by trying to adopt a lot of our language and some of our practices. The architects of the McDonald's turnaround were Denis Hennequin and Steve Easterbrook. They began in France, where Denis painted the restaurants green and created a culture that was in some ways similar to Leon's. He was a maverick in a very conservative system, who could see what was happening. I like him very much. He is bald, rides a motorbike or bicycle everywhere, and looks great in a leather jacket (he turns up in one to very formal global McDonald's meetings).

Denis told me that he stood outside our restaurant on Carnaby Street, having just eaten there, and said to himself, 'This is what McDonald's needs to be. Good food fast.' A lot of what you see in the global turnaround of McDonald's is because of us.

Steve Easterbrook ran the UK for him and acted as a good partner, sharing and then taking on a lot of Denis's vision. He implemented a similar turnaround in the UK and is now attempting to do this in America. But the story is not finished and the question I have is this: how big can Leon be versus McDonald's? Yes, I want to win in fast food. But most of all, I care about Leon – and me – being in the present, doing the right thing every day. Let's see where it takes us.

Where the Buck Stops

Legally, each board member must protect the financial well-being of a company and its shareholders and creditors. But the paradox is that they then must – from a day-to-day perspective – entrust this responsibility to the CEO. It is very important to get the dynamic between them right. And the reality is that the more freedom and responsibility they take away from the CEO, the less likely the company is to succeed.

The more a board of directors or investors constrains the movements or impedes the freedom of a chief executive, the more a chief executive will rightfully be able to turn around in the event of failure and share the responsibility for that failure with the board. I feel it is extremely important that, by giving account-ability to the CEO, they give *responsibility* to him or her. In other words, they must give both the power and authority to the chief executive to exercise responsibility. This will vary given the experience of the CEO – a chief executive who has a Biu Jee mindset must not be treated by their non-execs as if they have a Chum Kiu or a Siu Nim Tao mindset. A CEO who is still in the equivalent of the First Door will require and may seek greater controls.

It is because of fear that investors feel the need to control the chief executive. Because many investors work in the nice part of town, eat in nice restaurants, attend members' clubs and enjoy the things that come with the 2 per cent of the total money they manage that they charge as fees every year, irrespective of per-formance, it becomes easy for them to think they are the smart ones. That the CEO is a tool to be used or discarded. Because there are plenty more where that came from.

I am lucky that my investors think the opposite. But I see many CEO friends with investors who have become a little con-fused by the trappings of their corporate lifestyle.

If investors are frightened, deep down, that the CEO may not respond well to being managed, they may appoint a finance director who they see as *their* woman or man. They argue that this creates a 'healthy tension' within the company. It doesn't. It just creates tension. Most sensible chief executives will politely find ways to stop this happening.

Investors and board members who trust the chief executive,

and allow them to exercise freedom and responsibility, will end up doing a much better job for the pension funds and pensioners who invest in them.

Voice of the Beehive

Ottie is one of the superstars of Leon. In fact, she is probably one of the best people Leon has ever had. If I were prime minister for a week, I would have her be the receptionist at Number 10. She would get Putin to give her a twirl, remember everything about each visiting head of state and the names of their children, while also doing the same for the people who do the (possibly more important) job of emptying the bins.

Ottie is one of a number of personal coaches that I have across Leon. People who share advice and wisdom. If I say, 'Look at how many emails I've got,' she will reply, 'You would be very sad if no one ever wrote to you, so let's be grateful that all these nice people are emailing you.' Or, 'John, it's a full moon on Friday, so make sure you don't get angry with anyone.' Or some other such lunacy.

Ottie is Japanese and was sent to school in the UK because her dad wanted her to have creative schooling that he thought she wouldn't get in Japan.

She is certainly creative. Her thinking is instinctive, she has immense intuition and her mind is non-linear. In fact, Ottie is such a fan of non-linear systems and thinking that she studied it.

Think bees. Think ants. There is a queen, for sure – a boss of sorts – but she does not issue any orders. The bees work it out between themselves. And so do the ants.

If Leon is to grow, I cannot spend my whole time giving orders and being directive. I believe that the people in the restaurants know better than I do about running those restaurants. My job is to make the vision – and the customer – the boss. (Oh, and to create unexpected challenges that need fixing – when I offered, in a newspaper column, to give free salsa verde to everyone who tweeted me, we were left with about 500 jars to make. Much of the support team in Borough self-assembled without me needing to say anything and spent two days in the test kitchen chopping herbs and filling jars and wrapping them up as gifts. Thank you, Leon peeps.)

I first met Ottie when she was working in our restaurant on the Strand near Trafalgar Square. It was an amazing team – so I have asked Ottie to explain why. Remember, as you read, the story of Squirrel, Beaver, Goose.

Over to Ottie:

Justin, our then manager, gave each of us one task and told us what the most important thing was that we had to achieve – and not to allow that to be compromised by anything else. To me he said: 'Ottie, as a front-of-house team member, your most important job is to make sure that the customers are happy.'

That job of keeping the customers happy allowed me to do whatever I needed to do to treat guests like the humans they are. That meant listening to and understanding customers – we would recommend a competitor when we couldn't help them, or we would rustle up a cold-buster with the ingredients at hand for a sick guest with an important day ahead.

Ali, then a grill chef (now a manager at Canary Wharf), knew that his job was to make sure we had food to sell at all times.

Orlan, then in the kitchen (now a deputy manager at Canary Wharf with Ali), knew his tasks included organizing the kitchen, the fridge, keeping it clean at all times, but that his main job that he must not veer from was to make the food perfect every time.

It's fast-paced, serving four to five customers per minute, and at any one time 10 people are working on different jobs. Had Justin micromanaged the team it would have been slow and not sustainable.

In 2012, Starbucks introduced the names-on-cups concept in a bid to be friendlier. It was in fact something we'd started doing at Leon in 2007 to reduce complexity.

Not many customers had a standard latte or cappuccino . . . it was a 'single shot in half full-fat, half hot water' or '3/4 of a portion of chocolate with extra-hot milk mocha' for about 100 or more people every morning.

Many regulars were from the same office, and sometimes one would come in to pick up eight coffees for their colleagues, and they'd say 'I need to pick up coffees for Henrique, Louise, etc.', who all had their complicated preferences, so we ended up writing their names on the cups to indicate which drink was for who.

To sum it up, the responsibility and freedom we were given allowed us to serve more customers who we would have otherwise lost, and to make more money without costing too much time.

Justin had a goal, and it still remains the same today, which is to be the laziest GM in the business by empowering amazing people until he becomes redundant. This gave us the space to do other fun stuff.

We didn't chase sales – we knew that sales are the output of great people knowing exactly what their job is and having the freedom to deliver what they are responsible for.

Thanks, Ottie. Thanks, Justin. Thank you, everyone else who worked there. Bee proud.

Beehives for Schools

When Henry and I were writing the School Food Plan, there were many who said, 'Why do you need a plan? Just pass a law saying that the children have to eat good food and be done with it.' Now, I'm not saying that laws can't be a small part of the solution, but what we concluded was that the leadership of and the ethos created by the head teacher – i.e. the culture – in each school was far more important than any laws. And we concluded that the more freedom, accountability and responsibility a head teacher had, the better the food culture and school meals were in that school.

Before our plan, there were already very specific laws in place about the micronutrients (zinc, magnesium, etc.) that had to be provided on a rolling three-week set of menus. But they failed to account for the reality of what was being served and eaten in schools. There were huge discrepancies in the quality of food despite there being uniform legislation. The cooks (some now prefer the title 'chefs', but there are many of you out there happy to be called cooks, I know) were spending huge amounts of time calculating and adjusting the micronutrient content to conform to the laws and create the perfect theoretical set of menus.

The reality? Take-up of school dinners was on average 42 per cent, leaving 58 per cent of children eating (mostly unhealthy) packed lunches, or going out of school to grab fried chicken or crisps, a chocolate bar and an energy drink. The theoretical cycle of menus did not and could not dictate what each child put on their plate, nor what they then ate from the plate. Nor did the theoretical menus take into account which days the children ate school dinners on. Fridays, for example, were always French fries days or treat days on the weekly menus. And, unsurprisingly, take-up was always higher on a Friday. The reality made a mockery of the (false) belief that legislation was the answer.

This did not stop the press becoming agitated when the government gave academies the freedom to choose what they could provide, and thus not to have to follow the three-week micronutrient rules. The Local Government Association issued a press release which the media quoted pretty much verbatim, telling the public that children in academies were being fed junk food.

This did not tally with what we saw in the schools we visited. And each time we asked anyone and everyone to show us an academy providing junk food, we were told, 'Well, I don't know of one myself but I have certainly heard they exist.'

The reality was that the academies we visited were good, and often outstanding, on school food. At the David Young Academy in Leeds, the head teacher and chef worked together to create an excellent canteen and to make food a great part of school life – the rugby team got strong enough to stand up to the local private school, and students who were would-be chefs worked in the canteen alongside the professional chefs. And at Carshalton Boys Sports College in London, their students grew vegetables, studied them in biology, learned to cook them and ate great school meals.

At the same time, we also saw terrible food and drink, and low take-up in many schools that had chosen to stay under local government control and who in theory had to abide by the law.

We worked with ministers to simplify the law so that it was easier to understand and implement, including rules that you could understand if you were cooking at home. Meanwhile, we did all we could – including providing free meals for the first three years of school – to make the economics work, and to create a virtuous cycle of quality and reduced cost. And we made sure that what was working well was shared between schools.

The key to all of this? Making sure that the head teacher had enough freedom and responsibility.

In one school, the business manager (aka bursar) excitedly told us that they were putting a beehive on the roof. What would have happened if it had been the law to have a beehive? She would have grudgingly gone online, tutting to herself that 'the government now wants us to have a bleedin' beehive', and bought the cheapest one possible from 'Beehivesforschools.com' before sticking it somewhere to rot.

I spoke about the School Food Plan at a brilliant conference called 'Risky Business', which is all about helping hospitals and other high-risk industries learn about and share lessons from mistakes and successes in the airline industry and other sectors, or from significant events like the Deepwater Horizon oil spill in the Gulf of Mexico or the truth and reconciliation process in South Africa. And I asked Tim Baker, head teacher of Charlton Manor Primary School, to come with me so that they could hear from someone who was in the thick of the school food revolution.

Tim's school had also acquired a beehive. He told the Risky Business delegates: 'When we told the parents we were going to get a beehive, they said, "Won't the children get stung?" The children helped choose the beehive, painted it, helped me find the colony, and had the honey on their toast. And did the children get stung? . . . Of course they did – they're bees!'

Pirates

Steve Jobs once said that it is better to be a pirate than to join the navy. This has always struck a chord with me. I have frequently felt as though I walk a fine line between the two, but that I have a tendency that tips me towards the pirate ship.

As a Challenger, I am more likely to challenge the status quo than I am to support it. And I certainly like to disrupt. But the thing that keeps me slightly 'navy' is that I seek to disrupt positively – to make things better, not tear things down out of anger. So maybe like Captain Jack Sparrow, I am a pirate, but a kind of good-ish pirate?

One of the first things I did after becoming full-time CEO again was to organize a 'pirate trip' to the Isle of Wight, on the south coast of England. We dressed up like pirates, and we drank a reasonable amount of rum, and we danced on precarious tables and sang a whole lot (we sang 'Sweet Caroline' far too many times), and we went to lie on the beach when we were spent, but we didn't steal anything. Cos we are nice pirates, innit.

Aside from all this pirate palaver, the important thing was our discussion about what it means to be a pirate. We agreed that pirates:

1. Want to challenge rather than preserve the status quo (which is the job of the navy).
2. Think for themselves without the need to take orders.
3. Take responsibility for their own welfare . . .
   . . . whilst coming together, without asking, when a fellow pirate is in need.
4. Do not have the support of an entire infrastructure – they have one ship so they had better look after it.
5. Share the spoils.
6. Are resourceful – they find their own sword rather than wait to be issued with one.
7. Do not allow the institution to become more important than the individual.
8. Have a flat and democratic command structure.

And lots more things that I am sure you can think of. But it's not unlike the bees, don't you think?

I am reminded of my mum's teaching philosophy – treat every child as an individual and afford them trust. Children respond so positively to being treated in this way. At 82, my mum is still teaching and has thousands of former pupils who are grateful for her approach.

The way of the pirate supports our philosophy that, if we make the true objective of Leon to provide an environment in which people can live well and understand (and experience) what we mean when we talk about wholeness, we will make more money as a result. When people are treated this way, they are more ready and keen to serve others. Making money is not the objective, but it is a prerequisite if we are to fuel the adventure. The more we make, the more we will achieve this purpose, every day.

Every year we say, 'Let's do another pirate party', but that one was hard to beat. One day, maybe. But if I have done my job right, it won't be me who organizes it.

Go Fly!

Despite my belief in freedom, I have received feedback that occasionally I communicate with my team like this: 'Go fly . . . I believe in you . . . you can do it . . . you know what to do . . . make this your own . . . soar like an eagle . . . no, no, no not like that!'

Sorry.

The thing is: freedom and responsibility are not just nice words. They have to be lived with full commitment, so you must be prepared to honour these principles.

A good example comes from my favourite company Southwest Airlines. An individual made a verbal commitment to a supplier and, in keeping the verbal commitment, cost the company a significant amount of money. Other businesses would either have said that the individual did not have the authority to make that commitment, or would point to the fact that there was no written agreement. But Southwest Airlines took the high road, honoured the fact that it trusted its people to represent the company, and paid out the money. Of course, this was an expensive mistake on the part of the individual (and therefore the company), but the company was much stronger for the fact that it reinforced its culture of honouring both freedom and responsibility.

This recognizes the fact that it is not businesses that do deals. It is not companies that make commitments to each other. It is people. It is individuals.

Wherever we have a franchisee or partner or supplier, we make sure that there is one single person whose eyes we can look into. Whether it's David Park from our chicken supplier or Walter Seib from HMSHost or Simon from SSP, we make sure that there are individuals partnering with individuals, shaking hands and looking into the whites of each other's eyes. And, at the point of handshake, we are making a commitment to their success – to making their success work with our own.

The Emperor and the Prime Minister

Just as we cannot leap to the Fourth Door without experiencing the others, the wisdom of Freedom and Responsibility is part of a graduated process that begins with discipline. The model of 'situational leadership' developed by Paul Hersey and Ken Blanchard suggests that, when managing someone, you need to assess their confidence and competence, and adjust your management style or approach accordingly. When someone is new to the organization or to a particular task, they will possibly not know they are shit at it . . . for now. Many young people think they can drive a car because they have played driving games on their Xbox, or because they've seen their mum and dad driving for years. When they realize they don't have a Scooby Doo after the first lesson and their confidence plummets, they have low confidence and low competence. Then, slowly, they get better and have medium competence and fluctuating confidence. Eventually, they have high competence and confidence. At this stage, they can drive a car unconsciously – without having to think about every move.

When managing these four stages, the manager must begin by directing, then coaching, then supporting. Then, finally, they can delegate. By the time the person in their charge is at the fourth stage, they have won their freedom, like Russell Crowe in *Gladiator*. Sort of.

The student of Wing Tsun must go through the discipline and directive instruction of the First and Second Doors in order to begin to free themselves in the Third Door. What is inherent in Wing Tsun is an aspiration to move the student along the process – freedom is an objective. The teacher will move their student to a place where freedom increases as the student develops, and constraints correspondingly decrease.

One of the films we show to the Leaders of Leon is *Twelve O'Clock High*. It tells the story of a US Army Air Force Base in England in World War Two. At this base, the crews are enduring horrific casualty rates on every mission. Many aeroplanes and crew are being lost. And morale is plummeting. The commander tries to boost morale by giving the crews time off and not giving them a hard time over anything. It doesn't help performance or morale. A new commander is appointed who takes a different approach. He introduces a regime centred on discipline and order. A Confucian approach, if you will. Morale begins to edge up, and he is able to start giving more and more freedom as time goes on. Morale soars.

So, please understand that when we talk about Freedom and Responsibility, it is to be cherished and pursued, but at the right time. As confidence and competence grow, as you progress through the Doors, you will experience greater responsibility and greater freedom. Don't allow yourself or your teams to be stuck in a culture of rules and regulations, but equally don't rush to give freedom before it is deserved. People want to be 'held to high standards and treated with respect', as my friend Brad Blum reminds me – and this includes giving them freedom, and leading them from Confucianism to Taoism at the right time.

Freedom by Design

I have always been interested in the power of graphic design. At school, I liked to work on the branding of events we put on, and helped to design and create the school's first yearbook. At university, with my mate Richard, I created brand identities for dance events that we used to create, promote and produce. At Procter & Gamble, I was part of a team that rebranded Max Factor and created the first ever integrated marketing and brand role. And subsequently, at Whyte & Mackay – and of course at Leon – I have been heavily involved in the practice of graphic design. And yet I have very little technical design capability. I can see things in my mind, I can make an attempt at sketching out on paper what I've got in my head, but I am always reliant on fantastic graphic designers to actually produce the images (and I'd like to say a big thank you to those graphic designers I've had the pleasure of working with over the years).

It is the intellectual process of graphic design that fascinates me – the tension between creativity and the tightness of constraints driven by a brief. Norman Berry, the creative lead at advertising agency Ogilvy, once said, 'Give me the freedom of a tightly written brief.' I've always tried to understand how tight or loose the constraints need to be around a creative in order to produce magic. And I have come to realize that a graphic design brief is a very good example of the power of Freedom and Responsibility.

The cliché of the advertising creatives left alone to produce 'creativity' in a room with darts, a trampoline and table football shows you how much freedom is valued in the creative process. But there also needs to be some level of constraint to define the boundary within which the creative must work.

At Leon, we have tested the boundaries of the creative process. There is no one Leon logo. At this point, we probably have 70 or so ways of expressing the brand through a logo. Wally Olins, a very experienced brand expert who is no longer with us, was a fantastic friend to me and to others he mentored and partnered with. He and I were very clear when Leon was created that we didn't want to have a bullying relationship with the high street where – irrespective of the locality, feel, neighbourhood and local architecture – we would force the same design on every community. And the same goes for graphic design, bags, logos and so on. When you go into a Leon, you will hopefully see that there is a very single-minded personality and idea, but a very flexible way of achieving it. We wanted to create something that was instantly recognizable as Leon while remaining incredibly flexible.

However, given too much freedom, designers will often veer off course. The Leon design is intended to evoke freshness, flavour, Mediterranean goodness and joy, using fruit packaging as inspiration. We're not saying that we made this food – Mother Nature made this food – but we *are* saying that we bring the best ingredients to you at the right time of year, when they are at the top of their game. And the use of fruit-packaging-type imagery has inspired our creative direction. It gives our brand a visual unity in much the same way that our 'fast food in heaven' idea unifies our philosophy.

But because this design is quite timeless, designers that are new to working with the brand make the mistake of thinking that it is retro, which it is not. They use too much old-school, Americana advertising imagery. Or they make it look old-fashioned, in a scrolls and arts-and-craft-shop sort of way. Or they make it look too homespun. It's very important the brand is both timeless and is of the standard that only a professional could produce.

In widening the scope of a brief, we provide designers with a greater opportunity for creativity and innovation. But with that comes a greater level of self-responsibility for them too. They need to more precisely engage their own thoughts to understand when a design stops being Leon. The scope is not boundary-less. It is, in fact, the riverbank. And the designer is the river.

And it is not just at the briefing stage that one requires boundaries for creative freedom to flourish. The editing process, where I give creatives feedback and say 'no, thank you' to certain ideas, provides a riverbank too. Whether creatives agree or disagree in the moment, we are doing them a great service by having an opinion.

I once represented a recording artist (I have done a few things here and there, with my Enthusiast Seven-wing inspiring me to dabble) and I met the A&R man for the British singer Robbie Williams, formerly of Take That. He told me: 'Every artist needs an editor. If I released every song that Robbie brought me saying, "This is the next 'Angels'" [his biggest hit], you would think he is the worst songwriter ever.'

We Do It by Breaking Every Rule that the Company Has About How We Are Supposed to Manage Rotas

My friend Brad was intrigued. He and his colleague Bob Mock were looking at the people turnover data of their 500 Olive Garden restaurants. And one stood out. It had by far the highest 'retention' of people. So Brad and Bob flew to this restaurant to find out what was going on. The manager welcomed them, and after shaking the hands of everyone in the restaurant they took the manager for a coffee.

'You have the lowest team turnover in the whole company,' said Brad. 'Bob and I were hoping you could tell us what the secret is.'

'That's easy,' said the manager. 'I ignore every employment rule the company has.'

Now even more curious, they asked him to continue.

'The company says that people must work certain hours, that the manager must do the rota, that people can't swap shifts without the manager's permission, and that they can't go on extended leaves of absence. Well, that doesn't work for the actual people who want to work here. So I scrapped all of that, and people love working here. They like the freedoms they have and the ability to be flexible. I trust them. And if you trust someone, they will be trustworthy.'

Let's give people more freedom. And freedom to bestow freedoms. Let's trust them, and they will repay us with trustworthiness and responsibility.

Go Your Own Way

Although I'm hesitant to overplay this analogy, because of the bust-ups and countless personal relationships that make the band so fascinating, it's clear that we can all learn, at least in parts, to be a little bit more like Fleetwood Mac.

Fleetwood Mac is, of course, a single band. But it is also a band with fluidity, where people have come and gone at different times, contributed creatively, and shagged another band member and then taken a little time off.

The famous British comedy show *Fawlty Towers* had one writing team (John Cleese and Connie Booth) and 12 episodes. *The Simpsons* has been going for 30 years and has had over a hundred writers – coming and going, coming and going, coming and going again.

Yet Fleetwood Mac has always had both a clear direction and fluidity and flow within that direction. People are able to contribute when they want to, and in ways that they want to. The 'idea' of the band and the ongoing 'energy' that the band brings provides the 25 per cent – the boundaries that need to be set – and the creatives work in ever-changing ways to be true to it.

I have tried to replicate this – and I flatter myself that we've done it at times successfully – with Leon. Yes, Allegra and Henry and I worked together in the creation of Leon, but the menus and our plans had the input and hard work of Ben Peverelli, Nick Hales (who Allegra replaced when he decided to go and open a restaurant in Hastings in the south of England) and also Henry's mum. And so, even before launch, we had a whole bunch of creative input from lots of different people that knitted together to create something incredibly strong.

In the last 15 years many others have contributed, united by a shared vision and able to work freely within this vision. Among them are Jane Baxter, Skye Gyngell, Nellie Nichols, Kay Plunkett-Hogge, Scott Uehlein, Chantal Symons, Gizzi Erskine and Rebecca Seal.

All of them have operated with the same brief in mind, with the same riverbanks, but they have been able to flow freely within those banks.

Tiger Would

Tiger Woods, once the best golfer in the world, has just made an incredible comeback to win the Masters. Those Leon people who attend the quarterly Eat Well, Live Well sessions with motivational speaker Steve Head will have seen his genius mime of Tiger Woods missing a putt. (If you'd like to come along for the whole session, contact me – details are on the Leon and Winning Not Fighting websites.)

When Tiger (played by the wiry, white Geordie Steve Head) misses that putt, he blames everybody and everything. There was a clump of grass in the way. He looks accusingly at the crowd, as if someone has coughed at a key moment. He looks at his putter as if it is faulty. He looks at the sky as if the Lord himself has made him miss. Then, as he walks towards the ball for his next shot, his demeanour shifts – as if he has crossed a line, past which he walks taller again, with composure and a confident smile because he recognizes and concedes that it was in fact *him* who missed the putt.

It ain't a real line. No more than the equator is a real line. Or the border of Kenya and Tanzania. No FIFA referee will get a can of white spray out for you and mark a line in the grass the way they do for free kicks. But it is a line that is worth creating in your own mind – and crossing – when you are faced with missing a putt, or whatever the equivalent is in your life. Yes, by all means, spend some time getting frustrated and allowing your ego to blame everyone else. But don't do that for longer than necessary. Get over yourself. Put yourself aside. And cross the line.

And if you are hiring people, or looking to promote people or let them go, look out for those who blame others. If, in an interview, someone criticizes their current employers, you will find out before too long that they will do the same to you. So think carefully before hiring such a person.

In the first session the Leaders of Leon ever had with Steve on this topic, he asked us to draw a vertical line down the middle of an A4 piece of paper. On the left-hand side he asked us to write down what life involves on the 'it's everyone else's fault' side of the line. And on the right, what represents life on the 'I am responsible' side of the line. It is an exercise I do with new Leon people when we train on Winning Not Fighting. I find this simple exercise one of the most powerful.

On the left, people often write:

- Frustration
- Anger
- Aggression
- Shame
- Defeatism
- Blame
- Denial
- Moaning
- Rolling your eyes

And on the other:

- Accountability
- Acceptance
- Esteem
- Responsibility
- Fixing problems

I ask them how they would describe the person on the left. They quickly get to the word 'victim'. I then ask them the same for the person on the right side of the line. More often than not people will agree on 'winner'.

'So could we say that the left-hand side of the line is fighting and the right-hand side is winning?' I ask.

'Yes!' they say. And I feel like the defence lawyer delivering the final line in a John Grisham trial scene, or like Barack Obama as he dropped the mic.

But that's my ego talking.

Live as if Everything that Happens to You is Down to You

It is quite liberating to live on the right side of the line. Not blaming anyone else. Not meeting in small groups to complain about 'what the company has done now'. Being reassured that it is all down to you. If you are late for a meeting because of a traffic jam, know that if you really wanted to make sure you were there on time you could have left yesterday and stayed overnight. You didn't, that's okay. But you had the option.

This attitude leads to action. If you know that your actions decide your destiny, then you may as well start taking some actions, and working out which ones work.

Isn't it attractive being around or working with someone who lives like this?

Digital vs Humans

You are about to live through a pivotal time for human beings. You will have to decide what role you play in it. We will all have a responsibility to do so. Even by doing nothing, you will be playing a role.

The first question is: what are you going to do about the environment? The planet needs you to act, or conversely it will show all of us that it doesn't need us. The second question is: how will you respond to the 'opportunity' of digital data and 'intelligence'?

A friend was with someone from Silicon Valley who is pioneering new artificial intelligence in robots, and asked them if they had seen *The Terminator*. 'What's that?' said the Californian entrepreneur. 'Go buy the box set,' said my friend.

I attend conferences where experts, 'futurists', tech companies, and pharmaceutical, medical device and insurance companies come together to plan your future. They want the future to mean that you are monitored every day, all day. They envision implants to track your movements and all of your vital statistics. They'll be able to make a lot of money from this data.

They'll sell you drugs for prevention and 'cure'. And they'll know if you've taken your drugs or not. Insurance companies will be able to raise premiums for people at risk. And reduce them for people who drive less often. And lots, lots more.

And the government will come to the party too.

One day, a new mum will be invited to take part in a trial. It will be called something like 'The Gabriel Project'. It will be to 'improve the life chances' of her baby. Perhaps this new mum will be you or your own daughter. For the trial, and perhaps for all time following the successful trial (because the stats will show its success, I can assure you), all mums will be offered free nappies. And lower health insurance. And promises of lower car insurance when the child is old enough to drive. And the promise of freedom from abduction. And lower taxes, because we will 'need fewer police', because, over time, we will know where everyone is. And to achieve all this, all that is needed is a small device placed in the baby's neck. Or brain. Or thigh. Or wherever the focus groups say seems the least intrusive place. We all need to be ready to say *no, thank you*. And when they make it law, as many things are already today, we will need to be ready to overthrow the government.

We must not take our freedoms for granted. And we must remember that the promise of freedom *from* something (say from disease or from crime) comes with the erosion of freedom *to*. The more our actions are dictated by laws and by monitoring, the more we will see an equally dramatic reduction in responsibility.

You are responsible for stopping this happening.

9.

Expect to Be Punched
By John and Julian

Julian

Everyone gets 'punched' by life at some point. The question is, what happens next? In Wing Tsun, Expect to Be Punched gives you the ability to thrive despite the perceived adversity against you. It is the 'grit' that allows you to continue when everyone else has given up. Importantly, it also guides you back to reality. It is an additional 'check-in' to achieve an egoless state.

Expect to Be Punched is, perhaps, the single most important factor in achieving long-term success and happiness. In the West, this is often termed *resilience*, but Wing Tsun takes a deeper view and goes further.

The resilience of a material is its ability to return to its original shape after being compressed or stretched. In Wing Tsun this is not enough; we want the ability to expand, grow and develop. Resilience can also have a negative connotation, implying that the world is tough, against you, and that you have to learn how to battle through it as best you can. Wing Tsun feels no such thing. Life is neither tough nor easy. It is all about your perspective and what you do with it.

The purpose of Expect to Be Punched is to take the shock out of unexpected situations and give you the skills to win. In Wing Tsun you are taught this through practical training, where you become accustomed to what, otherwise, would be stressful situations, along with mental training exercises and a change of perspective. When you practise this in Wing Tsun you become accustomed to making 'behavioural stretches' and dealing with discomfort. Not for it to become your way of life, but to continually build your physical, mental and spiritual fortitude.

Expect to Be Punched also teaches us a valuable lesson: it is through difficulty that we experience the most growth. You go with the punch and learn from it. Without challenges, it is very difficult to reach the next stage of our spiritual and personal development. The same applies to our general well-being; our health depends on us being able to have contact with viruses and bacteria to be able to build a healthy and adaptable immune system. It's simply a question of balance and resourcefulness.

Expect to Be Punched is created through your ability to build self-reliance and self-trust. Whatever happens, you trust yourself to make the correct decision in that moment. You make yourself the known quantity in the unknown situation you face. It is both the systematic cumulation of the wisdoms you have read earlier and a distinct teaching in itself: that of 'positive pressure' and 'positive determination'. In Expect to Be Punched the six previous wisdoms are integrated as follows:

1. *Know Yourself*: Understand your triggers and how you react under stress.
2. *Staying Relaxed*: Stay calm under pressure, be responsive not reactive, and see the situation clearly.
3. *Don't Force*: Feel what is happening and adapt to whatever situation you face.

4. *Positivity*: See the gift and make the most out of every situation, no matter how bad it first looks.
5. *Simplicity*: Find the simplest solution and the easiest route out of the current chaos.
6. *Freedom and Responsibility*: Let go of your mental tension and previous attachments. Choose your way.

Expect to Be Punched is a 'grounding' principle in Wing Tsun. You spend all your time in Wing Tsun focusing only on how to win. Each wisdom builds another layer of skill and each Door transports you to a new level. By the time you reach the Third Door you are extremely fast. You're unbelievably power-ful. And you possess skills that most of the world could only dream about. This is not to mention your worldly wisdom and understanding that few others achieve. Furthermore, you know instinctively how to minimize every risk, and maximize every chance of success.

Apply these skills and you are guaranteed to win. There is only one caveat. You're human. And, therefore, fallible. You are a human 'being' not just a human 'doing'. And you need to remember that. Even the Roman emperors recognized this, having slaves whisper in their ear when on a victory parade, *'Hominem te memento'* ('Remember you are a man').

No one wins all the time, and no one wins without getting hit. So, the questions are: what happens when you don't win? What do you do? And how do you respond? And how do you turn a loss into a win?

Expect to Be Punched addresses these questions, and it starts by showing you how to understand the nature of life. Namely, the relativity of every experience. You cannot have pleasure without pain, or winning without losing. Every judgement is only possible in relation to the opposite feeling. So you only know what is good when you have experienced bad. Expect to Be Punched teaches you how to embrace this dualistic game.

This principle is known as Hsiang Sheng – the doctrine of 'mutual arising' in Taoism. It is summed up in the classic text *Tao Te Ching*:

> When everyone knows beauty as beautiful,
> there is already ugliness;
> When everyone knows good as goodness,
> there is already evil.
> 'To be' and 'not to be' arise mutually;
> Difficult and easy are mutually realized;
> Long and short are mutually contrasted;
> High and low are mutually posited;
> Before and after are in mutual sequence.

Understanding failure, and how you deal with it, is therefore crucial. And it starts with our own use of language. *Failure* is such a loaded, emotional term that we don't use it in Wing Tsun. As the wisdom of Positivity teaches, we concentrate instead on what we want to achieve and how we want to perceive ourselves. Failure is also an inaccurate label and an unhelpful societal stigma. Failure is not a reality. You're not defined by a single moment nor a single event. And similarly, winning is a continual process. Even by normal societal definitions, you have to fail to win. It is the nature of learning and experience. No one can win at everything all the time. No one can be 'on' all the time, nor can they be at peak fitness at every waking moment. Expect to Be Punched helps take the emotions out of tense situations and gives you the opportunity to reassess the feeling as to why you feel the need to always win. Where is that pressure really coming from? Who is it for? Is it positive for you? Do you really need it?

Being punched creates energy. The question is, where do you focus that energy? Negatively, in shame and self-pity? Or positively, to new growth, new goals, renewed focus?

Lessons of the Seventh Wisdom: Expect to Be Punched

1. Expect to Be Punched is the ability to thrive despite perceived adversaries.
2. Understand the nature of life – you cannot have winning without losing.
3. See the gift of the challenge – it is through difficulty that we experience the most growth.
4. Look at where your pressure comes from. Don't define yourself by perceived failure.

John

Stuff Happens

When we were preparing to open our first restaurant in the United States, we were keen to learn from all sorts of people. We spoke to the leaders of other companies who had launched there, and we spoke to people running American organizations.

The type of restaurants that have emerged in the US in the last 20 years and seen huge growth are called 'fast casual'. Think of a line of people choosing their burritos or bowls canteen-style: you're now thinking of a company called Chipotle Mexican Grill, founded by Steve Ells. It is *the* pioneer in this space, and one of the most successful.

Chipotle enjoyed unfettered growth for 20 years. Funded at one stage by McDonald's, and subsequently listed on the New York Stock Exchange, it was worth $7 billion at its height, and had over 500 restaurant sites. Then E. coli hit. More than once. And the company found that, all of a sudden, the halo had slipped.

Some felt that the business didn't respond quickly enough or in the right way, but whatever the reason, Chipotle found its sales per restaurant decline by a quarter – a huge figure, and a big drain on company profitability for a business with so many fixed labour and property costs.

Even so, at Leon we admire Steve Ells's achievement with Chipotle, and one cold February afternoon in New York, Leon's strategy director Cengiz and I went to meet him. We found him to be charming, human and willing to share the many layers of Chipotle history and the lessons that came from it.

The remark he made that struck me most, and that has stuck with me, was in reference to the E. coli events, and the idea that his organization had lacked the resilience to deal with it. 'Nothing had ever really gone wrong at Chipotle before. When it did, our people didn't know how to cope. The culture had been built on everything going well, and our people were unable to adapt to a world where we were on the back foot.'

Bowled Over

Alan Watts, in a recording of a seminar he gave in the late 1960s, talked about what he called a 'ceramic' view of the world.

He was talking mostly about the creationist Judaeo-Christian view that stems from the idea of God creating the world in seven days. Like you or I would make a ceramic bowl. (Though it would probably take me longer than seven days to make a bowl.) Preplanned, and as close to perfect as possible.

When we try to mirror this in our own lives and in our companies, we are doing ourselves and our teams a disservice. Nothing is that permanent, nor of itself perfect. The more perfect we try to make things, and the more we try to make them unchanging, the more brittle they become. Drop a ceramic bowl on the floor – or a Ming vase – and it *will* shatter.

The more rigid we make our lives and our thinking, the more likely they are to break when the wind blows. Flexibility – both physical and mental – can be lost with age. People and businesses that are too rigid will break where others bend naturally to the conditions. The *Tao Te Ching* remarks on the ability of bamboo or palm trees to flex in the wind without breaking. Be more bamboo. Be prepared to bend.

If one adopts the ceramic view of the world, a small setback can seem like a chip in a Ming vase, as a disaster from which you will never recover. As it was in Chipotle.

A perfectionist attitude can be profoundly damaging, both for a company and its people. When people lost their jobs in Japan after the Asian financial crisis hit, a huge number of Japanese businesspeople, mostly men, felt unable to tell their families. They would dress for 'work' every morning, and walk out of the house with their briefcase, then sit by the river until 'home time'. All to hide their shame.

But the shame, the worry, must be overcome.

Organizations and people must choose resilience and flexibility over perfectionism and rigidity.

Good in a Crisis

I wrote about the tale of Choi in the earlier chapter on Positivity. You will recall how, in the parable, the neighbour comments 'Oh dear, that's so unlucky' every time something seemingly bad happens, and 'Ooh, that's so lucky' when the reverse seemed to occur.

From what I have seen first-hand, organizations that experience and overcome big challenges in their formative years are more resilient and even grow faster and stronger than those that do not. It is like a broken bone growing stronger than it was before. Or perhaps like pruning a rose bush.

When I joined the management consultancy Bain in 1997, its London office had recently experienced near-bankruptcy as a result of financial and reputational challenges. A younger generation of partners had taken over the company and they were determined not to be beaten. The zeal, camaraderie and focus that rose from the organization's near-death experience is the reason, I believe, that Bain London has seen 20 years of successful growth. There was a determination never to experience such an existential crisis again.

One of our Leon investors and board member, Spencer Skinner (whose resilience and good humour have been invaluable to Leon), was once told by a sailing instructor, 'You're good in a crisis, but I wish you wouldn't get into quite as many.' I sometimes think about Leon like this. From the very start, we experienced all sorts of challenges. Our opening was delayed by three weeks because we couldn't fix our ventilation/extraction system. We had two rather rotund builders trying to fix the problem, and one of them literally got stuck in the ducting. (Don't worry, we got him out.)

We had to extend the training of the team so many times that, when the CCTV cameras were installed, the rumour went round that there was no real restaurant opening and that instead they were all being filmed for a reality TV show.

Since then, we have run out of money, been caught up in a massive street fire on Kingsway in the first week of that restaurant's opening, and endured a significant four-year consumer downturn that began in 2008 with the banking crisis. Restaurants have flooded, we have run out of all stocks of fries due to a poor potato harvest, and ceilings have fallen down onto team members. We have also helped rehouse managers after nearly fatal apartment fires, sat with the mothers of Leon people who have died of illnesses while being employed by Leon, and Leon and our people have been directly affected by terror attacks.

The Borough Attack

I was at home one Saturday evening in June 2017 when my daughter Eleanor came down to the kitchen holding her phone. 'Have you seen there's been a terror attack in Borough Market?' I grabbed my own phone to check Leon's emergency WhatsApp group, knowing that we had two restaurants in the area, including one newly opened site, and our head office was right in the market.

Messages began appearing immediately as we all tried to piece together what was happening and to coordinate our response.

Over the next few hours and days we were able to understand what had happened. And I am in awe of the way that teams across Leon managed themselves that night and in the week after.

At the time of the attack, one of our Borough Market restaurants still had guests and team members inside. While it isn't right to share all the details, I can say with confidence that the quick-thinking actions of one young female team member prevented the first knife-wielding attacker from entering. (We were on the first corner of the market the attackers came to.)

As soon as the Leon manager running the restaurant that night had gathered all the team and guests downstairs, on the advice of the police, he turned his attention to giving first aid to a man who had been attacked on our doorstep as he had been passing by. To this day we do not know whether this man lived.

Our London Bridge restaurant in the station nearby – exercising its own discretion – reopened to serve coffees and food to the emergency services and to people fleeing the market. There is a photo from CCTV showing a throng of people cloaked in silver thermal sheets (the sort marathon runners are given after a race to preserve body heat) and also members of the emergency services, being given coffee for free.

The next day, and for the following week, Vida, who was at the time helping with Leon well-being and who is trained to support people who have experienced trauma, began a programme of hosting the teams at our Kwoon on London's Eastcastle Street, to help them understand and process what they had experienced.

Owing to the police investigation, we couldn't access our restaurant and offices in Borough Market for a week. So, on the Monday after the attack, each 'head office' person went to their own 'buddy' restaurant to lend practical (the restaurants may disagree!) and moral support.

One young man in the Borough Market restaurant team had also been on Westminster Bridge three months earlier and had narrowly – by a foot – avoided being hit by the car that had mown pedestrians down. Next to him a policeman had been hit, and he stayed with the policeman, giving him first aid. As you can imagine, this young man needed special attention from us and I hope we gave him the support he needed.

To this day we still give emotional support to those team members affected. And the stories of that night, and of the following week, remind us that nothing in life is ever predictable.

Ultimately, all this comes down to culture. When Hurricane Katrina struck New Orleans, Walmart's culture allowed local managers to use discretion and freedom to self-assemble to do what they thought was right, distributing supplies for free to the people and locations they thought needed them most – in contrast to the response of most federal organizations, which were slow to respond and which relied on a top-down hierarchical chain of command that broke down.

Which Would You Choose?

Marion, my mum, is the wife of Leon, my dad. As you would expect. I am her only surviving child (if 'child' is the right word – some of you may say it is). And yet she was pregnant six times.

She tells me how she was sitting in her hospital bed, having lost her baby from her sixth pregnancy, when she realized she had a choice. 'I could have chosen self-pity and anger, or I could have chosen positivity. I chose the latter. And I decided then that I would be a primary school teacher. So, as soon as I was discharged, that's what I did.'

Mum, in her eighties, still teaches two days a week as an official member of staff. Anyone who has been taught by her will know that this decision has benefited thousands of people. And I have never met a more positive person in my life. Thank you for teaching your family and all your pupils so much. The maths and the English and the science and the French are all good. But love (and resilience) – that is the real gift.

Something Will Go Wrong, We Just Don't Know What Yet

When I train management teams at Leon, I ask them to read the chapter in Jim Collins's book *Great by Choice* about productive paranoia. Collins has identified the five or so things that make successful businesses stand out from the rest. And one of them is knowing that something will go wrong, even if you cannot predict what that will be.

Here, again, I find Southwest Airlines an inspiration. They do not rigidly overplan. In fact, their long-standing CEO, the late Herb Kelleher, once said, 'We have a strategic plan, it's called doing things.' Instead, they have a large number of scenario-planning sessions to ensure that the organization knows what to do if certain things go wrong. In 2018, Southwest suffered their first on-board fatality, and the news reports that followed praised the airline for their effective response.

Just as important as scenario-planning is the determination of the leaders of Southwest to maintain a strong and safe balance sheet. That means you are not going to run out of cash during a major jolt to the sector, as happened after 9/11 in the US, or in the event of the company itself suffering a crisis, like the one experienced by Chipotle.

I credit Jim Collins with an important decision that I had to make at the start of 2017: should Leon raise more debt or more equity to grow? We were offered two alternative packages by two groups of people I liked very much: debt from a US-based company which specializes in funding restaurant company expansions; and equity from a Brazilian-based investment firm.

Equity came at a cost – my shares, and those of my fellow shareholders, would be diluted, and therefore my share of the company would decrease. This would not have been the case with the debt, but that would come with a requirement to pay back cash to the lender each year, and that would make us vulnerable to losing all of the equity if we defaulted or if we broke the lending 'covenants' (profit-to-debt obligations) that inevitably come with it.

The board was split on which to go for, and it was my job to make the final recommendation. I'd just written the first draft of this chapter, and had also just read Jim Collins on productive paranoia, so I made the decision to go for the equity route. I was also swayed by the personal loyalty I felt to investor Fersen Lambranho, who had led the deal on behalf of the Brazilian team.

We agreed terms in May 2017. In the six months that followed, the UK restaurant industry saw a perfect storm of financial and market challenges. Half of the profit was wiped out by increases to the UK's legislated Living Wage, by rises in local property tax and by a leap in ingredient costs following a weakening of the pound.

And at the same time, sales across the industry decreased by 10 per cent from June through to September, and only marginally recovered to the end of the year. In a business that has such a high proportion of fixed costs, this had a big implication for our bottom line. If we had chosen the debt route, we could have lost the company.

I wear a number of T-shirts around the office. Not all the time, but when I want to get a message across without having to say it out loud. One says simply: *Something will go wrong. We just don't know what it is yet.* This was a classic case in point. And we prevailed.

Now I Feel at Home

Fersen is one of the reasons I continue to have so much energy for running Leon. Almost as soon as he had invested with us, both the revenue and costs went in the wrong direction. And at the first board meeting, just a few months after he had put his money in, we had to share our financial performance. It was a lot worse than we had predicted at the time of his investment.

This was a critical and pivotal moment – a test for us as management and for him as an investor. We presented the numbers and waited for his response. There was a pause. And then he said in his strong Brazilian accent, 'Now I feel at home. In Brazil, things are always shit.'

A message for all investors: this is how to get your 'management teams' running to work for you.

Emotionally Ready

So, the practical elements of Expect to Be Punched are scenario-planning and having the financial and other resources in place to survive. There is an emotional element to it too: preparing yourself to cope with the potential fear or worry when it happens.

In Wing Tsun, we are taught not to attach ourselves emotionally to the punch. Not to be surprised. I have learned that it is the same in business – not just from Leon, but also from other projects we have been involved in tangentially.

Our work on the School Food Plan, as I touched on earlier, led to attacks coming at us from a number of directions. An episode of Channel 4's *Dispatches* said we were producing a dish for children at Leon that was high in salt (they had bought lots of dishes from one of our restaurants and sent them all off for lab testing).

338

We offered to appear on the show and we were denied the opportunity. Instead, they read out a quote that made it look like we had refused to go on the programme. It taught us a lot about how not to get emotionally affected. As did diary items in a newspaper and that press release I mentioned earlier. All these things did not kill us, they did not kill Leon and they did not kill the School Food Plan.

The history of the largest restaurant operator in the world is a lesson in how to overcome punches. The founders of Subway (Fred DeLuca and Peter Buck) opened the first store and it failed.

'Move on,' friends and family told them.

'Nope,' they said. 'We're going to try again.'

And was the second store a roaring success? No, that failed too.

Most people would accept defeat. Instead they opened a third, which worked, and then went on to open more than 20,000 of them.

In Deep Water

Occasionally I see a movie that has so many lessons for us at Leon that I gather all the Leaders of Leon to watch it. On one such occasion, we gathered to watch *Deepwater Horizon*, the movie about the BP oil rig disaster. It was a powerful experience, and for ten minutes after the film there wasn't much conversation as everyone took it all in.

Leon people deal with life-and-death situations every day. Food safety, accident and injury risks. We have had major fires, floods and terror attacks. So while Leaders of Leon may try to take themselves less seriously, they take their jobs very seriously.

Deepwater Horizon shows how corporate greed on the part of the oil company and the maintenance company, wishful thinking, ego and poor communication led to the deaths of 11 people in a huge rig fire, and the worst oil spill in history. There are many things to take away from this movie, and we discussed it in the week afterwards in teams. My main messages to the Leaders of Leon: we never put profit ahead of safety; if you think I am doing the wrong thing in any way, speak up without hesitation or delay; tell your teams the same thing and respond in encouraging ways when they do; assume that people have misunderstood what you have told them and that communication has gone completely wrong – and act continuously to put that right; accidents will happen and your job in the moment is to not be surprised and to stay relaxed, and in the longer term to make sure that the organization learns all the lessons we can from what went wrong.

Learning to Fly

My wife Katie helped chair one of the most fascinating conferences I have ever had the pleasure of attending – Risky Business (as previously mentioned). The theme: Expect to Be Punched. Not that they put it this way.

It was initially created for the medical community to learn from events and people outside the world of hospitals, and has since broadened to help other high-risk industries. They had laid their hands on some truly outstanding speakers. They included: 'Sully' (aka Chesley Burnett Sullenberger III), the pilot who landed in the Hudson River after both engines were disabled by a bird strike, saving all on board; Albie Sachs, one of the leaders of the truth and reconciliation committee that helped heal South Africa after apartheid ended; survivors of the plane crash in the Andes where rugby players had to eat their dead friends to stay alive; and many, many more. They discussed how to prevent accidents, how to manage them as they are happening, how to learn from them, and how to deal with pain, grief and forgiveness after a tragedy.

Inspired by this, we held a 'Learning to Fly' conference, again with the Leaders of Leon and our key suppliers too. Our principal speaker was Guy Hudson, the pilot who helped lead the Risky Business conference. He reminded us that things WILL go wrong, that we WILL be punched, and that our job is not to let things spiral out of control in the moment, and to create a culture where we systematically learn and adjust. He was very strong on the danger of ego.

Two case studies stuck in my mind. The first was the story I shared on page 143 of the pilot and engineer who ganged up on a co-pilot who tried to raise a concern about the pilot landing too fast. The second was the story of Elaine Bromiley, who died during a routine nasal operation due to an unexpected closing of her airways. Her death could have been relatively 'easily' (I use this word with due care because hindsight is wonderful) avoided. Her husband, Martin, a pilot himself, was perplexed by the response of the hospital that from a procedural perspective it was 'one of those things'. This is not to say that they were not themselves devastated, it was just that they did not seem to have the culture of the airline industry when it came to analysing an accident and learning from it. So Bromiley set about, in a very constructive way (especially given his own grief), to work with the hospital and surgical team to understand what had gone wrong. It turned out that the team had missed a number of opportunities to recover the situation, and the film which describes these events is now used by the surgeon Atul Gawande as part of his efforts to improve procedures and checklists in hospitals.

One of the changes we have made at Leon as a result of the film and Gawande's work is for everyone to introduce themselves properly at the start of a shift. One of the reasons the surgical team failed to save Elaine Bromiley was because there were no established relationships. When one of the (female, non-British) nurses offered a solution that would have saved their patient's life, the (male, British) surgeons, it is said, looked straight through her. Both of them needed to act differently – the surgeons needed to be more receptive, and the nurse needed to be more assertive.

This was an opportunity for me to remind people at Leon, or rather to train their subconscious and their nervous system, about the need to maintain communication in a crisis. You will at some stage be punched. Don't crumble when you are.

The Opportunity to Learn

What is true for businesses and organizations is also true of people. At Leon, there are individuals who stand out to me not only for their deep strength of character but for the things they have overcome.

Shereen, who you've met before, has an emotional wisdom which seems to go far beyond her years. Shereen had a tough childhood but she had a determination to learn and, in her mum's words, 'to change her stars'.

When she was seven, she announced that she wanted to be a mermaid. When her mum explained that this was unlikely to happen, she said, 'Okay, in that case I'm going to be the Queen.'

Again, her mum gently managed her expectations.

'You're not making this easy for me, Mum,' Shereen replied. 'In that case, I'm going to be Judith Chalmers!' (who you may or may not know as the TV presenter who used to front a holiday programme called *Wish You Were Here*).

Shereen has not achieved her goal of being Judith Chalmers. She went one better: she has achieved the goal of being herself. She has changed her stars, and now, daily, changes the stars for Leon and all the people who work here. And she is loved for it.

She has learned to treat 'failures' and 'disasters' as opportunities to learn. 'I would swap my childhood for my mum,' she says. 'But I wouldn't swap it for me – it has made me who I am.' In this, she lives her life as Choi did.

Role Models – Be Careful

It is important for young people – in fact, for people of all ages – to understand that those they think are successful, who are often sold to them as role models, have actually endured many failures, and are often riddled with the same frustrations and insecurities as the rest of us. Their images and stories are literally and metaphorically airbrushed.

We explain to our team members that failure is a perspective not a fact. We remember Babe Ruth's truth that 'Every strike brings me closer to the next home run'. Many people, when punched, give up. Apart from maybe Arsène Wenger's Invincibles of 2004, no champions go without defeat.

When we're punched for real in a physical exchange, we are, for a moment, tempted to be shocked, or to attach some emotion to the punch. But then we must remember that everything that happens can be turned to our advantage.

My wife Katie has been a media and arts editor, a news anchor and is now a presenter for BBC Radio 3 and for The Proms, London's classical music season. But her career has not always gone steadily upwards.

A few years before she landed the role as presenter of The Proms, Katie read in the newspaper that she had not got one of the top news anchor jobs she'd applied for. Her agent told her, 'You have 24 hours to be miserable and upset. Then you need to get back out there and be positive again.' In combat, you may have milliseconds rather than 24 hours. If grieving for a loved one, you will need more than 24 hours. But in each of these situations, you are doing what Steve Head, our Leon coach, teaches us – crossing the line. And putting it behind us.

The Lessons of Lincoln

Julian's Wing Tsun journey has been, he says, built on perseverance over talent. In his first class there were others with more
natural ability, but he overtook them one by one because of his
commitment and decision to persevere.

If you were to go into the reception of Leon at our Borough
Market office, you would see on the wall the career and life of
Abraham Lincoln. Lincoln is seen as one of the most successful
people in history, and often it is only his glory years that get
taught in schools, reaffirming the myth that great men and
women are somehow born and blessed with a life of success and
little failure. But his life looked like this:

    1832 – Lost his job, and was defeated in run for Illinois state
           legislature
    1833 – Failed in business
    1834 – Elected to Illinois state legislature (success)
    1835 – Sweetheart died
    1836 – Had (alleged) nervous breakdown
    1838 – Defeated in run for Illinois House Speaker
    1843 – Defeated in run for nomination for US Congress
    1846 – Elected to Congress (success)
    1848 – Lost renomination
    1849 – Rejected for land officer position
    1854 – Defeated in run for US Senate
    1856 – Defeated in run for nomination for vice president
    1858 – Defeated in run for US Senate
    1860 – Elected president of the United States (success)

Suddenly, Lincoln seems like someone who could easily have
been unknown to us in the twenty-first century. There likely

will have been thousands of people like him (perhaps with more talent and greater credentials) who could have been president of the United States.

In his book *Great by Choice*, you'll remember, Jim Collins examines pairs of companies, one of which failed and one of which succeeded, even though they had similar starting points and almost identical conditions to work in. One of the handful of things that he identifies that makes a company great is the ability to respond and jump on lucky opportunities when they arise. Through analysis he showed that the successful companies had no more 'luck' and experienced no more 'lucky events' than the unsuccessful companies. They just did more *with* their luck. This led Collins himself to coin the phrase 'return on luck'.

It is my view that perseverance – or rather open-minded, open-hearted perseverance, in a way that lives up to the principles of Wing Tsun and Winning Not Fighting – is the ultimate meta-capability, and that all else follows on from this. Perhaps one could call it 'present-moment perseverance', because, of course, perseverance can only happen in the now. Perseverance is something that cannot be postponed.

If you choose persistence, if you see 'setbacks' as opportunities and do so consistently, you and your business will prevail.

Water Moves, Plants Grow

Those who have experienced plague or war are very aware of what it is like to be punched. And those of us who have parents or grandparents who grew up in World War Two will understand that this generation typically had a particular gratitude for the life they lived after the war.

Generations and societies who have not directly suffered such upheavals can quickly become used to a perfectionist view of the world. For example, so optimistic were the times in 1992 that the political economist Francis Fukuyama wrote:

> What we may be witnessing is not just the end of the Cold War, or the passing of a particular period of post-war history, but the end of history as such: that is, the end point of mankind's ideological evolution and the universalization of Western liberal democracy as the final form of human government.

Although even then his article elicited some scepticism and derision. I don't want to provide a spoiler, but it wasn't the end of history after all.

But the way in which America won the Gulf War, and arguably prevailed in the Cold War, imbued a sense of confidence and optimism in both the West and elsewhere (we've warned about that, haven't we) that extended into the economically successful years of the Clinton administration. And we weren't yet fully aware of the dangers of climate change or the forthcoming War on Terror.

The shock of 9/11 lay not just in the terrorists' horrific actions that day, but in the way it shattered that sense of confidence, and the feeling of vulnerability that came with it. And it was a shock that the right wing in America was able to use it to engender support for the subsequent wars in Afghanistan and Iraq. Perhaps the terrorists knew how brittle our collective confidence was.

I think we had created a ceramic view of the world and a perfectionist view of the end of history. Our egos had once again defaulted to a need for constancy in identity and constancy in events – whereas, in reality, the world and our lives were just as precarious and just as vulnerable to change and disruption as they had always been.

Wing Tsun recognizes change and inconstancy as inevitable and natural. In nature, water moves, plants grow and wither, animals are born and die. The same will happen to us. And we make ourselves sick by not recognizing that. Pleasure cannot be understood without pain, and victory cannot be understood without defeat. Failure is the other side of the coin from success, and 'down' cannot be understood without 'up'.

At the start of the twenty-first century, during the dot-com gold rush of 2000, and again in 2007, I heard the same phrase repeatedly: 'I think that we've solved boom and bust.' It was a suggestion that somehow (magically) economists and politicians had achieved the historic first of being able to tweak the dials available to them and create steady economic growth. Never again would we have to have the downturns, and associated upturns, in economic performance.

Of course, what followed these proclamations were the massive downturns of 2001 and 2008.

A warning: if and when you hear this phrase again, sell your shares and, if you're running a company, take out costs and shore up the balance sheet. It's even in the Bible: you'll have seven years of famine and seven years of feast. In Taoist terms, humans will never be able to dominate or control the natural order.

Laugh Along the Way

I love the saying 'If you're going to be able to look back on something and laugh about it, you might as well laugh about it now.' In addition to the need to Expect to Be Punched, we need to learn to laugh about the punches too.

No one who suffers at times from low self-esteem, anger, fear, grief and frustration should think that they are alone. I have experienced much frustration over Leon, and much anger too, and wavering levels of self-esteem. If you are ever asking yourself 'Why me?', the good news is that you are not special. Life is a series of present moments that come in all colours and shapes. Subconsciously, and sometimes consciously, we choose their meaning and how we want to feel about them. These sorts of books (especially this one) are written by humans who are imperfect and in no way better than you. No one's pretending that choosing to be positive, staying in the now and expecting to be punched aren't difficult things to do. But maintaining one's sense of humour makes it easier.

When we experience what we perceive as a punch, it helps to reimagine it as something else. Nine times out of ten, it's not as big a thing as it first seems. That one in ten – that's the important stuff. Someone dying? That's worth grieving over. A failed promotion or missing a train? Not so much.

The Fourth Door

Muk Yan Chong (Wooden Dummy) – Beyond Self
By Julian

The fourth and final Door of Wing Tsun represents living in a true Zen state. It is where you have transformed to being in a life of effortless action.

Through the teaching of Beyond Self you have a completely different awareness to how life works. Although it is not an outcome to be chased, you will have an inner clarity and perception that makes you an invaluable adviser, leader and mentor.

One of the oldest training apparatuses of the Shaolin Temple, it was also the final test before being fully initiated. Muk Yan Chong means 'pile used as a dummy'. It is a step change, as you practise on a piece of equipment, whereas in the previous three forms you practised alone. Most commonly known as the Wooden Dummy, it is designed to reflect the key movements and angles of a human.

To become a Shaolin monk, you had to successfully navigate your way through the legendary Hall of Wooden Men, skilfully defending against 108 mechanized dummies. After the destruction of the Shaolin Temple, this knowledge was taken by the founders of Wing Tsun and synthesized into one simple, but extremely potent, dummy.

The Fourth Door also draws all the various aspects of the art into one aligned whole. Representing Mastery in action, it combines the stability and relaxation of Siu Nim Tao (the First Door); the combinations and movement of Chum Kiu (the Second

Wooden dummy.

Door); and the power, precision and speed of Biu Jee (the Third Door). It's the near perfection of motion, angles, timings and dynamics. The whole of your body can be utilized as needed.

In Biu Jee, each motion is trained to its fastest and most powerful. You learned that physical tensions are caused by mental tension, and it is by putting these aside that you can reach your physical peak. The Fourth Door combines the previous separate movements into one simultaneous and coordinated movement. The Third Door taught you three different attacks against three different targets consecutively. Muk Yan Chong enables you to use three different limbs at the same time. This is a deceptively simple but remarkably challenging skill, taking you to the absolute physical limitations of what is humanly possible. While most martial arts can only concentrate on doing one technique at a time (either a block or a strike), from Muk Yan Chong's wisdom you can deflect an opponent's attack, counter-attack with the other hand, and provide a devastating kick – all in one motion, and all while remaining balanced, grounded, calm and clear.

Training on the wooden dummy.

Your skills are applied in such a fluid way that Wooden Dummy practitioners become known as 'ghost warriors'. It is where you embody the principle 'it doesn't matter how hard the person hits if you are not there'. For this reason, the Fourth Door is known as 'the door that has no door'. Every time a person attempts to 'open your door' to hit you, you effortlessly manoeuvre and counter-attack without giving them any clue as to how, or why, it happened. So startling is this for an opponent used to being resisted and fought, it is literally as if you dissolved before them. The door opened to reveal nothing. You were never there, yet always present.

It's not just sublime coordination and sensitivity that comes with learning Muk Yan Chong, but the mastery of a new force, the 'soft palm force', Yau Chau Lik. As you are now training on a solid wooden tree trunk, there is no way – despite what people may tell you – to punch it repeatedly without serious injury. Instead you learn how to send the force flowing from your palms, creating a highly potent shockwave. It is astonishing how little force you need to make it work. Repurposing the energy you learned in the Third Door, this is where the saying 'the palms are the weapons of the masters' originates. The least aggressive, yet the most effective, it is one of the easiest illustrations of the female origins of Wing Tsun.

Palm technique.

Forward palm. Sideways palm. Low palm. Reverse palm.

Muk Yan Chong, therefore, physically represents the ideal of Mastery, where you find the complete contentment of immersion in your practice, and your present-moment experience. Having been on this personal journey, it's also the time when the master returns to society to share his or her wisdom and compassion. This is Wing Tsun's version of becoming a Buddha – the 'awakened one'.

The Wooden Dummy provides you with a relationship and with feedback you haven't until this moment received before. It refines the 'mirror' principle that you learned in Chum Kiu (the Second Door) and applies it to all your senses. Just touching the wood provides you with a different insight. It's more than you, yet it instantly reflects you. We call this the 'talking tree'. At every moment you are shown how you feel, move and think. Any time you drift off, you are instantly reminded of it. Muk Yan Chong is a powerful tool to help you consciously live in the present. And it also brings in the element of sound meditation – the repeated motions on the dummy change the wavelength of your brain. It allows you to access the more primeval and tribal aspects of your being.

Spiritually, Muk Yan Chong is so simple that it can be hard to comprehend. It echoes the teachers of Zen, who state, 'I have nothing to teach.' This is because the Fourth Door is teaching you to just see life for what it is.

In the Third Door, you stripped away all the false layers of identity and fear that hid your true essence. Now, in Muk Yan Chong, you finally understand that your true essence is part of something much bigger than yourself. Everything is one, but that 'one' has infinite ways of expressing itself.

The Chinese best explain this realization with the analogy of the ocean. We are all the ocean, but our ego has told us that we are just a tiny drop of water, ignoring our part in the whole ocean. The Fourth Door widens your perception to see your part in the greater expression of the universe (Tao). When you truly realize this, it brings you to a state of complete harmony, where conflict doesn't even exist. A wave cannot fight against the ocean, it is just an illusion. This realization is known as Beyond Self.

To explain this further, you are an emanation of the universe – distinct, unique and different, but ultimately connected. You came out of it and you are part of it. Your definition of you is no longer limited to your physical body: you are you, but not the you that you originally thought. This concept is mind-blowing, as you are no longer confined by your mind. You experience life, rather than separating yourself from it by being trapped in your own thoughts.

That this wisdom was always within you is why the Fourth Door is known as 'the door that has no door'. You've gone through this structure to realize there are no 'Doors' or even 'reality' as we think of it. These were just clever constructs of the mind to help you consciously reconnect with your true essence.

Wood is used to allow you back in touch with your natural state and intuition. Muk Yan Chong provides a tangible way for you to experience Beyond Self.

The more you train with the Wooden Dummy, the more this becomes spiritually apparent to you. When you first start it feels like it's you against the dummy, but as time progresses this relationship changes. You go from feeling like you are hitting a piece of wood to feeling more and more connected to it. You get to the stage where you don't know where the Wooden Dummy ends and you begin. You move in a deeply unconscious way, without premeditation, for the next move. Step by step, hit by hit, kick by kick – your perspective and reality are shifted. Just like the Zen archer or the master swordsman, the feeling becomes that 'the force flows through you'. The old masters described this state of awareness with the saying 'In the beginning you do Wing Tsun, but eventually Wing Tsun does you.'

So how is Beyond Self helpful for you? Aside from showing you the true nature of life, it changes your behaviour, alters your perception. You act very different when you no longer feel removed from the world around you. Furthermore, it brings you a beautiful sense of harmony which transforms your whole experience of living.

However, the power of this Fourth Door comes with a warning: be careful before you open it. If you're truly enjoying the game of life, stay where you are and don't enter. The Third Door has taught you the ultimate in self-realization; it is where you are so much in your power that it is the achiever's dream. There is very little you cannot do or have when you attain this state.

The Fourth Door is not this. It's not about you being so successful that you are unstoppable. The first three Doors taught you to recognize the game of life and how to win in it. The last Door shows you that the game you have been trying to win doesn't exist. It's why Samurai warriors were forbidden from studying Buddhism in-depth too early, as it would make them question the whole system of martial law and their purpose. The Fourth Door shows you that the need to achieve in the Third Door is still a form of suffering. It shows you how to find your peace.

Muk Yan Chong is about the ultimate freedom. And that means

letting go of those final attachments. It doesn't mean that you can't have success by other people's definitions. It doesn't mean that you can't have material objects. It just means you are no longer attached to them. And it no longer means success for *you*.

This is why it is the Fourth Door. Typically, four is a number avoided in Chinese culture as it has associations with death. Here, this death is no longer negative. The death of the idea of self is replaced by wholeness. It takes the fighting adage 'act as if you are already dead and then you never fear dying' to a more profound degree. You cannot in fact die; you can only re-form. You are, and always have been, pure energy (and, as we all know, energy cannot be made, only transformed or transferred). It was the attempt of the ego to persuade you otherwise.

By shifting this final illusion you have now reached everlasting life – the Way of the Golden Elixir (known in Chinese as Jindan Zhi Dao).

Finally, in relation to our wellness, the Fourth Door is about directly experiencing the world around us. It's about tuning into the natural rhythms of life. We have the tendency to become artificially disconnected from this – especially in cities, with their man-made structures and artificial lighting. If you can just start taking short walks in nature, it allows you to increase this feeling of relaxation and reconnection.

In business, the Fourth Door helps you tune into your innate sensitivity and natural intelligence. It creates a genuine gravitas and a connectivity with everyone around you. Practically, it teaches you about reading situations, cues, energy and the people around you. It shows you how to make positive, far-reaching decisions, and focus on win–win scenarios.

Lessons of the Fourth Door

1. Understand that your true nature is part of something much wider.
2. To be wise and successful you need to let go of attachment to success.
3. Connect with nature to improve your vitality and mental health.
4. Beyond Self creates ultimate gravitas and connectivity.

10

Mastery
By John and Julian

Julian

The final wisdom of Wing Tsun, Mastery, consists of three elements: focusing on one thing, practising in the present moment, and letting go of the need for outcomes.

Mastery, on the face of it, appears to be something to be attained. And a master appears to be someone who is the best they can be. What you are about to discover in this chapter is that this is not the case. The opposite is true. Mastery is an approach, a mindset and a practice, but it is not an outcome.

Indeed, by practising Mastery, it is essential to be in the present moment without grasping for an outcome. There is a supreme irony to Mastery – the more you focus on your present-moment experience, the more likely you are to achieve the outcome. But when it does come, you will be less fixated on the result or its value.

Although it is the eighth wisdom, Mastery is to be practised starting from the First Door, and in this chapter you will discover the process that will allow you to flourish throughout your life and your Wing Tsun journey. The reason that Mastery can seem a little contradictory is that in the first three Doors you practise Mastery for the outcome (in the same way someone who is learning the piano does). You want to get better, be better and see a tangible output. In these three Doors Mastery teaches you the power of your intentions and your determination to constantly improve. In Wing Tsun, this is known as Continual Mastery.

Ever realistic, in Wing Tsun the structure of the Doors is graduated because it acknowledges that achieving the three elements of Mastery from the outset is pretty difficult. Mastery takes practice. Anyone that begins a martial art is doing so because they are chasing an outcome, whether it is becoming fitter, stronger, more spiritually aware or better able to defend themselves. Giving up the desire for an outcome when you are so hardwired by society to achieve is not something that you can easily switch off.

As you go through each Door, and the more you begin to experience a deeper level of Mastery, the more you understand your ego and put it aside. So by the time you get to the Fourth Door, Mastery is no longer theory for you. You will be so immersed in the practice that you will have an oblique and indirect opportunity to achieve the sort of clarity that Zen describes as enlightenment, or Satori. You go from practising in the first three Doors to a state of experiencing in the final Door (Beyond Self).

Masters of Zen dialogue – the classic conversation between master and student in Zen – recognize that we suffer in life because we desire. So the student is set the task of not desiring. It then becomes apparent that you cannot stop desiring if you are desiring not to desire. The only escape is to let go of the attachment to mind and instead focus on experiencing life. In the same way, the student of Wing Tsun becomes progressively able to put practice before outcome through the experience of Mastery.

Mastery begins by advising you to replace desiring with aspiring. You paint a picture of what you want to get, but you soften your grip on having to achieve it. By focusing on what's in front of you, you are moving towards your aspiration. As you progress, you increasingly realize that the more you give up desiring outcomes, the faster you achieve them. This, indeed, perhaps indicates that the universe has a sense of humour . . .

So you have a choice of going round and round, continually feeling unfulfilled in the search for achievements, or doing away with the need for the game completely and achieving enlightenment.

As the practice of Mastery continues, the desiring subtly decreases and the ability to stay with the present moment increases. This persists until you have reached a state where you are truly not attached to the outcome. At that point, someone looking from the outside would say you have achieved a breakthrough level of Mastery (known in Wing Tsun as Mastery Realization).

As you go deeper into Mastery at each Door, you go through a number of transformations. You reassess what winning means to you and increasingly learn not to fight. You progress from wanting to achieve to a desire for longevity to a feeling of wholeness – revealing and understanding your whole self. These changes occur at each step as you progress from being driven by ego and fear to a sense of completeness.

The Fourth Door shows you that Mastery provides harmony. It provides you with a way of being in flow that trusts instinct and intuition rather than thinking. Importantly, Mastery is never a status to be attained. It is only ever something that we do right now. A master is not something we call ourselves, otherwise it's too easy to become caught in another 'self-identification' ego trap. Becoming a master is realizing that the more you learn, the more there is still to learn. So instead we can say that we are attempting to do our best to practise Mastery – and it could, perhaps, be said there are no true masters.

The way that we practise Mastery in the Fourth Door provides the physical practice for us to truly live and understand the importance of being centred and grounded. By the wisdom of

Staying Relaxed, the master can see things more quickly and clearly. Because of our Western interpretation of the word 'master' (such as a 'schoolmaster'), we have a sense that the master has a disciplinary approach to the student. And while this is true in some expressions of twentieth-century martial arts, where the relationship is quite Confucian, this is not so for Wing Tsun. It is instead in the vein of ancient Zen teachers, who had a much more nurturing, familial and familiar tone.

These philosophical and physical characteristics are linked so closely (as with the whole of Wing Tsun) that they are two sides of the same coin. Although we like to separate them, the physical manifestation and philosophical wisdom are one and the same. But the very practice of Mastery and how it is trained in Wing Tsun, and its relationship to Winning Not Fighting, is what fuels us through the different Doors.

In Wooden Dummy and Mastery, we perfect the art of the centre line, omnidirectional movement, staying grounded, and balance. This combination is, again, physically and fundamentally different from other martial arts:

- The centre line shows you to follow your path. It is different from other people's and one only you can be on.
- Omnidirectional movement (the ability to defend/ strike/move in any direction) represents the ability of the master to see in all directions.
- Staying grounded teaches you the importance of not grasping and throwing yourself off balance.
- Physical balance represents the ability to use both left and right equally – harmonizing both/all sides of your being, creating wholeness and harmony.

Mastery creates unity of the body and mind. As the First Door taught you, when you train the hands, you train the brain. By practising each technique equally on the left and right sides, you develop highly competent ambidextrous abilities. The benefits of these are profound: studies have indicated that ambidextrous people are, typically, more adaptable, emotionally resilient and determined in problem-solving.

Mastery, therefore, seeks to create synchrony between the right and left hemispheres of the brain, with the practices containing many key elements: cross-lateral movements, cross-sensory experiences and deep meditative states. Mastery also proves a valuable counter-balance to the extreme value the West places on the logical left side. An imbalance which has left us feeling isolated and disconnected from others.

Wing Tsun Mastery similarly gives you real-world skills. Through your harmonization of motions and ergonomics, you develop the ability to improve almost any system you are faced with. Whether training in the military or making coffee, it all stems from the same place. With Mastery, you will see how to distil to the simplest elements that can be enhanced.

Finally, Mastery is like a beautiful Zen circle:

Zen circle.

You cannot progress through the First Door without Mastery, and the last Door brings you back to it. When Grandmaster Leung Ting was asked by a journalist why my Sifu should still learn from him upon completion of the art, he simply replied,

'The first time he learned Wing Tsun he saw it was like a temple. Now he sees it is a golden temple.'

Lessons of the Eighth Wisdom: Mastery

1. Mastery creates contentment through a single-minded focus.
2. The Mastery mindset creates continual learning.
3. Mastery creates opportunity.
4. Mastery ties together the three aspects of winning: be yourself, enjoy the present and achieve longevity.

John

In Which John Attempts the Impossible

Not only does the Fourth Door of Wing Tsun reflect the teachings of most of the world's religions and examine the fundamental challenge of humans' separation from – or connection to – God or the universe, but to make matters worse, if you try to write about it, you grapple with the challenge of describing in words something that is meant to be experienced unconsciously, without words.

So, let's try that, then.

The way to true enjoyment is through the wisdom of Mastery.

This is choosing one thing to focus on, one thing that you love and that you feel you are meant to do, practising it unconsciously in the present moment, and not chasing or obsessing over the outcome.

This is a choice available to everybody, right now – not to a chosen few. But it requires us to not overthink, to give up the need for certificates or status or ego.

It recognizes humanity's fundamental task is to rediscover wholeness, to realize that we are not really separate from everyone and everything else, and that this wholeness is synonymous with love.

You do not achieve wholeness by trying to be all things to all people, by trying to overstretch yourself to solve everyone's problems or 'change the world'. You achieve wholeness through mastery. You serve all by being true to who you are. By recognizing that you are distinct and unique, but not separate. In the same way that a proton, neutron and electron are distinct from one another but fundamentally part of one thing. If they stop being true to what they are, the atom – the whole – no longer functions.

That's it. Thank you so much for reading. Good night!

. . .

. . . and here's the encore.

The Beginning

Some strange people like to skip to the end of a book to find out the ending before they begin. Unless you're one of them, you've nearly made it – but it may come as a surprise to you that this last chapter is also actually the first. You will discover that mastery is not so much an end point but a practice to choose now. And to do so in what Wing Tsun calls the 'eternal now' that we experience when we stop rushing into the future and enjoy the present moment in a way that does not compromise the long term.

In the First Door, we bent down to pass through it. As a low door, it required us to put aside ego. By understanding and practising the concept that Wing Tsun calls Chu Ming, we learned to face ourselves. To become conscious. Now in this Fourth Door you must face yourself once more, but this time by experiencing yourself unconsciously.

In the same way, by practising Chu Ming, you will in this Fourth Door face yourself again and realize that you are, as Grandmaster Leung Ting describes, the equivalent of a golden temple. You have come full circle. But the process of travelling the circle has given you new insight into where you are now.

In the Third Door, you were winning, you were on top of your game. The Fourth Door is called 'the door that has no door' because, when you step through, you turn around and see that there is no Door. You transition from winning the game to realizing that there is no game. That the game was one of many false ideas that you and others conspired to fabricate.

Some people leave the Door ajar, unable to give up the feeling of winning the game. Because this is heady stuff. So, while we wrap our brains around it, I am going to tell you that the way to true enjoyment is through mastery.

As mentioned above, mastery is the decision to choose one area of focus, to focus on practising it now, in the present moment, and to give up the fruits of money or fame or anything else that the ego desires. They may come. They may not. It doesn't matter. Because they are not the point of the endeavour. You suffer because you crave things, says Buddhism and its friends. But you can't consciously give up desiring or desire not to desire. You can only put yourself aside and live unconsciously in the present moment, immersed in the process of mastery.

A person entering the Fourth Door will learn more in the next given period than they did as a student. The learning curve is exponential. Not just because they have more skills and ideas to build on, but because they have learned to master the act of practising.

The Fourth Door is not something to leap to. Each Door must be fully explored before moving to the next. It is like exploring the levels of a computer game – each brings new adventures, insights and powers. You began the process by becoming conscious of the nature of your distinctness, and you experienced and began to understand conflict. At the same time, you learned to understand the fear, anger, shame and desire to grasp that all come with ego. You learned that anger and fear are made possible by a lack of love. And you began slowly to put these aside. You learned to engage with others with love and positivity, and to free yourself, thrive and win the game.

Having discovered and explored 1-ness in the First Door (the desire to be number 1, exploring and discovering your 'I'), in the Fourth Door you will now discover oneness. This oneness does not turn everything into a milky, hazy soup where everything loses its self-identity. It recognizes and respects the distinctness of your I-ness, just as in any marriage both people must respect and love themselves, and then shows that, while distinct, you are not truly separate. And by the Fourth Door, you will have worked through the different layers to get to your true self. You will have felt and expressed anger, conflict, greed. You will have experienced the feelings of separation that accompany these emotions of the ego. And you will learn to find something pretty cool beyond them. *You*. A true you that is distinct – and is also a part of the whole.

And you will discover that the way to your true self is through mastery.

It's Time for a 'Dad Joke'

I know it's a 'dad joke' for a fact, because my dad used to tell it, and it goes like this . . .

A guy takes a violin and a painting to the *Antiques Roadshow*. The expert examines them closely and says, 'This is amazing! You have a Stradivarius, and a Rembrandt.' The guy, of course, is beside himself with excitement. 'The thing is,' says the expert, 'that Rembrandt didn't know much about making violins and Stradivarius couldn't paint.'

Neither Rembrandt nor Stradivarius set out to be famous. But they became two of the most renowned people in history. They both loved what they did. They did it repeatedly. And there is no record of them having five-year plans.

This is why Julian's teacher, Grandmaster Maday Norbert, says to him, 'Never practise for glory – practise for practice's sake, and glory may or may not come.'

Do you remember where we came in? I told you the story of

how my coach Aimée suggested that I might not be a general, that I should probably come to terms with that, and gave me an alternative metaphor with the story of Arthur Stace.

Aimée also showed me how to be comfortable with focus. As an aid to this process, she gave me homework in the form of *The Great Work of Your Life* by yoga master Steven Cope.

Cope's book is a modern-day exploration of, and commentary on, the *Bhagavad Gita*. The story of this Hindu text is a dialogue between the prince Arjuna and his charioteer Krishna, in which Krishna must advise the prince on a seemingly impossible decision. In the army he must now destroy, Arjuna sees his own relatives, dear friends, and teachers he admires and respects. What, then, must he do?

The insights in the book can be simplified to three main messages. First, decide on your one Dharma, or sacred purpose. Second, practise it properly, and with focus. And third, which Cope rightly identifies as the most difficult, 'give up the fruits'. Don't chase fame, or success, or certificates, or money, or happiness. For happiness, paradoxically, does not come from the pursuit of happiness. It is something achieved indirectly, through immersion in the practice of one thing – in other words, through mastery.

The first lesson of Cope's book, about focusing on one thing, came for me at the right time. Two years before, I had created for myself a life that was too complicated and stressful. Back then, I was part-time at Leon, responsible for the food and restaurants and marketing, co-writing the School Food Plan with Henry, trying to keep a new flatbread pizza business above water, and helping start a food business in Ethiopia while also being on the board of a fast-growing beer business in the north of the country doing $35m profit (and serving as its CEO for three months).

This on top of trying to build a consumer brands investment business, and help grow a UK-based chocolate business with the name of Choccywoccydoodah.

Oh, and trying my best to be an okay dad and husband and son. And friend. And walking the dog now and again. And feeding the chickens. And writing some cookbooks.

This wasn't good for my blood pressure. Sleep and exercise were two things that got the least attention. Katie and I were both hitting our overdraft limits regularly. Leon was taking all the cash we had and more. We found a bank that would extend our mortgage further on our house, but we were still maxed out at the bank and on our credit cards. And the Tax Man had a surprise for us too. It wasn't cake.

In July 2013, we published the School Food Plan and were able to hand over its executive management to Myles Bremner, who had previously led a great charity called Garden Organic. This relieved a little pressure, but I was still doing too much.

And then, at the beginning of 2014, Leon hit some rather large financial problems. Henry and I met, the board met, we all debated and discussed, and I ended up with an opportunity to take the reins at Leon. But I would need to give up everything else. To choose one thing. To stop trying to have my cake and eat it too. Yes, I was driven partly by necessity. I wasn't prepared to let Leon go under. But the time had come for me to stop dabbling and start focusing.

Fancy a Dabble?

Many of us have experienced what it's like to dabble. Sometimes we do it because we want to try new things; or sometimes parents, family members or friends encourage us to take up new pursuits.

As a young teenager, I tried to learn the clarinet. My father had an image of me in the swing band, delighting audiences. But I only got as far as a damp-smelling music room where the end of the clarinet gently dribbled saliva onto my geeky school shoes, and my goofy front teeth continually banged the wooden reed of the mouthpiece. It did not sound good.

I also tried to learn the piano, took up and put aside bird-watching, and at a young age decided to be a detective. I recently found a small exercise book, on the front of which was written JOHN VINCENT, DETECTIVE. On the first page it has a date and *Saw nothing suspicious*. This is the only entry in the exercise book. In short, I was a dabbler.

Dabblers envy masters. Masters achieve an ever-increasing and compounding satisfaction from learning one thing. I've never been to a party where someone said to me, 'John, meet Simon, Simon is number 450 in the world at tennis and chess *and* baking.' Jacks of all trades don't achieve much momentum.

George Leonard, author of *Mastery*, is himself a master of Aikido, a martial art which, though much younger when compared to Wing Tsun, shares some of its philosophical strands. And the Dabbler is the first of four character types that he describes.

The Dabbler is the guy you meet at a dinner party who shows you his new GPS watch and explains, 'I'm going to do an Iron Man race,' then the next time you bump into him and ask how the training is going, he says, 'Iron Man races weren't for me, I've taken up golf instead. Here, I have a photo of my clubs, they're the same ones that Tiger Woods uses . . .' And so on.

The second is the Hacker, who gets to a certain mediocre level and stays there, quite happy to hack their way round the golf course every time.

The third character could on first pass seem similar to a master but is actually very different. This is the Obsessive, who is focused so much on the outcome that they shortcut the process, the training, and fixate on beating their friend Adam at tennis. They seek the result quickly and at all costs. They may achieve a short-term spike in capability and short-term results, but ultimately they never enjoy the steady journey of the master, because this fixation is not true focus. In the *Bhagavad Gita* this is the person who is grasping for the fruits. Off balance, desiring, taking shortcuts with the practice.

By now you will have figured out that the fourth character is the Master. She or he focuses on the practice. On the journey. According to Leonard, they accept the plateaus in performance, enjoy but don't obsess about the occasional and unpredictable improvements in performance and outcome, and work hard without making it hard work.

There is one nuance I would like to introduce here. My practice of mastery is, like yours is for yourself, about finding out what is faithful to my true self. Yes, I was dissipating my energies across too many projects, and yes I have since focused on Leon. But my repeated skill, action, character, Dharma and mastery is to innovate and create, and to recognize that I have a skill in seeing new opportunities and ideas. This is a skill that is more repeatable than the role of 'running Leon', and if this takes me or Leon into new areas, so be it.

Wing Tsun applauds the sentiment. And by the Fourth Door, you will see mastery in this light. But Julian and I have come to the conclusion that, in reality, many people come to martial arts with an outcome in mind, and switching this off, or replacing such desire with aspiration, or doing away with the desires completely, takes time.

The journey through the doors of Wing Tsun recognizes this reality. Over time we desire less, and we start to redefine what we mean by 'winning'. We can only progress into and through each door if we put aside fighting.

Kung Fu itself means 'working hard'. The challenge of the master is to be sufficiently in flow, sufficiently in the present, that working hard does not feel like hard work.

Where Leonard, Julian and I agree is that we see mastery as a process, not a status to be attained. Anyone who practises properly is practising mastery.

Like this man . . .

'I Walk the Line'

When my dad died, I went to meet the CEO of the hospital where he spent his last days. Dad went into hospital in November 2017 for an operation that we thought he would recover from. This first hospital had great doctors and nurses, but they were let down by a system that was not joined up and which, in my opinion, had no sense of itself. By contrast, the hospital where Dad died four months later, following the complications experienced in the first, was very well joined up and run. So I went to thank the CEO and to find out if there was any way I could offer financial or other support.

The CEO had the air of a master. He had the wisdom to know that turnarounds take time. He had started the job around six years earlier, and had told everyone at the time that things would not be transformed overnight. At the same time he set about making changes immediately. He didn't stay in his office, he walked the corridors asking each department what they needed to improve. He came across one in-patient department with incredibly low daily admissions and treatment rates. They were seeing a third of the number of patients a day compared to other hospitals. So he went to find out why. He watched as the front desk checked people in. He saw them take the patient's details, and then disappear for at least a minute or two down the corridor and return holding a piece of paper to then finish the registration process.

'What do you need to make this process go faster?' he asked them.

'Well,' replied the woman on the front desk, 'it would be really handy to have a double computer screen, because I have to transfer the patient's details from one system to another and I can't get both systems up on the same screen at the same time, so I have to print the details off, walk down the corridor to the office, then type all the details into the other system. If I had a double-screen computer I could have each system on a different screen and copy and paste the details.'

The CEO straight away called the head of IT and told him, 'Go down to the PC store and buy this woman a double computer screen. Here's the money for it.'

'I can do better than that,' the head of IT replied. 'I have one downstairs in the storeroom.'

Within 15 minutes the department receptionist, with the help of IT, had her screen up and running. Within a day the department was seeing four times as many patients a day as before.

This hospital CEO was not born a master of his craft. But he had over time developed a wisdom and a mastery that all of us can learn from.

This reminds us that the wisdom of Mastery is about exercising patience (not exercising patients, you understand) while also taking action right now; about breaking challenges down into simple problems and simple solutions. Having done this, it's about making the right thing the easy thing. About having no ego or grandeur that stops you going to see what the issue is for yourself, and talking to the people who experience it – whether it's the janitor, the hospital porter, the lab technician or the receptionist.

It's about knowing that, on the one hand, the future will not be safeguarded unless we act now. And, equally, that the big turnaround will take time.

You Are Not a Slot Machine

Penny-pusher machines, one-arm bandits, chocolate vending machines. They are all coin-operated. No coins, no game. No coins, no chocolate. Not even chocolate coins.

You, however, are different. You are not coin-operated. You

are not mechanical. There is something a little less transactional going on with you. It's just that the way you are incentivized at work hasn't quite cottoned on to this. Yet.

In my practice of Wing Tsun, my understanding of mastery has deepened, as has my belief that much of Western culture runs contrary to its principles.

Wing Tsun, and the Taoist and Zen Buddhist philosophies that inform it, provides an ancient antidote to this. As with many aspects of life, Western science is starting to catch up to what Eastern wisdom has known for millennia.

In his book *Drive*, Daniel Pink proposes that 'cutting-edge social science' has 'discovered' that people are far less driven by money than they are by solving problems and becoming good at something. This really shouldn't have been a revelation. It is something that lies at the heart of how Wing Tsun understands human nature. When people discover something that they love as true amateurs (and it is worth noting that amateurism means doing something you love, not being bad at something), it becomes the thing they think about in the bath, when they wake, and that they read about before they go to bed. For some lucky people it may be sailing or tennis, or building model railways, or cooking.

These pursuits provide so much more delight than the transitory pleasure of cashing a cheque.

Success is the Preparation

When you are passionate about your mastery – your Dharma – work does not feel like work. Yes, you put the hours in. Many of them. And it can take a toll on one's family. Even on holiday I find myself thinking about Leon.

When I visited the house of my friend and collaborator Brad Blum, I found on his bookshelf a book by the renowned

American college basketball coach John Wooden. It has become a core text for all new managers at Leon, and a great topic of discussion at many of our gatherings.

The message at its heart is that one should define success as preparation and practice, not as winning the match. Wooden ensured that he and his players defined success as tying their shoelaces properly, as practising their moves and executing their game plan properly, and as being mentally prepared. He made sure that his team dressed smartly and turned up on time.

Wooden's approach is echoed in the 'critical non-essentials' that Rugby World Cup-winning England coach Clive Woodward insisted upon. But, unlike Woodward, Wooden didn't just win the one tournament. As the coach of the UCLA team, he won ten national championships in a 12-year period. But this was not how he kept score. As he described it: 'There were times when we lost the game that I knew we had been successful because we had prepared well – and there were times when we won the game but I knew we had not been successful because we had not prepared well.'

At Leon, there are factors outside our control and events we cannot predict. Our job is to prepare well and focus on what we *can* control. If I know that we have a menu that our guests value, that we are giving each guest a big welcome, making the food with love, serving it within 30 seconds in the world's cleanest restaurants, then I cannot ask any more. Of course, the daily sales figures matter. A business that doesn't make money dies. But I cannot force a customer to choose us (by 'aggressively driving sales'). By hiring great teams, I can create a welcoming space which serves great food, fast, that the customer wants to experience and enjoy.

At Leon we have concluded that the only true fundamental driver of success is the speed and consistency of how we learn. And this is the result of what we do in the present.

Mastery is Not Your Job Title: Corporate Dabbling vs Transferable Mastery

Our investor Fersen shared with me his view that, in the UK, we tend to pigeonhole people, not realizing that people can be generalists who move from one thing to the next, or one role to the next.

It struck me that this could be perceived as a challenge to the principle of Mastery. But on reflection, looking at my own experiences and at other businesses, I have concluded that there are – crudely – two types of generalists in business: ineffective dabblers and master generalists. Master generalists specialize in *being* generalists.

The first, the dabblers, are the type I often experienced in big corporate multinationals. People who did six months in finance, then nine months in marketing, and then were switched from the light bulb division to the cosmetics division. With few transferable skills, they cost the company a lot in relocation costs.

By contrast, a master generalist is still, in their own way, a specialist. This is someone who seemingly works across sectors but who has a repeatable skill that they get better and better at. At Bain, we used to call them 'athletes'. They may not have the domain or industry knowledge, but they know how to get things done repeatedly, how to analyse situations or to inspire other people to get things done.

Which brings us to Fersen's mentors and colleagues, who founded 3G Capital, one of the most formidable success stories in business right now. He was referring to them specifically when he talked about businesses unnecessarily pigeonholing people.

After running a number of successful investment companies, 3G's founders chose to buy and run a beer business in their home country of Brazil. They became so good at it that, through a combination of mergers and purchases, they now run beer brands on four continents.

This same team has now bought Burger King, the Canadian coffee business Tim Hortons, and – teaming up with Warren Buffett – the food group Kraft. They have Coca-Cola in their sights.

What is clear to me about their wide-ranging commercial success is that it has been achieved by Jorge Paulo Lemann, Carlos Alberto Sicupira and Marcel Herrmann Telles performing very distinct roles pursuant to their characteristic skills and individual masteries, and doing so consistently and repeatedly.

Lemann, the most senior of the three, explains that when all is said and done, he is first and foremost a teacher. Someone who identifies talent, inspires it, and provides a meritocratic culture in which it can thrive. He states that the reason why they continue to buy more companies is to provide opportunities for 3G people to grow.

Clearly, Lemann has deeply impressive additional skills, including the ability to structure the finances of major acquisitions and mergers, and to raise the money to fund them. However, it is clear that at his core he is a specialist teacher. And that he is repeating this skill, and this passion, to get repeated results.

The Wisdom of Foolishness and Childishness

There is a certain 'foolishness' to Taoism. And by foolishness I mean two things. The first is the ability to play the role of the fool, who turns weakness into strength and who sees things in situations that others do not; and there is the other sense of foolishness as 'stupidity'. As in adopting a 'stupid mind', which might be seen as the ability to keep one's mind uncluttered by knowledge and to maintain a childishly open view of the world.

It is not to be confused with Jung's idea of the *puer*, the man who never grew up nor developed the character required of a grown-up. It more describes a man who refuses to be jaded by cynicism, who is prepared to trust his intuition like a child, and to put aside inhibition like a child. The *Tao Te Ching*, in its 55th verse, describes how a person who maintains the softness and flexibility of a child achieves wholeness:

> He who is filled with Virtue is like a newborn child.
> Wasps and serpents will not sting him;
> Wild beasts will not pounce upon him;
> He will not be attacked by birds of prey.
> His bones are soft, his muscles weak,
> But his grip is firm.
> He has not experienced the union of man and woman,
>   but is whole.
> His manhood is strong.
> He screams all day without becoming hoarse.
> This is perfect harmony

In Annette Moser-Wellman's book *Five Faces of Genius*, and in her and Jane Melvin's adaptation of it into a training course, as you may remember, the Fool is the person who turns weakness into a strength – a problem into an opportunity. They provide ideas that other people are less likely to come up with. For a good while Leon, and therefore I, had a Fool in Saskia Sidey, who would challenge the thinking of the group. Leaders love Fools. They make the leader laugh, they challenge thinking because they cannot help but do so. Saskia would often look at me quizzically as I was speaking to a group of people. And for a good while she looked after our social media, giving it quite the foolish attitude. When a guest complained there wasn't enough *gobi* in her Leon Gobi (a cauliflower curry), Saskia posted her a whole cauliflower saying she had found the missing *gobi*. The Fool has a special mastery and is in touch with their real, spontaneous self.

And we could all do with having a little 'foolishness' in us.

Supposedly, when Buddha gave his first sermon to explain his enlightenment, rather than speaking he instead pointed to a flower, to demonstrate the uselessness of words. One of his disciples laughed, seeing the ridiculousness of the situation. It was this person who Buddha effectively chose as his heir.

The master is happy to maintain a stupid mind.

Mastery and the Surprising Danger of Knowledge

As we learned earlier, Lao Tzu said, 'To attain knowledge, add things every day. To attain wisdom, remove things every day.'

This is a classic case of describing the wood and the trees. Lao Tzu is not saying that knowledge should be shunned, but that knowledge should not be pursued to feed the ego, nor should it be allowed to cloud judgement and wisdom – which is the ability to see clearly and see the truth in situations.

While I cannot bring myself to fully embrace the *Tao Te Ching* and shun knowledge altogether, I am well aware that the accumulation of knowledge can have the power to get in the way of common sense.

Recently, I spoke at a conference in Hamburg, and the organizer was adamant that I had to have 'lots of content'. 'Give people lots of facts and figures they can't get elsewhere,' he said. I began by telling the audience that I was hoping to share what I think humanity's fundamental challenge is and what enlightenment might look like, but that I wouldn't have time because the organizer wanted me to spend more time than I'd planned sharing facts.

What I should have done was project the above Lao Tzu quote, on a slide, and just lain down on the stage for 45 minutes.

One day.

When questions seem to cloud our minds at Leon, we are careful not to add more data. Returning to our single touchstone of 'if God did fast food' requires not complicated knowledge but a balanced emotional state that ensures we remember this and allows us to see clearly.

Mastery is Not Status, nor Certificates

The desire to accumulate certificates and diplomas can sometimes come at the expense of common sense. And potentially at the expense of free thinking or proactivity.

Somebody with unencumbered clarity of thinking is just as able, if not more able, to see this than someone who has two degrees and an MBA. These qualifications can sometimes bind the recipient into a rigid, dogmatic way of thinking, and blinker them from seeing alternatives and lateral paths.

And often it is the 18-year-old, fresh out of school, who asks the straightforward question that dumbfounds the room. Or, alternatively, an older person retiring from the Confucian structure of formal employment.

A friend once said goodbye to the tea lady, Irene, who had worked in the company for 15 years. Let's call him Mark. On the day of her retirement, he presented her with a leaving gift in front of the rest of the management team. He delivered a short speech and then asked Irene if she wanted to say a few words. Humbly, she accepted the offer. Over the next ten minutes, she offered up the most perceptive insights on the company and its detailed workings. She dissected the pros and cons of Mark's management style, explained the shortcomings of the interpersonal dynamics within the senior team, and pointed out that they had been foolhardy to enter China with their current strategy. And she criticized the business for not investing sufficient money to support their US operations. She offered probably the best critique of the company's strategy that had ever been offered by anyone, including expensive management consultants.

There is huge wisdom in people who have achieved distance and clarity, unencumbered by the pursuit of minute facts and formulae.

Mastery is Not 'Promotion'

There are many organizations where people constantly want to climb the ladder of promotion *as fast as they can* in order to gain more 'seniority'. This construct of organizational hierarchy does not necessarily represent the true terrain.

We draw the Leon organization as a progress flow. It is not top-down, nor is it hierarchical. There is no command-and-control structure. As you've seen, I often think of Leon as a tree, or a garden, or a river.

The key to any healthy organization is to develop people's expertise and constantly give them important and rewarding challenges that they are well suited to solve. It is not healthy, in my view, to promote people from positions in which they flourish, and which they are very good at, to managerial or administrative positions that take them away from the action.

At one point, after Vivian sold Whyte & Mackay, we set up an investment business and invested in the Ethiopian beer business I have referred to. We also looked to buy a Turkish spirits business called Mey. We didn't get it, but Diageo did. When their recruitment team went out to look at Mey's HR practices, they were horrified to learn that there was very little promotion from sales executive to sales manager. So they asked why not, and the CEO of Mey replied, 'Why would our best salespeople want to become sales managers? Sales is what they're good at. Sales is what they enjoy. And sales is where they are continually developing.'

I agree. I'm continually trying to explain to people at Leon that if I were going to rob a bank, I would much rather be driven away by the best getaway driver rather than by the head of getaway driving who has probably not driven a getaway car for a few years.

When someone from the support team says they would like a promotion, I explain that a promotion means becoming a restaurant manager. We should not create a sense that a manager should be angling for a 'promotion' to being an area manager or to work in 'head office'. This is why we call the place people might think of as our head office 'the Borough Market support team'. The job of the restaurant manager is like being the CEO of a business unit. It is critical. Being an area manager or in the Borough support team is like having a 'group' role. Nice, but much less important.

We make sure at Leon that the managers have opportunities to contribute more widely to things that will affect all managers and restaurants. For example, one of our managers, Nirav, has spent the last three months leading the development of our delivery business.

We do not want to create an overblown bureaucracy where people try to get out of important roles to be in supervisory or administrative roles. So we make sure that the managers can earn more than their area managers. Last year, 14 managers achieved a £25k super-bonus for what they achieved.

The Ability to Unlearn

If we cling to past knowledge, we will not be able to take on fresh thinking. So the master must be able to unlearn old things to learn new things. This takes practice and a lack of ego.

When Galileo concluded that the earth orbits the sun, and not the sun around the earth, very few said, 'Fair enough, let's change our minds.' Instead, they tried him for heresy. It took a generation for the new paradigm to be adopted. Those that thought one thing died, and the new generation were taught that the earth rotates around the sun – heliocentrism, if you fancy the technical term. (But, as we know, a clever-sounding term can get in the way of mastery.)

Today, in the field of nutrition, any idea that challenges the current orthodoxy is deemed 'unscientific'. People are attacked when they offer up plausible hypotheses that they think should be tested. This has led to the creation of a scientific journal where people publish their ideas anonymously because they believe that their reputation will be unfairly attacked or their funding withdrawn if they offer alternatives to the current thinking.

Current thinking is often ego by another name. While scepticism is vital – the whole purpose of hypotheses is to disprove them – many remain untested for the wrong reasons.

Today a master needs to have their wits about them, to look at themselves in the mirror and ask whether their ego is getting in the way of their mastery. To follow Jung's rare example: 'I shall not commit the fashionable stupidity of regarding everything I cannot explain as a fraud.'

The Psychotherapist Waiting Beyond the Fourth Door

After finishing what I thought was the final draft of this book, my head was full. So I briefly went away to Austria to try to clear my mind, or rather to separate myself from it.

I walked around a lake, hiked in the forest and met some interesting people as I did so. There was a Swede who now owns sustainable forests in Brazil and Colombia, a student at Bristol University, a property developer from Chicago, an art dealer from London, and a bar and hotel owner from Ireland. It was like an episode of *Lost* – the TV show that you thought would never end.

In my conversations with these rather fascinating people, and with others in the town where I was staying, one name kept coming up in conversation – people repeatedly spoke with great admiration for a psychotherapist called Claudia Waldner, and they recommended that I see her too. Doing so led to my rediscovering something that supports the wisdoms learned in the Fourth Door – the work of the psychotherapist Viktor Frankl.

It was strangely similar to that moment when I was writing about the Third Door, Biu Jee, and right in the middle of it I was introduced to the teachings of the psychotherapist Alfred Adler – very much one of those 'yellow budgie' moments when the right thing turns up at just the right time. Adler provided me with a twentieth-century explanation of what Wing Tsun has taught for centuries – that you can free yourself from the patterns that you inherit from your past and your ancestors.

My conversations with Claudia provided further validation of the power of Winning Not Fighting and of the Four Doors of Wing Tsun – and in particular an incredibly timely new addition to this last chapter.

We met in Claudia's corner office overlooking the lake I had explored in the previous few days. If you have written a book, or a dissertation, or even an essay that has absorbed you, you will know that – having submitted it – you experience not just a sense of relief but also of mental and physical decompression. I had been reflecting on Alan Watts's caution that words can be 'a great servant but a poor master', and it was not lost on me that in attempting to use words to describe how one must and can go beyond words, I had been putting myself through various mental contortions.

My time with Claudia, in Austria and since, has not only provided new ways to explain the ideas in this last chapter, and in the book more broadly, but also helped me to *do* the things I describe – to take myself beyond words.

At our first meeting I experienced the exhilaration that we all feel when we encounter someone with whom we quickly connect. It was like we were taking a thousand-piece jigsaw and working together at speed to complete it.

Claudia explained the journey that she takes her clients on to discover what both Wing Tsun and she describe as one's 'true self'. It is a process, she told me, that happens in stages. We must first become aware of our own self, before experiencing a series of steps in which we connect with our own bodies and feel, process and understand our emotions.

To illustrate, Claudia drew a diagram that looks like a dartboard – but where the bullseye is the starting point rather than where one aims. One's journey, Claudia explained, is to expand outwards from the middle. At the centre lies our mind – which Claudia described as being 'very limited'. At the outermost of the circles we discover our true essence, infinite and limitless. In between are a circle that represents our body and another that represents our emotions. (We have reproduced this at winningnotfighting.com, and if the Internet still exists when you are reading this, you can find it there.)

Claudia explained that we are tempted to bypass our body and emotions to get to our true essence – and cautioned that it is important not to take such a shortcut. We must, Claudia explained, explore each in turn. We must begin by exploring our mind, and then become attuned through physical activity – and also sometimes by sitting still – to what our bodies are telling us. Then we must be prepared to examine our emotions: the conditioning, patterns and beliefs that have shaped us. Only by passing through each circle can we hope to arrive at our true essence in a state that allows us to fully understand it – or rather, ready to immerse ourselves in it unimpeded.

Claudia described, in terms that clearly echoed in the experience of the Four Doors of Wing Tsun, how: 'In order to get to who we truly are – at the outer, infinite circle – we need to create awareness about our conditioning, patterns and beliefs on the mental and emotional level, and thereby release and transform. Psychotherapy allows us to understand and become aware of how we became who we think or believe we are, and thereby reconnect to who we truly are.'

And so, in the most timely of manners, I was given this gift from I know not where. A meeting with someone who was able to offer a model that is consistent with the fundamental belief of this book and of the Four Doors of Wing Tsun – that we must take each form or Door in turn to experience our mind and our body, to free ourselves from the emotions that have held us back, and finally in this Fourth Door to experience our true and limitless self.

Therefore I say again, without any qualms about repeating myself, enter each Door one at a time, and do not rush through to the final Door. In Siu Nim Tao, stop and break away from the way that you are unconsciously living. Learn about who you have become; not what your true self is, but what your personality has become and how your mind has been shaped. And begin to tune into your body, which is perhaps something you have not done for a long time. In Chum Kiu, continue this process by exploring how you relate to others and how your emotions have been shaped by your relationships, and be prepared to feel these emotions intensely before you say goodbye to them. In Biu Jee, feel what it is like to be on top of your game, respectful of others but not bound by their views of you, and free from the emotions that have been restricting you.

When the time is right you will walk through the Fourth Door, and you will turn around to realize that there is no door. That there is no game to win. And that winning is discovering and immersing yourself in your true self, and finding meaning in what you are doing right now – thus achieving a new and very different form of unconsciousness.

My sessions with Claudia gave me exactly what I needed, exactly when I needed it. Not only did our conversations give me a perfectly timed denouement for the book, they gave me what I needed right then personally. Having just finished this final chapter, and therefore having used words and the rational mind to explain that one can only achieve peace by putting these very things aside, my mind was chasing its own tail. I needed someone else to help me just 'be', and to get me out of my mind. Thank you so much, Claudia, for helping me do this.

But from where had Claudia learned and developed this thinking? Claudia Waldner belongs, it transpired from our conversations, to a school of psychotherapy that was born from the teachings of the twentieth-century psychotherapist Viktor Frankl, and the subsequent expansion of his thinking by his student Alfried Längle. Our discussions sparked in me a memory of stories about Frankl from school. Those stories had in my teens provided staple and powerful school assembly content (told by the rather alternative – and I thought rather cool – school chaplain), especially for a school in North London with a mix of ethnic backgrounds and a good share of people whose families had been directly affected by the Holocaust.

Although I referred in previous chapters to Adler as the Third Man (after Jung and Freud), Frankl's thinking is more often referred to as the 'third school' of Viennese psychotherapy, after the first school – Freud's psychoanalysis, of which Jung was a part before growing somewhat distant from it – and the second school of Adler's individual psychology.

Frankl graduated from the University of Vienna's medical school in 1930, and joined the staff of the city's Steinhof psychiatric hospital before opening a private practice in 1937. But in 1938, the Nazis annexed Austria, and Frankl was permitted only to treat his fellow Jews, going to work at Vienna's Rothschild Hospital in 1940 before being deported in 1942 to the Theresienstadt ghetto in Czechoslovakia, and then to Auschwitz two years later. His mother, father and wife were all killed in the camps. Of his immediate family, only he and his sister survived.

As soon as the war was over, he returned to Vienna and

immediately wrote – in just nine days – and published his seminal work *Man's Search for Meaning*, based on his own experiences and observations in the camps.

Frankl's thinking supports many areas of this book. He believed greatly in our freedom to choose how we think, and encouraged his readers and clients to value both freedom and responsibility, writing: 'Everything can be taken from a man but one thing: the last of the human freedoms – to choose one's attitude in any given set of circumstances.'

The fact that he had endured the horror of life in a concentration camp gave him particular authority. He concluded that 'Human freedom is not a freedom from but freedom to.'

Claudia later explained to me: 'This is certainly one of the most fundamental quotes of Frankl. He wanted to make clear that we cannot always free ourselves from the conditions or circumstances we are in, but we have the freedom to choose how we react to those circumstances.'

And the following words by Frankl demonstrate that he was aligned very clearly with the principle of Freedom and Responsibility in the Third Door: 'Ultimately, man should not only ask what the meaning of his life is, but rather must recognize that it is he who is asked. In a word, each man is questioned by life; and he can only answer to life by answering for his own life; to life he can only respond by being responsible.'

But he is particularly instructive with regard to the Fourth Door, and to mastery. He concluded that we find fulfilment as a result of seeking and finding meaning and purpose, arguing that this should be the primary purpose of psychotherapy. 'Seeking to find meaning in one's life is the primary motivational force in man.'

In so doing, Frankl undermines the presumption inherent in current economic theory that you and I and everyone else is primarily motivated by money. My experience of working with people in Leon is that they are motivated by contributing to the lives of our guests, and by solving problems or rising to challenges as part of a team. Sure, bonus time is nice. But it pales in comparison to when a manager turns a restaurant around or sees one of their team members promoted. And although we seek to pay very well, having this sense of meaning and taking on these challenges, to a Leon person, is what it is like to be rich.

It became clear as I read his works that Frankl provides 'modern' (albeit 70 years old) support for Wing Tsun's belief in mastery, the power of understanding and following one's purpose, and the ability of people to find meaning in the most joyous or most difficult of situations.

He also advocates for the value of immersing oneself in the practice, in the present moment – having established one's own personal and particular meaning – just as we do when we pass through the Fourth Door. And he agrees that we must 'lose' ourselves in the practice and the daily tasks associated with meaning and purpose. And that this focus on the task in front of us, and on the present moment, helps to prevent us from being self-absorbed or put off balance by attempting to achieve a goal.

Frankl warned against hyper-reflection, where one is preoccupied with how one looks through the eyes of others, and suggested a process of 'de-reflection', where you focus on others rather than on how others see you. He offered the example of public speaking, where a person must focus on the task of speaking and on the meaning of what is being said and on the audience, not on how others see them.

Be present in the experience itself, he suggested. Focus on the music, on your love for another person or on whatever you are doing – and then, through losing yourself, you find yourself. In keeping with the entire oblique nature of mastery, Frankl explained that you 'actualize' yourself only when the goal is not self-actualization – and when you are not thinking about yourself at all, but only about the value and meaning of the task at hand.

Also in keeping with the Fourth Door, Frankl concluded that people have not only a mind and emotions (*psyche*) and a body (*soma*), but a 'spirit' (*noos*) that is our true, unique essence and also has to be considered – the outer ring of Claudia's diagram. Each person has, he believed, a healthy core that is unique and irreplaceable.

Claudia described it like this: 'Frankl speaks from three dimensions of human life, adding a third dimension to the description used by Freud or Adler: body, psyche (mind and emotions) and spirit. Frankl's term, "spirit", has no spiritual meaning in this context, although he was a quite spiritual person.'

In Zen terms, it is akin to our true nature that is waiting to be uncovered. Modern humans, modern medicine and modern culture have ignored and misunderstood the power of spirit, Frankl argued. Our role is not only to discover our spirit and meaning, but also to enlighten others to the existence and power of theirs.

For Frankl, psychotherapy was meant to help people uncover this spirit and the particular personal meaning or purpose that each of us seeks to uncover. He called the process 'logotherapy', from the Greek word *logos* – λόγος – that itself can be variously translated as not only 'meaning', but also 'truth' or 'word', and which is as such similar to the use of the word Tao in Taoism (check out the first verse of the *Tao Te Ching* and you might see an uncanny similarity to the opening bit of Genesis), or Dharma in Hinduism or Buddhism, which I referred to at the start of this chapter.

In keeping with Wing Tsun, Frankl is careful to state that he does not have a one-size-fits-all solution to the meaning of life. His respect for human individuality does not allow it. And so he encourages each of us to find our own unique meaning of life. When asked how this might be done, Frankl referenced Goethe: 'How can we learn to know ourselves? Never by reflection but by action. Try to do your duty, and you will soon find out what you are. But what is your duty? The demands of each day.'

This is the power of Wing Tsun: using physical movement and action to generate personal insight, with the four physical forms of the Four Doors, twinned with the wisdoms of Taoism and Zen Buddhism. Respecting the relationship between (or rather the unity of) our mind, body and spirit. Meditation in action.

Is Capitalism the Problem? Or Are We?

Winning Not Fighting has big implications for how we organize ourselves, how we manage our own lives and how we organize society. Having learned the wisdoms of Wing Tsun, when one looks at the world one recognizes that much of the economic theory taught in schools and practised by governments – what we call capitalism – assumes that we are motivated by the grasping desires of what we in this book call ego. This informs the way that we consume, the way we are sold to, and the way we are incentivized and motivated at work. It is a perversion of Darwinian thought that would always have us fighting – fighting for more, fighting for change, fighting each other.

We assume that, since Adam Smith coined the term 'the invisible hand', that capitalism will somehow regulate itself as we go about making money and competing. If we focus on increasing our bank balances, and on fighting, somehow everything else will take care of itself. Experience tells us that this simply isn't true. And it forces me to ask: what if some or many of us manage to move beyond ego and discover a true self based on meaning? What if we embark on a journey towards wholeness? What would be the implications for the economic and social structures we build for ourselves?

Today we are faced with two competing economic ideologies. With the first, capitalism, 'greed is good' and money is the scorecard by which people measure success. (Notice that whenever anyone says 's/he is very successful' they never mean 's/he has found a vocation that fulfils them and has a nice family life'.) In the second – socialism, or even neo-communism – the majority of an individual's earned income is transferred to the state, and our commercial and individual freedoms are constrained.

There must be an alternative choice between these two extremes.

And before you dismiss my thinking as unworkable, consider that neither capitalism as we have constructed it nor socialism have shown themselves to be sustainable. Neither offers a model where humanity's motivations and the needs of the planet can be balanced and addressed. As long as we are dominated by ego, as long as we are fighting but not winning, we will not be able to resolve this bitter tension. To safeguard the planet but also allow us to live in harmony with it – in line with our true nature – we need to heed the lessons that I believe I am lucky enough to have learned through Wing Tsun and in writing this book. I am personally of course some way off perfection, but I believe that if we can rid ourselves of the mind virus, *wetiko*, then we have a chance. We cannot change who we are, but we must learn to act not through ego or fear but rather through what Claudia Waldner and Wing Tsun call our 'true essence'. Begin first with yourself, and start to see the world through this new lens. You might start to see that the emperor has no clothes indeed.

Taoism has always promoted evolution over revolution. So I ask: can we create or evolve a new system, enshrined in personal freedom married with responsibility, where making money or creating economic growth is not the end goal? Where we exercise responsibility to win in the way we describe in this book? Where we learn to put aside ego and to act in a way that protects our future and that of the generations to come?

The Great Law of the Iroquois holds that we ought, with every decision, to consider its impact over seven generations. If we were to draw inspiration from this and to apply it today, the implications would be profound. It would require business leaders guiding their organizations to put meaning before money. And the irony is that they would likely find themselves making more money in the long run.

Governments need to learn not just to create jobs but to create meaningful jobs, and to make GDP and growth the enablers of this rather than ends in their own right. We should learn to think of money as being like the fuel in an aeroplane. It gets us where we want to go, but it is not a goal in itself.

This requires different and better leadership across society, and better self-leadership too, because all change begins with ourselves. And it requires governments and businesses to understand and account for the natural world. Pursuit of economic gain without regard for the planet cannot continue.

It will require, too, active partnership between business and governments, but both must safeguard personal liberties and serve the individual rather than the institution. My work with the government as co-developer of the School Food Plan and as chair of the Council for Sustainable Business has shown me on the one hand how rare it is for business and government to work in tandem, but how powerful it is when they do, especially when they put the child (in the case of the School Food Plan) or the individual and planet (in the case of the CSB) first.

The problem may well not be capitalism itself but the way in which we are currently incentivized to use it. The values we adopt as human agents determine our behaviours. If we can learn to value meaning, and to see the making of money as an enabler rather than a goal, perhaps we can begin to change the course of the supertanker our society has become.

Every Master Needs a Master

If, as a CEO, I have to be a role model for Leon's people, it's only fair that I should tell you a bit about one of mine, who to me was like the older shaman I described in the chapter on Simplicity (the one who said about the younger, flashier one 'he hasn't learned yet') – the late brand 'guru' Wally Olins. We had many rich conversations over the years, and I am not just better at business as a result, I am richer in spirit.

Wally certainly saw the value of making money – he made some here and there, lost some here and there – but his biggest preoccupation was always his craft. He advised many big companies on their brand positioning and he and his brilliant partner Michael Wolff, who I have recently been very fortunate to get to know too, created – and elsewhere recreated – some of the most interesting corporate brands in the 1980s, 1990s and 2000s, as well as publishing seminal books on the subject. And he advised me on the rebranding of Whyte & Mackay and on Leon.

Like all of us, Wally was no saint, but he knew who he was and was a master of his craft. Where younger brand people sought to create complicated 'brand onions', with a long list of core benefits, USPs, functional benefits, emotional benefits, core values, conceptual benefits, and on and on and on, Wally explained brands in plain English with short but whole sentences. He relied not on data but on his unconscious and his intuition.

And he taught me a valuable lesson: the master stays an apprentice for as long as they can. Warren Buffett said that the key to life is knowing whose bag to carry. People we perceive to be the masters of their trade have spent many years putting aside ego and learning from others.

Today, many people are obsessed with getting to the top quickly. The true master will be patient. And will serve their own masters with humility. Be prepared to be the person in the room who takes the notes. It is not beneath you.

A year ago, I met Michael Markowitz. In many ways, he's something of an American Wally. And he has helped me bring the Leon brand even more into focus, which has coincided with the completion of this book in a powerful way. For quite a portion of its writing, Julian and I borrowed a beach house on Florida's east coast, where we'd work and train in Wing Tsun. I carry a notebook to all our training sessions, and one morning, as we discussed how we'd describe the path through the Four Doors, I wrote, 'Wing Tsun provides a journey from separation to wholeness.'

An hour later, we stopped and I checked my emails. At the exact same moment I had written that down, Michael had emailed me out of the blue. 'I have been thinking,' he wrote, 'and bear with me here because it might be a little bit left field, but I think that the Leon mission is best described as *nourishing the journey towards wholeness.*'

The Master as Destroyer

I have noticed a pattern when it comes to the building and unmaking of movements. Often a master will choose to destroy the movement they have created. Wally, for example, helped create – or certainly formalize – the rules for corporate branding from the 1970s to the 2000s. By the time we worked together, around 1998, Wally was beginning to look beyond the rules he had helped create. 'Branding has become bullying,' he said. 'Brands impose their identity on the high street with no sensitivity to the architecture or feel of the place or the people who live there. And there is no space for self-expression or creativity.'

Brand books or visual guidelines published in, say, Seattle (like Starbucks') set down how a designer of a coffee shop in Cheltenham or Shanghai or Brixton should design the external and internal identity of the shop. Both Wally and I wanted to rewrite this script, and we recognized that in understanding (or, in Wally's case, having helped create) the rules, we were in a better position to break them.

'Branding' specialists have a tendency to construct brands from the outside, and consciously. With smart visual identities and rationalized ideas. While in reality strong brands grow for the most part unconsciously from the inside out. I think that Wally came to increasingly recognize this, and wanted Leon to have the opportunity to do so. Wally was tearing up some of the rules he had helped to write.

As a result, when we created Leon in 2004, we wanted to give freedom to designers to reflect both the local dynamic and energy of the location, and their personal take within a set of parameters that defined the personality of Leon – but with much more freedom and sensitivity than brands are typically allowed. This is what led to there being no one Leon logo, and each restaurant having its own feel in terms of frontage and interior design.

The master can be Brahma the creator, Vishnu the operator and, in this case, Shiva the destroyer.

The desire for masters to challenge and reinvent the movement they have created is made more intense by an Enneagram Eight because our biggest fear is being controlled by others. We can therefore feel constrained by the very people we work with and by the organization we have created. We have taught the rules of the game and we are then surprised that we're expected to live by them. 'Screw that,' we say. 'No one's going to control us.' So we might create a rival company or a rival movement – or worse, destroy what we have created from within.

In Wally's case, destruction was a force for good, like the forest fire that clears the way for new growth. But for it to be so, we must – as we have seen – understand our dark or shadow side.

When I was separated from Leon from 2009 to 2012, I created a new brand called Flat Planet. I intended it to be radical and disruptive, a brand that could tackle many of our economic and social challenges. When I came back to help at Leon in 2012, I stopped working on it. But, for a while, I was quite happy for it to grow into something bigger than Leon.

What's My 'Mastery'?

I do not believe I am a master in the sense of master as imagined expert. Rather, I believe that I am trying to practise mastery and therefore to identify and focus on what exactly it is that I love doing and that I'm good at doing.

I believe that the roots and inspiration for what we should attempt to master – i.e. to practise – based on our passions and capabilities, are there to be seen in our late teenage years. Or maybe sooner. At university, I organized and promoted dance events with the founders of the British drinks brand Innocent. Richard Reed spent his holiday writing out TV-inspired ideas for names and brands for our events, including 'Rainbow' (inspired by the British children's programme) and 'Freeway' (tagline 'When They Met It Was Murder' – prizes for guessing the title of the TV show he was referencing). He couldn't stop himself; to ask him not to would be to ask a dog not to bark. Adam Balon volunteered to be in charge of drinks purchasing and sales. He drove his car to the cash and carry, and made sure that we sold the drinks at the event. (Jon Wright, the third founder of Innocent, was at this time the Treasurer of the May Ball.)

Wind the clock forward nearly a decade to Innocent's launch – in fact, wind it even further forward to the day they sold the company – and they played the same roles they did at university: Richard was responsible for the brand and the marketing at Innocent, Adam for sales and distribution of the drinks, and Jon was the company's organizational and financial backbone.

So I think it's probable that the roots of who you are and what you want to master are to some degree found in the 19-year-old you. If I look back even earlier, to my school years, I tended to be the one who was agitated at the thought that things were not as they should be. Be it the way events were organized at school, how athletics training was run, or how disciplinary sanctions were handed out by prefects, I wanted to make these things *better*.

As an Enneagram Challenger, I . . . challenged . . . and I was able to offer alternative ways in which they could be done.

Whether it's in organizing events, captaining athletics at school, skippering yachts when I was 16, organizing our first-ever school yearbook, creating a rival event to the May Ball at Cambridge, turning around Max Factor at P&G, re-engineering consumer brands at Bain, organizing events at Bain, turning around Whyte & Mackay, starting Leon, or helping invest in and grow an Ethiopian beer business, there is a repeatable skill that I believe I have been attempting to master.

My Jungian Insights profile begins by saying that 'John has a natural instinct for spotting trends and future developments, often before others are remotely aware of them.' But it ends with: 'He feels constantly drawn to begin many projects, yet by failing to complete many of them he allows his energies, inspirations and insights to become dissipated.'

Which explains to me why I used to be a Dabbler. And still have the potential to be so. My Enneagram Seven-wing explains this too. (Both the Enneagram and the Insights profiles describe the conscious self we have created as well as hinting at the unconscious, spontaneous, true self that lies underneath – but as you see here my Jungian Insights profile understands the truth that my instinctive self can see the 'future' before most.)

Even when I was spreading myself too thin as a Dabbler, there was a thread of mastery running throughout. I am not an administrator or an analyst, nor a great manager. My repeatable thing is this: I exercise a vision, select a team and create an environment in which they can flourish. And as I have hinted above, and outlined more in the section about corporate dabbling versus transferable mastery, it is this skill that I see as my mastery more than running

Leon. So if I can run Leon and still follow this Dharma, great. But if it means doing this in other ways or in new businesses I must be true to that. Sometimes what can be perceived as dabbling is actually the practice of mastery, if it is the same repeated skill.

It is now my job to continue to bring myself back to the present moment and be comfortable in who I am. And it is, of course, your job to do the same for you. I am comfortable that I am not the best administrator or the best manager. But with continued practice, I want to create a situation where I can be free enough to have and exercise a vision, and to share it with those around me.

I believe that my ability to see a brighter, more positive future is something I have been able to improve and develop repeatedly. And I believe that, in attempting to develop this mastery, I am not just using my rational mind. I have come to things indirectly, when I am relaxed enough to best use my peripheral vision. And I have learned to trust, in those precious moments of clarity that lie between sleep and waking, that my subconscious will paint the picture my rational brain needs to see. Like 'If God did fast food' for Leon, 'Taste island life' for Jura, 'Express masculinity' for Whyte & Mackay, 'Connoisseurship' for The Dalmore.

The big picture comes to me at once, not in some flash of genius but because I have practised trusting my subconscious. I have practised the power of not forcing, the power of staying relaxed, the power of being yourself, the power of being in the present, the power of tapping into your unconscious brain, and of keeping things simple. And I have learned to balance enough creative constraint with the right amount of creative freedom.

Mastery also requires you to know the boundaries of your abilities. I have a repeatable ability to visualize new concepts in detail. But this only goes so far. I can conceptually see a new business in my head. I can see with clarity the way I want to communicate its brand through design and visual identity. But I do not have the ability to take a building and turn it into a restaurant that works. That is why I am blessed to have partners like Adam Blaker, the Leon property director. Where I can visualize a brand, Adam can visualize space. He can see and then create a restaurant that works, from something you'd think could never function.

The Greatest Street Sweeper

After one Winning Not Fighting conference, one of the Leon managers said to me, 'How do you know all this stuff?' I genuinely didn't know the answer. But I have been reflecting on the question. I think the answer is that I treat every meeting, every experience and every conversation that I have with anybody as a chance to enhance my thinking. I see every opportunity as a chance to learn my craft.

When I was last in New York on a scouting visit for Leon, I went to the same restaurant two nights running. On the first night, the toilet attendant was sullen and clearly did not want to be there. The next night, there was a different man on shift. He was cheery, and took every opportunity to do whatever he was doing well – be it folding the towels or arranging the soaps – and he engaged with each guest as an equal.

Martin Luther King put it like this: 'If a man is called to be a street sweeper, he should sweep streets even as a Michelangelo painted, or Beethoven composed music or Shakespeare wrote poetry. He should sweep streets so well that all the hosts of heaven and earth will pause to say, "Here lived a great street sweeper who did his job well." '

This is mastery.

Singin' in the Rain

At Leon I am always thinking about how to shrink what Leon does as much as possible, almost to the point that it stops being 'Leon'. If I just sold the baked fries, it would no longer be Leon. But I could probably take the menu down to 17 items, and still be happy that it represents who we are. When I ask myself what is the repeatable thing that I can do at Leon to lead the company, I try and shrink it as much as I can.

Here I have a certain master of the silver screen in mind: the director Stanley Donen, who received an honorary Oscar in 1997. At nine years old, he saw his first musical – *Flying Down to Rio*, with Fred Astaire and Ginger Rogers. And it set him on a journey that would lead him to directing arguably the best movie musical of all time, *Singin' in the Rain*. If you have never seen it, be prepared to witness mastery expressed in light, music and dance.

In his acceptance speech, he gave a small insight into how he did it:

> I'm going to let you in on the secret of being a good director. For the script, you get Larry Gelbart, or Peter Stone, or Huyck and Katz, or Frederic Raphael. Like that. If it's a musical, for the songs you get George and Ira Gershwin, or Arthur Freed and Herb Brown, or Leonard Bernstein, and Comden and Green, or Alan Lerner and Fritz Loewe. Like that. And then you cast Cary Grant, or Audrey Hepburn, Fred Astaire, Gene Kelly, Sophia Loren, Richard Burton, Rex Harrison, Gregory Peck, Elizabeth Taylor, Burt Reynolds, Gene Hackman, or Frank Sinatra! Like that. And when filming starts you show up and you stay the hell outta the way. But you gotta show up. You've gotta show up, otherwise you can't take the credit and get one of these fellas.

All of them, masters of their craft.

I find this inspiring because it speaks to what I think my mastery needs to be at Leon: to have a vision for a future, to bring in the best people I can, teach them the Wing Tsun principles contained in this book, and give them the room to flourish. Which, it turns out, is what Gene Kelly did with Donen, apart from the Wing Tsun bit. They met in New York on the Broadway production of *Pal Joey*. Kelly was the star; Donen a hoofer in the chorus line. But Kelly saw Donen's potential, and took him out west with him when Hollywood called.

'Show up and stay out of the way' is probably the best explanation of how we foster mastery at Leon.

From 1-ness to Oneness

Draw a circle on the right-hand side of a blank piece of paper. Then ask: what does it mean to you?

A wedding ring? Completeness? Totality? The score achieved by the typical Norwegian Eurovision entry? A dinner plate?

I go with oneness, because the circle has been used in many cultures to signify the whole. Recognizing that all things are in one place at one time. It is a notion inherent in Taoism.

Now, on the left-hand side, draw the number 1. What does this mean to you? Perhaps 'I'? Or being number 1?

I call it 1-ness, as introduced earlier in this chapter. It is very different from the circle's oneness. It is about 'looking after number 1'. It is about ego and separation. Understanding this in the First Door is very important: you need to know where and how you are separate from and different from others. But you need to know too how you are connected, and part of a whole.

Mastery recognizes the dualistic and simultaneous need for both, held together in harmony.

Each Door and each wisdom of Wing Tsun has provided you

with a new lesson as you progress. You keep each lesson with you as you move forward. And you find yourself winning.

Now the Fourth Door reveals that there is no door, there is no game. Mastery requires you to give up the fruits of your win. And as you do this, you will feel not separation, but will experience more connection to everyone else, and to the planet.

The circle is the symbol that represents the Fourth Door. It serves to remind us that we are, and come from, one thing. It reminds us of the connection between mind, body and spirit. Between gut and brain. It recognizes that our body and mind mirror each other. It is a symbol of what Jung calls psychic totality – the coming together and balancing of our conscious and unconscious, and the balancing of whatever is our own superior function (e.g. thinking) with the 'hidden gold' of our inferior function (in that case, feeling). It reminds us of our true relationship with each other and our world and hints that there is no separation between past, present and future.

And the circle is love. Not that fake comfort blanket for the emotionally needy, but an idea that links everything in one thing. A synonym for wholeness.

We Are Dying from Separation

I am struck by the idea that today no one person knows how to make a pencil. No one person on the manufacturing line knows how to make an entire car. The process requires many different people doing different bits along the way. Businesses have been built on outsourcing or on breaking down each individual part of a manufacturing line so that one person is doing one particular task, like installing wing mirrors on a car, all day.

Modern business, by which I mean business as currently taught in many business schools, is actually built on separation. We mustn't confuse mastery with excessive specialization.

Whatever you choose to master will *add up to something* whole in and of itself. The person who does one step in a manufacturing line is not a master. Someone who can make a whole pencil is.

This idea of separation really struck me when we were working on the School Food Plan. We were attempting to replace that with a 'whole school' approach to food, as we've seen. It's a process that has left me with a question: how do we move from separation to wholeness?

Since the School Food Plan, Henry has worked with his own school, Gayhurst Primary School in Hackney, where one of the chefs from the famous Ottolenghi group in London, Nicole Pisani, has taken her skills into the school kitchen. Gayhurst provides a fantastic case study (though not a perfect one) for anyone looking to bring their catering in-house. Nicole stood by the bins to see what was being wasted, and asked the kids why. She has worked hard to solve this conundrum of how to provide food that kids like that will also do them good. And how to make food central to school life.

Hers is a practical example of going from separation to wholeness, an approach that we need to rediscover across society. Soon.

Actually, right now.

Even without adding the adversarial nature of politics, or the way that rich people separate themselves from others in their mega-yachts, or in their gated communities with their private security guards to keep the rest of us out, we see that we are no closer to finding and reconnecting the shards of the shattered vase. The desire to hoard, to spend £250k or more on watches, is a disease of the mind and an extreme distortion of ego. The irony is that the more we hoard, the more we are destroying the natural capital, the shared abundance of natural wealth and beauty, that we inherited. We are committing generational theft because our ego is out of control.

We have on a wall in our office these words from Jung: 'Where love rules, there is no will to power, and where power predominates, love is lacking.'

Love as Wholeness

This is the section where my wife Katie and my mum Marion have given me the sternest talking to. Loving, but stern. 'It's pretty dense,' they say. The trouble is that I feel I'm only just scratching the surface of the relationship between love and wholeness. And it is pretty important!

Repeatedly, through different philosophies and religions, we see a thread, a concept, that supports the Wing Tsun idea that the Fourth Door offers wholeness, one-ness and love. And that it is man's task to achieve or regain wholeness.

In Plato's *Symposium* the comic poet Aristophanes argues that 'Love is the name of our pursuit of wholeness, for our desire to be complete'. He then spins a fable about how, in the distant past, humans existed as conjoined pairs until the gods split them in half. Thus we are condemned to spend our lives seeking our 'other half'. And thus our pursuit of love is a yearning to reconnect, to regain our lost wholeness.

Plato uses Aristophanes to describe love as the drive to rediscover wholeness: 'Love is born into every human being. It calls back the halves of our original nature together. It tries to make one out of two and heal the wound of human nature.'

He suggests that, in some mythical time and place, we knew the wholeness we seek. And such archetypes repeat across religions, many of them defined in this time period, named the Axial Age by the German philosopher Karl Jaspers. Broadly concurrently, Plato writes down his memories of the philosopher Socrates in Greece; Zoroastrianism is born in Persia; Siddhartha Gautama creates Buddhism; and Confucianism and Taoism arise in China.

The concept that Aristophanes and his fellow guests were discussing is that of 'Eros', the root of the word 'erotic'. But the meaning goes way beyond what we may today understand. There is something more spiritual and noble than simple physical desire in the word. Contemporary sociologist James Hunter has described the role that Eros plays across our life. The relationship between Eros and sexual pleasure, of course, but just as importantly, the one between Eros and all types of human relationships, between Eros and the creation and maintenance of a family, between Eros and personal psychological growth. He argues, in the *Journal of Religion and Health*, that if we neglect any of these connections we ignore what makes us 'whole' as a human: 'We become empty when our understanding of love is not informed by a clear vision of the wholeness towards which it aims.'

There is a belief in modern Judaism, rooted in its ancient mysticism, that mirrors the *Symposium*'s notion that love is synonymous with wholeness. *Tikkun olam*, which roughly means 'repairing the world', describes the idea that life is about acting with love and kindness in order to rejoin the shattered pieces of broken vessels, and thus to make them and the world whole once more. It derives from something you might have read before . . . and no, it's not by Oscar Wilde . . . 'Let there be light.'

According to the myth, God sent forth ten vases, or vessels, filled with light he had breathed into them, only for them to shatter on their way, scattering both light and shards of the vases. Your job in life, apparently, is to find the pieces and superglue them back together. Which is one for the weekend to-do list.

Buddhism, too, places the instinct to return to wholeness at the heart of its thinking. The cause of suffering (Dukkha), Buddhism explains, is 'Anatman', a sense of separation. We suffer because we crave things and because we see ourselves as separate from each other and from nature. Living in a gated community with CCTV is not in my opinion a sign of being wealthy but of being in spiritual pain: on some level people who live in these houses are suffering. They may not be consciously aware of it, but their subconscious knows for sure. When Wendy lived in Nairobi, hers was the only house on the road that did not have security or gates, and it was the only house that did not get burgled. A rich city is not one where the rich drive expensive cars, it is one where the rich take the bus.

In Christian thinking, atonement is the act of becoming one with others and with God by making amends . . . and yes, it does mean 'at-one-ment', just like your religious studies teacher told you, though its specific derivation is from medieval Latin – *adunamentum*, meaning 'unity'. And as the great Bono said, 'We're one, but we're not the same. We get to carry each other.' And the wise prophet Johnny Cash agreed.

Jung, too, was informed by an understanding of wholeness. As we grow older, he writes, we understand and experience the union of both masculine and feminine resulting in a larger, richer self. 'Man's wholeness,' he continues, 'consists in the union of the conscious and the unconscious personality. Just as every individual derives from masculine and feminine genes, so in the psyche it is only the conscious mind, in a man, that has the masculine sign, while the unconscious is by nature feminine. The reverse is true in the case of a woman.' In Jung's thinking, Eros takes on a new and potentially more creative meaning when understood as a drive towards wholeness, especially in later life. As one seeks a union between the masculine and feminine aspects of one's nature, one can bring about a larger, richer self.

Here, in love, in this notion of wholeness, lies Mastery. Love is the end and the means.

Shine Bright Like a Diamond – Your Mastery Serves All

One of many paradoxes of the wisdom of Mastery is that the more you focus on one thing, the more you find you are serving the whole, and the more connected you become to the whole.

There is a Hindu fable that describes the universe as a series of jewels held together and interconnected by string. Each jewel shines with its own innate brilliance, and with the reflection and refraction of the other jewels. Each jewel must be its own true self to help create the whole. The universe is well, this fable teaches, when everyone lives and acts in tune with their own true nature and lives spontaneously in accordance with who they truly are, and they must be allowed to do so without interference. The more you are you and the more others are themselves, the more the 'whole' is in balance.

Do not try to compete with the brilliance of others. You are serving the whole by being you and by recognizing and celebrating (not trying to compete with or diminish) the value of others.

Just as the tree trunk looks as if it is separate from the leaf, or from the apple, the whole thing is really one. I reflect often on the idea that humans' problems started when Adam and Eve started naming things – *apple, branch, root* – and created a sense of separation that undermined their sense of whole. At the same time the tree, the garden, the land, the universe – all need each item within them to do its job as part of the whole. By mastering the thing that is your passion or your Dharma, you are not being selfish. The leaf is not being selfish by not being a root. Everything would stop working if we all tried to become something that we are not. Mastery feeds wholeness.

This paradox of mastery explains that, to achieve wholeness, you must look inside and understand yourself. You are a mirror of – a hologram of – the whole universe. Just as a reflexologist believes (or perhaps knows) that the foot is a representation of the whole body, you are a representation of the whole universe. The solutions to the problems of the planet are inside you. Just as your demons are inside you, just as the shadow is inherent in you, so are the ways to achieve wholeness and to choose love. Wing Tsun is special among martial arts because it recognizes this. When you realize that there is no one else to blame, you achieve liberation. When you face the Wooden Dummy, you realize that when you face the world you are only facing yourself.

The reality is that, just by being you and immersing yourself in the practice unconsciously and in the present moment, you are not only doing what will bring enjoyment, happiness and fulfilment for yourself, you are doing the most powerful thing you can to achieve wholeness and help others – without forcing. You will inspire others in ways that you are not even aware of. People will be drawn to invite you to participate in all sorts of projects because you are being true to who you are.

The *Tao Te Ching* describes it like this: 'If you have truly attained wholeness, everything will flock to you.'

In leading Leon, or rather in trying to create an environment where everyone can be a leader, I am mindful of the role I have in encouraging everyone to reveal their true selves. In Don't Force, I described the danger of forcing yourself to be something that you're not. People who persistently do this at Leon do not stay. Authenticity is critical. If everyone is open about what size and shape jigsaw piece they are, the better I can solve the giant jigsaw puzzle that is Leon. Carl Jung said that 'the privilege of a lifetime is to become who you truly are'; the opportunity to achieve this is what I seek to give people at Leon.

Count to 10,000: A Game of Hindu Hide-and-Seek

While Zen and its parents, Buddhism and Taoism, see the universe as unconscious and growing from within, Hinduism approaches the idea of separation from the standpoint of God. It sees the universe as God playing hide-and-seek with himself. Without sounding flippant, it is based on the idea that God got bored being by himself (with no iPhone, I guess, to keep him occupied, or maybe no Wi-Fi) and decided to split himself into 'separate' things to understand what it might be like to try to divide himself or lose himself. (*Coming, ready or not!*) So when a Hindu says 'I am Brahma', he is not saying 'Hey, get me, I have become God' – he is saying that he and everyone and everything else around us *is* God. And when you are truly you, you are being the exact part of God you are supposed to be.

Beyond the Self-Ideal

When we passed through the Third Door, we explored Alfred Adler's concept of the self-ideal – the idea you have created of the you you'd like to be. We talked about choosing positive coping mechanisms and of readjusting your self-ideal, if helpful, to something more realistic.

Here we are going to take this further. To achieve wholeness, do away with the self-ideal. It's totally made up, anyway. It may have been helpful in motivating you to win the game. Now you know there is no game. This self-ideal is a story that you have told yourself and must not be confused with the true self that is always within you.

The pursuit of your self-ideal is one of the 'fruits' that mastery invites you to give up. The irony is that the more you give them up, the more likely you are to achieve them. And the more you realize you do not need them, the less you will value them if you do achieve them.

You have, Wing Tsun says, a true nature that is revealed and experienced when you do away with the self-ideal. You experience it when you stop trying to control or force, and when you allow things to flow in and around you. Living both in the present moment and less consciously. At this point, you show the truth of what size and type of gem you are.

Whole, Not Homogenous

Mastery does not require us to give up our individuality. In fact, it encourages us to embrace it. For it is only by being the best individual we can be that we serve the whole. What we must do is to remember that, although we are distinct, we are not separate.

Thus, wholeness does not demand we create a homogenous global culture, nor every high street be an identical replica of every other high street with the same identikit shops. Differences do not need to lead to a 'them vs us' dynamic. And in rejecting aggressive nationalism, we must not lose the value – and necessity – of each country being confident in its own culture, and contributing to the world in a way that respects its own contribution. (Jokes that start 'A European, a European and a European walk into a bar' won't quite have the same effect.) The more each country knows what or who it is, and can specialize in doing best what it does best – in terms of skills and expertise – the more we will create a world of wholeness. Wholeness is not putting your starter, main and pudding in the blender and serving it as a smoothie. It lies in celebrating the difference between each course.

And just as a capitalist system built on ego and separation must not be our future – or rather is not a sustainable future – nor is socialism, with its suppression of competition and its futile attempts to limit distinctness or the ability of the individual to grow or blossom. And in schools, do not try to create games lessons where nobody 'wins'. This is not wholeness. Let the fastest runner show themselves and others what they can do, just as the scientist will discover the wonder of their capabilities. And speaking of races, let's stop political correctness getting in the way of recognizing the special and innate talents that people from different cultures and countries can bring to the table. Yes, we must not stereotype, but we can and must create a wholeness where differences and unique contributions are not ignored.

A Separate Summary

The idea that we separate things in our mind that are not truly separate has two strands.

In the first, the suggestion is that, in our minds, we divide things that are actually one distinct thing. For example, we divide land into acres or distance into metres or history into defined time periods. Or, as I have explained, we separate things like 'apple', 'branch' 'trunk' or 'root' that are part of a whole (like a tree or forest).

In the second, the suggestion is that all of the objects and things that we see as distinct are in fact from one source. In Hinduism, as we have seen, they are all God playing hide-and-seek with himself; in Taoism they at the same time are, and are from, the 'eternal Tao', which is the nothingness that scientists today might equate with the form of the universe before the Big Bang.

Mastery is Now . . . and Here

Many people go to India, or some other exotic place, to find themselves. The reality is that you don't need to take yourself somewhere to find yourself. You are geographically pretty close to the real you already. Our daughter Natasha has, as I write this, just left school. She had the choice to go travelling, but instead chose to help direct a musical of *The Addams Family* at her old school. After the last night, she said, 'I've learned so much more directing this show than I think I would have done by travelling.'

As it turns out, we went to India for the first time last year. And, as part of our trip, I wanted to take a detour to Sarnath, the place where Buddha gave his first sermon after his enlightenment. I wanted to get a feeling of the place, to see if I might find a little bit of the something that his followers felt or understood. And you know what struck me as I stood under the tree where Buddha preached?

Nothing.

Not. A. Thing.

The irony is that all of the people we met in India talked of visiting this certain magical place that they had heard about and seen images of. They hoped one day they might be able to save enough money to visit this far-off promised place. Maybe to find themselves.

The place?

London.

It struck me that we might all be looking for salvation in the wrong places. Wing Tsun suggests we look within. That, to practise mastery, you have whatever you need inside you, and wherever you are right now.

From A to Zen

The Fourth Door of Wing Tsun is deeply influenced by Zen Buddhism and its idea that we achieve a state of enlightenment when we stop the mind trying to chase itself round in circles, and when we stop using our thinking brain and our ego to control, classify and measure the world around us.

Zen can, especially to the person who has just discovered it, sound like semantics that leave you tangled up in knots. And in a funny way it is.

Zen Buddhism is a dialogue, between the master and the student. And it can at times sound like a riddle. But the point is that you will never find sanity through words or literal discussion. You can edge closer to the answer, but when you finally reach the point of true understanding, words will become unnecessary. They are inadequate.

It is just such a dialogue that we encourage the Leon managers to have with their teams, and the dialogue that I have with the managers and the other Leaders of Leon.

Consider this response from one of the leading students of one of the great Zen masters when asked 'What is Zen?'

'Zen is just a trick of words.' That is to say, it seeks to confound the practitioner, to tie them in knots, with the ultimate goal of showing them the danger of confusing words, and conventional notions, with reality.

Central to Zen, and to the Mahayana school of Buddhism that influenced it, is the conviction that as soon as we have to name, classify or measure something, we lose it. That our words, and the conventions we create in order to be able to have a common ground to discuss, agree or argue about things, create an abstraction and distortion of the thing itself. Thus when Buddha was to explain what he had discovered in becoming enlightened, he merely pointed at a flower, believing, as Zen does, that any rational conversation about the truth of life and humanity is bound to fail because of the inadequacy and misleading nature of words.

Words, either gently descriptive or deeply scientific, allow the ego to think it is in charge of the situation, or in charge of emotion, or in charge of nature – just as classifying species gives us a subconscious reassurance that we are the supreme beings. But all words and all classifications are doomed to inadequacy, given both the complexity and impermanence of nature. Things must simply be experienced, with as little judgement as possible, exactly as they are.

In the same way, Zen believes that our desire to measure things necessarily creates subdivisions and separation that does not exist.

When Zen talks about enlightenment, or the revelation that is called Satori, it means the sudden or gradual process of understanding your true nature, your real self. It is a self that Zen says was always there. You do not become transformed, you just free that real self from the prison of your conscious brain and from all the false ideas it has created. And, as part of this, one realizes that what they thought was separate is really whole. Zen refers to the word *maya* to describe all of the objects and animals that we see around us. What Taoism calls the 'ten thousand things'.

When somebody experiences Satori, it is said that he or she suddenly realizes that *maya* is an illusion. This does not mean that we suddenly find ourselves, like in *The Matrix*, seeing the world digitally collapse into a bright foggy nothingness. It means we see that we have separated in our minds things that were really part of a whole. Because *maya* is the very act of measuring and falsely separating and classifying things into little drawers that don't exist. The word is related to the Sanskrit *mata*. From which we English-speakers have via other languages inherited the terms 'measure', 'metre', 'material', 'matter', 'metrics' and, yes, 'matrix'.

This process of measuring and dividing breaks whole things down into parts that we feel we can comprehend and 'own'. Thus we are dividing things. The Sanskrit word *dvar* (related to the English words 'divide' and 'duo' and 'dual') describes the process of breaking things down into bits – at least as we perceive it.

This extends beyond physical measurements to how we perceive events and ideas. In a lecture where he explained our desire to date things, Alan Watts challenged whether it can truly be said that World War One began on 28 July 1914 and ended on 11 November 1918, given that the roots of the war can be traced back to many earlier events and that the war continues to have ramifications today.

The fact is that, however reassuring or convenient or expedient we find measuring, dividing and classifying, it is doomed to only ever create a misleading sense of reality.

Satori, then, is not so much like putting on weird goggles and seeing things in a strange light where everything disappears and merges, it is that we see the same things but they now have new meaning. We realize that what we thought was separate is actually whole. We realize that all of the ten thousand things really are, at the same time, one thing. Rather than the dual idea that they are at the same time many and one, it is more that they were never truly separate in the first place – that we created a false sense of separation.

There is clearly something in our collective unconscious, in our shared archetypes, that creates the constant preoccupation to re-find wholeness and move beyond our sense of separation. It is perhaps the ancient memory of a time before we created consciousness and speech, and thus created this false sense of separation.

Phew!

Buddhism describes three states that we experience before we finally achieve the release that it calls Nirvana. The first is Dukkha. There are lots of words that we can use to try to describe this. 'Suffering' is often a favourite. Or 'sorrow'. Or 'the frustration that comes from grasping and desiring'. It is sometimes said that life is fundamentally 'suffering', and that we need to get real about it. However, I have come to the conclusion that this is a misunderstanding. It is more that *the way that most people live their lives* leads to suffering, and that this is not inevitable.

The second is Anitya. This is the truth that the more we

grasp, the less likely we are to achieve anything. The world is transitory, impermanent. It is certainly uncontrollable. It is like us trying to overtake our own shadow, or like a donkey trying to bite the carrot dangling in front of its nose.

Now we get to some better-sounding stuff. The third truth is Anatman, the ability to get 'beyond self'. It is not that you don't exist, it's just a realization that your mind cannot understand itself any more than a hand can grasp itself. Yes, we have made many breakthroughs in psychology. But no matter how far we get, Zen says, we will never get far enough. The mind will exhaust itself trying to understand itself. And the mind can't force itself to see itself. There is no 'self' that can be understood or grabbed hold of by measuring, analysing or creating conventions that we can discuss and understand. At this stage, one has achieved Wu Shin – no-mindedness. And here, being out of your mind ain't a bad thing. (I may have to leave this bit with you to . . . NOT think about.)

Then there is Nirvana. It has no direct translation, but I like Alan Watts's description that it is like the exhalation of relief. Like '*Phew!*' The moment of release when you stop trying to grasp your own mind. And stop trying to use thought to understand thought. It is the point when you become unconscious again, and learn to access and trust a true self that is unencumbered by conscious thought. Zen cherishes spontaneity, the childlike self that is not confounded by the distortions of thinking. Nirvana reveals a true world that is whole and not separate. A true you.

But, crucially, both this world and the real you were always there. Satori is not seeing another world or a transformed you. It reveals what was always present. It is the world that we can only point at and not describe. If we do, we use the word *tut* ('that'), which is the first word of a baby as it points to something in the very first stages of consciousness. It is the gentlest way we can introduce a sound without taking away from the full reality of the thing itself. Things are 'thus'. And rather than experiencing life as rapture, we experience the relief of realizing that life, and we, are 'nothing special'.

We have achieved in this state *moksha*, which is liberation from *maya*, the false world of measured and explained things.

Zen is somehow often seen as a state of perfection. But it is only a permission to be perfectly as we truly are. Unlike most monotheistic religions, Zen and Wing Tsun have no mistrust of our innate nature. Our true self is something to be uncovered and released. And it is not a state to be achieved to then achieve something else. It is 'it'.

Deeply Practical

Understanding the experience of many people who believe they have achieved this bliss, the *'Phew!'* of release (we may call them the lucky phew*), is one way of glimpsing the state that one experiences in Nirvana. And to know that Zen goes beyond confusing wordplay.

What takes us beyond the semantics of the Zen dialogue is the very practical nature of Zen. And here Wing Tsun plays a key role in rooting both Taoism and Zen Buddhism in something physical and real. By *doing*, we understand more than we can by *talking* or *being shown*. And the more we practise with the Wooden Dummy, the more we will understand our true self and the more we will achieve no-mindedness.

By engaging with the world practically and physically, through Wing Tsun or any other activity that involves the hands and our senses, we experience the world exactly as it is. Farmers, fishermen, firemen, it is said, can often glean more wisdom than mere academics.

---

* I am pleased with that one, which shows you how far I must be from letting go of ego today . . .

In the Buddhism that is most practised in southern Asia ('Theravada Buddhism') the most revered Buddha ('enlightened one') is one who stays away in a monastery. In northern, Mahayana Buddhism, which influences Wing Tsun, this is seen as all rather selfish. The Chinese admire most the Buddha who returns to society and honours their responsibility to their family and community. The Chinese way is deeply practical.

Wing Tsun provides the combination of what one might call spiritual aspiration with a realistic appreciation of how the majority of humans are 'programmed'. So while it offers in the Fourth Door the ability to understand and hopefully experience being Beyond Self, it recognizes that we begin our journey at the First Door full of mental maps that separate us from our true selves, and that, in beginning our journey, we are seeking, desiring and grasping. Perhaps we want to get fit, or to feel more secure when out and about. And this is why Wing Tsun brings us full circle, back to the First Door, so that it may reveal not only how far we have come, but that we have reached a Nirvana because we never knew that *that* was what we were doing.

In this, we realize that Wing Tsun has taken us through a graduated process where our definition of winning changes at each step. Where first winning required 'the fruits', now it does not. Thus ego no longer clouds our true self, and we are set free.

The Acid Test

There is no better test of your ideas than standing in front of 200 or so new Leon people. I attempt to boil into words (an impossible task, as we have seen) that we try to create a vibe and environment in which people can begin the process of putting themselves aside.

I explain that, at Leon, people will bestow on them new knowledge. And rules (how to make a dish in a way that is precise and keeps the customer safe; when to come to work; how to use a knife . . .). And that despite our very best efforts to describe the organization like a process flow, not as a top-down hierarchy, people will alas inevitably talk about 'promotions' and 'the boss coming in this afternoon'. I explain to them that this Confucian approach (structures, rules, shared conventional etiquette) is necessary. But that it must not at any stage obscure the true 'them' that they already possess – or 'are' – and that is more powerful than anything Leon can give them. I explain that I hope that Leon can be a place that allows this self to be continuously revealed.

The world of grown-ups can be seen by young people as the 'real' world, where common sense rules and the understandings of youth must be put aside, or discarded as naive or impractical. This must never happen or be presumed. I implore my young Leon colleagues to stay as spontaneous as they can while keeping themselves and the guests safe. To say very loudly if we are doing something that is hurting the guests, each other or the planet.

I will not be able to build an organization that fully achieves this. But I hope I can edge closer and closer.

Shit! I've Forgotten to Meditate

Mastery gives us a practice that allows us to do something that is true to our real self, to engage ourselves unconsciously in the practice (to 'lose ourselves' in the doing) and to be right here in the present, right now. But as we progress through the Doors we must put aside any desire for gain or outcome. Practice must be done for its own sake for it to leave us balanced, not off balance, as we try to grasp what we think may be ahead of us.

You may have a meditation app on your phone that you reach for when you need it. They are often now classified as 'stress relief' or 'for focus and concentration'. Meditation can be used in this way – with a purpose in mind – to help bring focus and concentration or relaxation. Or to contemplate in order to find an answer for something that you would like to solve (yogis meditated on the question of what we need to do to replace desire and landed on the gentler 'aspire'). But not in the Fourth Door. Here it must be experienced purely, without any outcome in mind.

The mind cannot try to focus on or achieve stillness. This must be achieved obliquely, indirectly. Sitting and letting the mind wander, or rather not having any regard for mind, is just 'that'. Just *tut* with no goal. Your mind will not be empty – it will have thoughts flying through it like particles in an atom or stars in space – but you will not be entertaining the thoughts. You will just notice them from a neutral standpoint, choosing wherever you want to be in space to view them from.

Meditation must not be done with the objective of achieving Satori. Satori is not something that can ever be grasped or sought after. It will happen, or not happen, when you stop trying.

Like You, but Just with More Apps

My wife Katie was once talking at an event for schoolchildren with Joanna Lumley. And she came home full of praise for Joanna's ability to communicate and empathize with the children. She had apparently said to the kids, 'I am just the same as you, except I have more apps.' Meaning, of course, that we all share the same operating system, but that we have each added our own apps – our own knowledge and experiences – over time.

The trouble is that we may not have as clean an operating system as Apple. I think we may be more Microsoft. More of an open-source system, prone to viruses.

Nirvana, when we achieve the state of *moksha* that dispels *maya*, is like getting rid of the viruses that have corrupted our operating system.

A Word from Albert Einstein

Perhaps you are totally with me. Perhaps you want to be but have this nagging doubt that I am being naive or that, when you talk about this book at your next dinner party, you might be laughed at by all the 'serious' people there. You know, the realists who do proper jobs in the REAL WORLD. So if you want a little back-up, here's something from the world's greatest-ever physicist (though who's ranking it?), Albert Einstein:

> A human being is part of the whole, called by us 'Universe'; a part limited in time and space. He experiences himself, his thoughts and feelings as something separated from the rest – a kind of optical delusion of his consciousness. This delusion is a kind of prison for us, restricting us to our personal desires and affection for a few persons nearest to us. Our task must be to free ourselves from this prison by widening our circle of compassion to embrace all living creatures and the whole of nature in its beauty.

The End . . .

. . . is really the beginning. And you already know it. Because if you were raised in the East, it is an immediate part of your culture. And if you were raised in the West, it is too. 'A new commandment I give unto you,' said Jesus. 'That you love one another.'

You have now read this book. Julian and I have written it. With these two actions, we three have embarked together on a journey from separation to wholeness. And here, at the journey's apparent end, we have begun again. For we find here, in mastery, a virtuous circle where mastery equals wholeness, which in turn equals love, which equals mastery. Again and again and again.

The *Tao Te Ching* tells us in its very first verse that the Tao is the unnameable nothing from which all things came, come and will come. Unnamed, the Tao is the beginning of heaven and earth. Named, it is the mother of ten thousand things. Ever-desireless, it is mystery. Ever desiring, it becomes manifest. It both is and is not.

In the same way, mastery makes us both a part of and separate from the whole. This is distinct from the notion of separation, from which we have come. Here we are separate in the way a proton is separate from an atom: distinct, but of the whole. A positive held in balance by a negative. A mind balanced by a body; a soul by a spirit; a conscious by an unconscious.

We are both of the universe and a universe in ourselves. When we come to know ourselves, when we become whole and walk a path true to our whole self, we give service to the universe. To do so, we connect our mind, body and spirit, and we balance our conscious and our unconscious to achieve psychic totality. To do so, we must live in the present, knowing that we are respecting and protecting the future. To do so is to remember our right relationship with ourselves, each other and our world. Indeed, with universe.

To do so is a choice.

Choose what you do and what you want based on a conscious understanding of who you are. Practise it without conscious judgement and in a state of unconscious joy, without chasing an outcome. Allow your conscious and unconscious mind to converge, converse and balance without forcing. This is your task: for you, your community, your planet. For you are both the Tao and the ten thousand things at one and the same time.

This way lies mastery, wholeness and love.

You cannot succeed in life without love. You cannot build a successful business if you don't love it. Every day, seven days a week, I go to work at Leon, and I love it. Julian feels the same about Wing Tsun. It is not obsession. With obsession, you make no time for anything else. And karma will catch up with you. I cannot tell you how many people I have seen this happen to.

It turns out that The Beatles were right after all. All you need is love. Although is it blasphemous to say that the tune, while catchy, can get right on your nerves?

Love is wholeness. It requires us to become conscious, to know ourselves, to stay relaxed, to remember our right relationship with others, to not force, to be positive, to keep things simple, to accept our freedoms come with responsibilities, to expect to be punched. And to bring all of this together in a way that recognizes the fundamental paradox that we are at the same time a key part of the whole *and* the whole.

This is your path: to remember your true relationship with yourself, others and the planet. You need it. The planet needs it.

So you need to put ego aside and not be hurt when the people say, 'We did it ourselves.'

When you have and you aren't, *that* will be when you know you are practising mastery.

Acknowledgements

As with any book, this has only been possible thanks to the support of many people. The first person we would like to thank is our editor Martina O'Sullivan at Penguin for providing us with a magical mix of support, clarity, faith, advice and patience, for knowing when to apply strength, and when to guide without forcing.

When we first thought of this book, we rang LEON's cookbook agent Antony Topping and told him what we wanted to write. He told us Penguin was the right publisher. We met them, agreed with him, and they agreed with us. Thank you all.

Thank you to Andrew Davidson and Fred Hogge, who both provided editorial support. Andrew for providing early direction and in particular for encouraging us to break down the chapters into bite-sized paragraphs. Fred – an advert for the 'power of yes' – for helping us get this book in on time for our final-final deadline with a minute to spare.

Our fact-checking and proof-reading heroines, Gemma Wain and Alison Rae, who have been through the manuscript with a magnifying glass and sharp minds. Celia Buzuk for helping with clearances, co-ordination and with the import of the illustrations. And Natalie Wall, the conductor of this mini-orchestra, for wrestling everything out of our hands and into these pages. Matt Crossey for your belief in where we might take this book. And Sam, Nicole and Lucy at Catch Comms, for your disciplined and cheery support.

Many thanks to the gifted Si-Hing Kit Liu for the beautiful illustrations, putting up with frequent last-minute requests for changes and additions with magnanimity and grace.

From John

Happy Fast Friends

In writing this book we have made new friends. They are, in order of appearance . . .

Sir Lawrence Freedman (Emeritus Professor of War Studies at King's College London, author of the seminal book 'Strategy' and military advisor to the UK government) whom you and I encountered in 'The (St)Art of War' chapter will, I hope, agree to have more coffees.

Professor Ranjay Gulati of Harvard Business School, with whom I struck up a conversation while trying to spot leopards in India (they were already spotted, it turned out), gave me important pointers about the history of business's adoption of the war metaphor.

Heather Rook, retired Detective Sergeant in the Met Police and all-round super sleuth, will be a collaborator and friend for many years, I predict.

Psychotherapist Claudia Waldner, she of Mastery/Frankl/ Logotherapy gave me a lot of her precious time and wrote many late-night, post-work, emails for which I am very grateful.

Vanessa Youngman, although not a new friend, has shared her always-expanding knowledge of Jung. Any errors or errant ideas are mine not hers.

My teachers

This book, Leon, and I are the products of many people who continue to teach me many things.

I would like to thank Wendy 'it doesn't not hurt' Mandy. Aimee 'what makes you laugh' Heuzenroeder, and Marion 'that's my mum that is' Vincent.

Steve Head – Mr. Glimpse of Brilliance/Act As If – has provided stories and advice that live everyday in my head, and in the heads of most Leon people, and that make us live and work a little more healthily.

Both the late Wally Olins, and now his business partner Michael Wolff, have provided me with wisdom that I attempt to put to good use and perhaps, in turn, pass on (as in 'hand down', not 'say no thank you' to). Separately, Michael Markowitz reminds me of Wally and has helped give me an important new clarity around Leon's mission to help people re-achieve wholeness – at exactly the same time, to the minute, that Julian and I were coming to the same conclusion.

Donna Lancaster, alongside Wendy, gave us the gift of the Enneagram and much more.

Jane Melvin for the magic moments, and bringing tales and insights from magical kingdoms. You will remember my description and examples of her work on the 'Five Faces of Genius'. Your ability to join the dots and then colour the whole picture in (and even add rhinestones) is unparalleled.

Jimmy Allen for his groundbreaking business advice every time we meet for dinner. And for great personal advice too.

Our wellbeing (one day we will all have to find a less tired word for this essential idea) programme relies on the generous participation of practitioners like Jesse Mandy, Ged Ferguson, Chris Enser, Jorge and Beatriz, and Alex Olds. And the leadership of Laura and Julian.

Thank you to people who wrote about us early on, getting our first Carnaby Street restaurant on the map – Giles Coren, Jay Rayner and Richard Johnson in particular.

My client/colleague/boss/teacher Vivian Imerman for giving me opportunities, lessons and insights that I carry with me.

Steve Coltrin who shares my number one principle for communicating – tell the truth.

Thank you to Chantal for your culinary brilliance in developing Leon food, and in what you do at Leon summer and winter wellbeing events. You will be known by many more people

Acknowledgements

before too long. And thank you Dave, the secret Taoist. And Victoria, the most organised person I know.

I have learnt a lot from my peers Richard Reed, Adam Balon and Jon Wright who built drinks company Innocent – they are an inspiration to me and to many, as was Becky from the Buttery.

Procter & Gamble, Bain and the Whyte and Mackay turnaround provided many teachers including Paul Geddes, Karen Higgins, Stuart Gent, Michele Luzi, Richard Carr, Julian Critchlow.

This book has inevitably been influenced by my teachers at Chase Side Primary School, at Haberdashers' and of my supervisors at Cambridge: Rosemary Kirk, Miss Harper, Miss Bland, Bert Hart, Andrew Rattue, John Lotherington, David Griffiths, Mrs Hackford, Mr Parr (you were right about meat), Mr Hayler (top man), Mr Dawson, Robert Tombs (thank you for the belief), Peter Clarke, and Christopher Andrew.

People who have taught me personal lessons that have informed this book include Matthew Gordon, JP, Yiannis, Evi, Charlie Hayward, Danai, Martin, Miek, Nick and Bob Binnendijk, all the Blakers, Nick Parker, Gabby and Kenny Logan, Lew Kornberg, Dave and Sumi Jeffery, Roger Wright ('and it is a partnership') and Angus Graham and to a huge degree Brad Blum who I mention multiple times in this book.

Some of the Wizards of Westminster

Our work with government has brought us into contact with, and allowed us to work with, many hard-working people.

The ever-popular Michael Gove (whether you like him and his reforming policies or not) is the most effective and hard-working government minister I have met. He has a desire to surround himself with good people and placed his belief and trust in them, and has a knack for working across government to get things done, and a very engaging sense of humour. He is not every voter's cup of tea, but he is refreshing, even on a hot day.

Labour's Sharon Hodgson, with whom we worked on the

School Food Plan, and Lib Dem leader Nick Clegg and minister David Laws also gave vital support to the Plan. Along with Ed Balls, they helped us create unprecedented political consensus for a plan based squarely on love – something I am not sure people expected from 'those two businessmen' (Henry and me). There is a correlation between faith in one's leaders and the happiness of the nation – people would be happier if they knew how much commitment and love and hard work you brought to your roles.

Our work with government as part of the School Food Plan and Council for Sustainable Business has required the active participation of many civil servants and political advisors – Matthew Purves, Nick Barter, Ian Kelly, Emma Howard Boyd, Charlotte Baly and Henry De Zoete are six people I would like to single out for thanks. And Charlotte, thank you for helping with the bit about the squirrels.

Of the business people on the Council for Sustainable Business many have shown particular dedication, giving their time for nothing and in the hope that we can save our planet. I would like to particularly mention Liv Garfield, Eugenie Mathieu, Kate Wylie, Justin Francis, Richard Kirkman and Hayden Wood.

Leon peeps

Although Allegra was at Leon for just a few years and Henry stepped down in 2014, your finger prints and energy will always be a part of any success (correctly defined) that we may enjoy.

Henry is a person of great character. Any room that Henry is in becomes more interesting, and every conversation he is part of sizzles with great potential. Henry, you open up many intellectual avenues that are always worth exploring. Thank you for giving birth to Leon with me.

My colleagues who work hard in our Leon restaurants and in our grocery business every day are the heartbeat of our company – thank you to each one of you. The Mums and Dads, aka managers, are responsible for the safety of their teams and of their guests. You are, as you know, the leaders around which everything does and must revolve.

The team who work with me most closely (Glenn, Adam, Shereen, Antony, Rebecca, Gemma, Erica, Chris, Nick and Nick, Beth, Clara, Lob, Charlotte & Charlotte, Dennis, Phil) thank you for choosing to be part of this and for helping us win. And thank you to your partners who support you and therefore us. Others have contributed much and are no longer at Leon – in particular Nellie, Cengiz, Kirsty and Simon.

We have many great franchise partners and of those Walter Seib and Stuart Fitzgerald stand out as exemplars of Winning Not Fighting. Thank you to all who work at HMS, Autogrill, SSP, Cibus, UMOE and Roadchef.

The wider team of committed outriders including: Laura Chandler, Chris Salt, Neil Treadaway, Ian Tandy, Rishi Khosla, Valentina Kristensen, Mo Sondhi, Ben Barbanel, Akeel Sachak, Elliot Moss, Jane Baxter, Kay Plunkett-Hogge, Gizzi Erskine, Jasmine Hemsley, Ted Young, Gavin Billenness, Lucy Knowles, Dar, Matthew Gwyther, Mel Aldridge and Robert Verkerk, Carole Symons, Megan Rossi, Pat Fellows, and Tina Taylor.

Young Jack Burke has supported me with research and good company during the writing of this book. And he has taught me some things about music. Look out for his Leon cookbook, *Happy Fast Food*, in the near future.

Fersen Lambranho has come into my life and that of Leon as a major source of essential energy and inspiration. And with him came the wonderful Paloma, Catarina and Mateus.

I have variously shared stories of Leon Chairman Tim Smalley and of investors and board directors Spencer Skinner, Nick Evans, Rodrigo Boscolo, Gavyn Davies, Jacques Fragis – all and many 'friends and family' investors, such as David Dimbleby, Belinda Giles, James Horler and Ian Neil, have been critical to our growth and all share the values of our team members, managers and support team.

And finally, for the past twelve years there has been Ottie. I discovered the wonder that is Ottie when she worked in our Strand restaurant. I cooked a cake for her and her fellow team members when they hit a record and Ottie has made sure that that tradition has stuck.

When Ottie is around great things happen. To me, and to many, she embodies the spirit of Leon. Ottie embraces the spiritual, and in Kung Fu style works hard without making it hard work. She has become part of the family. She sleeps in my daughter Eleanor's bedroom when she stays at our house, but recently the height differences have been reversed as Eleanor has grown.

There are few people as fun or as caring. We have travelled together to Japan, Ethiopia and Greece – you can tell a lot about someone when you are travelling with them. I am yet to find something that isn't a complete life-enhancing joy.

Thanks Ottie for all you do for me and for everyone else at Leon.

The Vincents and the Derham

Now for the most important people – my wife Katie Derham is my biggest source of energy, peace and courage. Katie has had to put up with quite a lot as I have tried to build Leon, turned around whisky businesses, written School Food Plans, and written this book. Writing it has taken up most holidays, many weekends and many evenings. As I type this we are on holiday and we are supposed to be going for dinner. Katie, the support you give me whilst being so busy with your own career(s) and family life is immense. When it looked like we were going to lose our house you said 'hey, we were happy before we moved here, we will be happy again'. This despite the fact that I know you would have been quietly gutted.

Natasha and Eleanor, I dedicated this book to you because ultimately if you are the only two people who read it, it would have been worthwhile. I love you.

Mum you are incredible. The editors suggested I take out one or two of the references to you being the most positive person in the world (it was a bit repetitive) – if you are reading this, they haven't taken out this one.

Dad, you were Leon. Not only does it bear your name, it bears your spirit. You were determined to always have fun (horse-racing, poker, sailing) and to always act with integrity. I still think you might answer the phone when I ring your/mum's number.

And to all the guests who choose to come to Leon and support what we do, thank you. There's more to come. What you see is not yet our best work.

Julian

Julian has taught me a lot, and we have had huge fun together along the way. Julian combines intelligence, determination, wisdom and an ability to stay very relaxed and very effective in combat. There have been some incredible and inexplicable moments of synchronicity. Julian, Leon is a better place for your massive contributions. And for my part, I owe you this adventure we are embarking on. Let's win, and not fight.

From Julian

This book would not have possible without my teacher, Grandmaster Máday Norbert. Nearly 14 years after he first suggested I write about the philosophical aspects of Wing Tsun, I'm honoured to begin to represent some of this art. His tireless contribution to Wing Tsun is the making of legends.

No art is an island to itself, it exists on the great work and dedications of countless masters. Each lifetime has given Wing Tsun an immeasurable depth and wisdom. From the nameless monks of the Shaolin Temple who gave their lives so that this knowledge could be passed on, to the modern masters who spread it to the West, I'm eternally grateful for the opportunities, experience and life that this has given me and many others.

Special thanks are due to my wife, Toni, for the endless conversations, timeless wisdoms and inspiring me to learn more from the art and myself. In many ways this book began with her. And to my daughter Sienna for putting up with my writing absences, and making my return the more joyous – bringing me straight out of my head and into the present with a smile.

Particular mention to my senior students, all gifted teachers in their own right for their boundless passion for this book. Their dedication and Wing Tsun practice truly made this book a reality: Si-Fu Vinnothan Balakumarasingham, Si-Hing Armani Leroy, Si-Hing Calum Thornicroft, Si-Hing Kit Liu, Si-Hing Gordon Man, Si-Hing Gideon Morris, Si-Hing Tyronne Perera, Si-Hing Nauris Sadovskis, Si-Hing Tom Reynolds and Ahimsa Ravi.

Over the last 20 years I've been supremely fortunate to have a large number of students and teachers who've gone far beyond what could ever have been expected. The time, effort, loyalty, kindness and acceptance you have shown me is both inspiring and humbling. It because of you that Wing Tsun has been able to live on – every master would be so lucky to have such students. Thank you.

Where my Sifu started, Bill Ayling continued. The debt I owe Bill over my own transformation of consciousness is immense. From helping me to see my own gifts, to understanding better those of Wing Tsun, Bill is one of those 'silent' Buddhas who helps without asking reward, and I'm blessed to have him in my life.

The Wellbeing Ambassadors, who trained with me in the lead up to this book, have helped us make Wing Tsun and its teachings relatable, accessible and so much more enjoyable. Thanks to Henrietta Kennedy, Oreke Consin Moshehe, Ifeoma Akpuaka, and Jen Christie and to Laura Hill, Marc Antoine and Patrik Zub. Additional thanks to Jen Christie for helping to take the learnings of Wing Tsun even further with The Conscious Coach.

A special thanks to the Leon family for being so open and warm to the learnings in Wing Tsun and taking part in what must have seemed a rather far-fetched idea.

Even martial artists need TLC and many thanks is needed to Hughie Morris for his physical treatments, patience, travel and great laughs. Similarly, my good friend and osteopath Paul Kyte for fatherly advice and his long support of my sometimes extreme physical exertions. Aaron Mattes for his unbelievable work, kind words and furthering my knowledge and understanding of the body. Dawn Golten and Sue helped hold me together during the long days and early mornings. Tony Riddle provided outstanding coaching and general life support. And thanks to Dr Robert Verkerk and Meleni Aldridge of the Alliance for Natural Health for their nutritional advice and friendship.

Writing a book is an unusual blend of collaboration and solitude. And in modern life, solitude can only be facilitated by the patience, kindness, time and understanding of others. Thanks is due to my mother Celia for her unbelievable generosity, love and putting up with constant change. My sister Claire has been a phenomenal editor of all things Wing Tsun for 17 years. And I'm grateful to my father Alan for installing drive, determination and the courage to do things differently. My in-laws Sue and Russell Marais, require much thanks for their repeated kindness – from supporting Sienna and last-minute requests, to looking after everything from toy boxes to Christmas trees. Lauren and Nettie Atkinson have been an inspiration in their love and support of Toni and Sienna.

Despite my rather single-minded focus on Wing Tsun at school, three teachers at Dulwich College helped shape my passion for writing and teaching; Dr Stephen Farrow for his precision and clarity; Titus Edge for his passion for history; and Ian Brinton for his kindness, inspiration and brilliant teaching methodology.

Acknowledgements

Additional thanks go to Roger Palmer, my first student and best friend who was always there when needed; John Scott, and wife Michelle, for unbelievable loyalty, friendship and love; Jasmine Hemsley and Nick Hopper for their friendship, fun and creative thinking; Daniel Eccleston for his passion and kindness; Janko for his specialist and gifted CT training, which tested my boundaries and furthered my skills and understanding; Baranyai Janos and Gal Istvan for the countless adventures in Hungary; Molnar Gabriella for introducing me to my Sifu; Tunde, Botond and Csenge Máday for welcoming me with so much love as part of their family; Mark Bellhouse and Andrew Cameron for providing me with the opportunity to find my purpose in Wing Tsun; Sarah McAllister for her gifted and patient Feng Shui advice; Jim Bulley for so much unconditional support in the early years of my teaching career; Les Barber, my neighbour, friend and Judo legend; Rupert Bullimore who is one of the most loyal and noble men who has been with me throughout my life; Allan Vousden for his excellent advice, keeping me grounded and putting up with my numerous requests; the gifted team at WelltoDo Global for facilitating and sharing many of our exciting initiatives; the great soldiers of 3 Para, the PF, and other units I cannot name, for their support, humour and adopting the Wing Tsun wisdoms and; the inspirational Benjamin Zephaniah for our conversations and companionship. And no acknowledgement would be complete without paying tribute to the wonderfully gifted Millie Ralph, who kept me sane, organised, productive and happy – I wouldn't want to imagine a life without your support.

Finally, John, my co-author, should be acknowledged for courage, vision and enthusiasm in making this book, and incorporating its wisdom into Leon and elsewhere. His contribution to Wing Tsun, and seeing its wider relationship and applicability in the world, is truly a first in world history.

PENGUIN PARTNERSHIPS

Penguin Partnerships is the Creative Sales and Promotions team at Penguin Random House. We have a long history of working with clients on a wide variety of briefs, specializing in brand promotions, bespoke publishing and retail exclusives, plus corporate, entertainment and media partnerships.

We can respond quickly to briefs and specialize in repurposing books and content for sales promotions, for use as incentives and retail exclusives as well as creating content for new books in collaboration with our partners as part of branded book relationships.

Equally if you'd simply like to buy a bulk quantity of one of our existing books at a special discount, we can help with that too. Our books can make excellent corporate or employee gifts.

Special editions, including personalized covers, excerpts of existing books or books with corporate logos can be created in large quantities for special needs.

We can work within your budget to deliver whatever you want, however you want it.

For more information, please contact
salesenquiries@penguinrandomhouse.co.uk

馮道德 FUNG DOU DAK

至善 JI SIN

伍枚 NG MUI